Other Books by Joey Green

Joey Green's Fix-It MAGIC

MORE THAN **1,971** QUICK-AND-EASY
HOUSEHOLD SOLUTIONS USING BRAND-NAME PRODUCTS

JOEY GREEN

RODALE

The author has compiled the information contained herein from a variety of sources, and neither the author, publisher, manufacturers, nor distributors can assume responsibility for the effectiveness of the suggestions. Caution is urged in the use of cleaning solutions, folk medicine remedies, and pest control substances.

The brand-name products mentioned in this book are registered trademarks. The companies that own these trademarks and make these products do not endorse, recommend, or accept liability for any use of their products other than those uses indicated on the package label or in current company brochures. This book should not be regarded as a substitute for professional medical treatment, and neither the author, publisher, manufacturers, or distributors can accept legal responsibility for any problem arising out of the use of or experimentation with the methods described. The J.M. Smucker Company does not endorse any uses for Jif Peanut Butter other than as a food.

For a full listing of trademarks from the companies, please see page 384.

Direct and trade editions are both being published in 2008.

Rodale books may be purchased for business or promotional use or for special sales. For information, please write to:

Special Markets Department, Rodale, Inc., 733 Third Avenue, New York, NY 10017

Printed in the United States of America

Rodale Inc. makes every effort to use acid-free ∞, recycled paper ♻.

Illustrations ©2008 by Connie Stern

Book design by Design Works

Library of Congress Cataloging-in-Publication Data

Green, Joey.
   Joey Green's fix-it magic : more than 1,971 quick-and-easy home solutions using
   brand-name products / Joey Green.
         p.   cm.
   Includes bibliographical references and index.
   ISBN-13 978–1–59486–784–2 hardcover
   ISBN-10 1–59486–784–4 hardcover
   ISBN-13 978–1–59486–785–9 paperback
   ISBN-10 1–59486–785–2 paperback
   1. Home economics.   2. Brand name products—United States.   3. Cleaning.   I. Title.
II. Title: Fix-it magic.
TX158.G67815 2008
643'.7—dc22   2007052731

Distributed to the trade by Macmillan

2   4   6   8   10   9   7   5   3   1   paperback
2   4   6   8   10   9   7   5   3   1   hardcover

We inspire and enable people to improve their lives and the world around them

For more of our products visit **rodalestore.com** or call 800-848-4735

For my father,
who taught me
how to fix anything

Contents

But First, a Word from Our Sponsor

When I was a kid, my grandfather owned a furniture store called Furniture World in Miami, Florida. My father worked at the furniture store and would occasionally take me to work with him. To me, spending the entire day with my father at the furniture store was a real treat. I'd hide between boxes of furniture in the dark warehouse, get lost in a maze of furniture in the showroom, and play with paper clips, mess around with rubber stamps and ink pads, and pound away at the keys of a manual typewriter in the back office to test five sheets of carbon paper at the same time.

We would start the day in the warehouse, where a crew of burly, kind-hearted men would load furniture onto the truck to be delivered to customers that day. But before they moved the furniture onto the truck, Billy, Earl, Armando, Lee, and my father would thoroughly examine the furniture for any damage. If they discovered any defects, they would quickly repair the marred furniture using an odd assortment of products on the workbench beneath a wall decorated with centerfolds of pinup girls from a bygone era. In seconds, they'd reattach legs to chairs with Elmer's Glue-All. They'd cover up scratches in a dining room table with Crayola Crayons. They'd lubricate the runners on dresser drawers with a bar of Ivory Soap. I'd stand nearby speechless, watching in awe, dazzled by their inventiveness.

To me, everything that happened during those early morning hours in the Furniture World warehouse gave me a wonderful glimpse into a secret world of American ingenuity. These guys could fix anything. Aside from knowing all the tricks of the trade, my father was also exceptionally handy at home. On Sunday afternoons, when he made repairs around the house, I served as his assistant (compelled by my rank as the eldest of four children), handing him whatever tool he requested or running to the workbench in the garage for whatever tool he had forgotten. I not only learned the difference between a pair of pliers and a wrench, but as a keen observer, I beared witness to some amazing shortcuts when it comes to home repair. My father taught me to wrap a strip of Scotch Transparent Tape around the drill bit to create a flag to know when to stop drilling—so I wouldn't accidentally drill a hole through the other side of the wood. He showed me how to lubricate the blade of a handsaw with a bar of Ivory Soap. And he demonstrated how to slow the drying time of plaster of Paris by simply mixing in some Heinz White Vinegar.

Whenever anyone asks me how I come up with all these tips, I usually explain that I was asked to come up with alternative uses for Nestea Iced Tea Mix in a meeting while working for an advertising agency in New York City. One of the account guys in that meeting said he had gotten badly sunburned one summer day, went home, emptied a jar of Nestea powdered mix into his bathtub, filled the tub with water, and soaked in it. We all looked at him like he was crazy, but he swore that the tannic acid in the tea had relieved his sunburn pain. That story inspired me to contact the manufacturers to find out other alternative uses for the many brand-name products we all know and love. But as I continued researching these tips, I realized that I had learned many of them by tagging along with my father, who proudly recalled that in college he had poured Coca-Cola over the battery terminals under the hood of his stalled car to fizz away the corrosion and get the ignition to start up.

Over the past twenty years, I've put many of these tips to work. As a homeowner, I've painted nearly every room in our home, removed wallpaper from walls, tiled bathroom floors, deodorized pet urine stains from carpet, installed shelves, repaired faucets and toilets, and best of all, I've wallpapered one of my daughters' bedrooms together with my father. I've fixed a broken dishwasher with Tang, cleaned oil spills from our driveway with Coca-Cola, removed water stains from wooden furniture with Miracle Whip, and cleaned grape juice stains from carpet with Canada Dry Club Soda. I owe it all to my father.

And so, I decided to put all these incredibly quirky yet practical tips together in one handy book, so you too can use brand-name products you already have in your kitchen, bathroom, laundry room, and garage to fix things around the house—saving time, money, and aggravation. But I had to know more. I locked myself in the library and researched hundreds of helpful ideas, contacted companies to obtain their secret files, talked with dozens of home improvement experts, and sifted through hundreds of e-mails that I receive through my website, www.wackyuses.com.

I uncovered some astonishingly helpful hints. L'eggs Sheer Energy Panty Hose strains lumps from a can of paint. Pam Cooking Spray lubricates the sliding racks in a dishwasher. Efferdent can clear a clogged drain. Wilson Tennis Balls erase scuff marks from floors. Listerine kills mold and mildew in a shower stall. Purell Instant Hand Sanitizer cleans tomato sauce stains from the insides of Tupperware.

This book is the result of my obsessive journey into the world of home improvement. But it's also a happy trip down memory lane into the recesses of the Furniture World warehouse, where my father first taught me the tricks of the trade. Thank you, Dad, for teaching me everything I know.

Cooking

- **Forster Toothpicks.** Identify rare, medium, and well-done steaks on your barbecue grill by using colored Forster Toothpicks to mark steaks on the barbecue.
- **Maxwell House Coffee.** A clean, empty Maxwell House Coffee can doubles as an excellent disposable pot to be used on the grill to cook bratwursts in beer.
- **Morton Salt.** After barbecuing, sprinkle Morton Salt over the smoldering charcoal to prevent the embers from flaring up into a roaring fire again.

Grill

- **Arm & Hammer Baking Soda.** To clean a barbecue grill, make a paste by mixing equal parts Arm & Hammer Baking Soda and water, apply with a wire brush, wipe clean, and dry with a cloth.

- **Cascade, Glad Trash Bags, and Parsons' Ammonia.** To clean caked-on grease from an outdoor barbecue grill, place the grill in a Glad Trash Bag and add one cup Parsons' ammonia, one cup Cascade dishwasher detergent, and two gallons hot water. Secure the bag closed. (The fumes from the ammonia help weaken the bond of the baked-on food and grease.) Let sit for forty-five minutes, then hose down the grill and wipe clean.

- **Dawn Dishwashing Liquid and Glad Trash Bags.** Mix up a solution of one-half cup Dawn Dishwashing Liquid and one gallon water. Place the grease-coated barbecue grill inside a Glad Trash Bag, pour the soapy solution over the rack inside the bag, seal the bag shut, and let sit overnight. The following day, scrub the rack with a wire brush and rinse clean.

- **Easy-Off Oven Cleaner and Glad Trash Bags.** Place the grill in a Glad Trash Bag. Wearing protective eyewear and rubber gloves, spray the racks thoroughly with Easy-Off Oven Cleaner, close the bag, and secure with a twist tie. Let set for four hours in the sun. Rinse well with a garden hose.

- **Glad Trash Bags.** When your outdoor barbecue grill cools down, cover it with a Glad Trash Bag to protect it from the elements.

- **Pam Cooking Spray.** To make cleaning a barbecue grill easy, coat the grill with Pam Cooking Spray before barbecuing. After cooking, when the grill is cool to the touch, scrub the grill with a wire brush. The cooking oil enables baked-on food to slide off much easier.

- **Reynolds Wrap.** To make cleaning baked-on food from a barbecue grill easier, place a sheet of Reynolds Wrap on the hot grill immediately after you finish barbecuing and close the lid. The next time you use the barbecue, peel off the foil, crumple it into a ball, and scrub the grill clean, easily removing all the burned-on food.

- **WD-40.** To clean baked-on food from a barbecue grill, remove the grill from the barbecue, spray with WD-40, let set for five minutes, then wipe clean. Then wash thoroughly with soap and water.

- **Windex.** To clean baked-on food from a barbecue grill, spray with Windex while the grill is still warm, then scrub with a wire brush. Let cool, then rinse well with water.

Igniting

- **Conair Pro Styler 1600.** After lighting a charcoal fire in a barbecue grill, carefully use a Conair Pro Styler 1600 hair dryer set on cool to fan the flames until the charcoal briquettes catch fire.

- **Maxwell House Coffee.** Using a can opener, remove the top and bottom of an empty Maxwell House Coffee can. Use tin snips to cut a few tabs around the bottom rim of the coffee can. Stand the can in the center of your barbecue grill, place one sheet of crumpled newspaper inside, fill the rest of the can with charcoal briquettes, add lighter fluid, and light the newspaper through the punched holes. When the coals glow orange,

remove the hot can with tongs and set in a safe place to let the can cool.

- **Tidy Cats.** Prevent grease fires in barbecue grills by covering the bottom of the grill with a one-inch layer of unused Tidy Cats cat box filler.
- **Vaseline Petroleum Jelly.** Apply a thick coat of Vaseline Petroleum Jelly to a cotton ball to start a fire in a barbecue. The cotton ball will burn for a long time.
- **WD-40.** WD-40 works as a substitute for charcoal lighter fluid. As with lighter fluid, be sure to let the charcoal fire burn off the WD-40 before cooking food on the grill.

Insects

- **Aunt Jemima Original Syrup.** Lure insects away from a barbecue by coating a few small pieces of cardboard with Aunt Jemima Original Syrup and placing them around the perimeter of the yard. Wasps and bees will be attracted to the homemade flypaper instead of your guests.
- **Budweiser.** To attract bees and wasps away from a barbecue and your guests, place open cans of Budweiser beer around the perimeter of the yard. Bees and wasps love beer. They fly into a can of beer, get drunk, and drown—which, if you're a bee or wasp, probably isn't a bad way to go.
- **Heinz Apple Cider Vinegar.** To keep bees and wasps away from your barbecue, fill a large bowl with Heinz Apple Cider Vinegar and set near the table of food. By the end of the barbecue, you'll have a bowl full of floating flies, mosquitoes, and moths. (For more ways to repel insects, see page 169.)

Pots and Pans

- **Ivory Soap.** To prevent barbecue soot from sticking to the bottom of pots and pans, rub the bottoms of pots and pans with a bar of Ivory Soap before putting them over an open fire.

- **Reynolds Wrap.** A crumpled-up piece of Reynolds Wrap makes an excellent pot scrubber to clean pots and pans used over a barbecue grill.

Strange Facts

- No one knows the origins of the word *barbecue*. Some linguistic experts say the Spanish derived the word from the Native American Taino word *barbacoa*, meaning a framework of green wood used as a grill for cooking food over hot coals. Others believe French pirates of the Caribbean cooked animals on spits that skewered the animals *de barbe a queue*—meaning "from whiskers to tail."

- Three out of four households in the United States own barbecue grills.

- In the United States, the most popular holidays for barbecuing are the Fourth of July, Memorial Day, and Labor Day—respectively.

- The most popular food for barbecuing in America is hamburgers—followed by steak, chicken, and hot dogs.

- A barbecue is called a *braai* in South Africa, a *churrasco* in Brazil, and a *barbie* in Australia.

- People in St. Louis, Missouri, consume more barbecue sauce per capita than people of any other city in the United States.

- Barbecue Bob (Robert Hicks) recorded for Columbia Records from 1927 to 1930 and became the most popular of the Atlanta blues guitarists of his time and Columbia Records's best-selling bluesman.

Caulking

- **Clorox Bleach.** To clean the caulking around the rim of a bathtub, fill a trigger-spray bottle with a solution of three-quarters cup Clorox Bleach and one gallon water, spray the caulking, wait five minutes, and wash clean. The bleach kills the mold and mildew. Repeat if necessary.
- **Smirnoff Vodka.** Clean the caulking around bathtubs by filling a spray bottle with Smirnoff Vodka, spray the caulking, wait five minutes, and wash clean. The alcohol in the vodka kills the mold and mildew. Repeat if necessary.

Cleaning

- **Arm & Hammer Baking Soda.** To clean a bathtub, sprinkle Arm & Hammer Baking Soda on a damp sponge, scrub, and rinse clean.
- **Cascade.** For a powerful way to clean grease, grime, and rust stains from the bathtub, fill the tub with hot water, add two

tablespoons Cascade dishwasher detergent, and let stand for about ten minutes. Use an abrasive sponge to scrub any stains and then rinse clean with water. The phosphates in the Cascade whiten even the dirtiest tubs. Repeat if necessary.

- **Dawn Dishwashing Liquid.** To clean soap scum from a bathtub, pour Dawn Dishwashing Liquid on the stained area, let sit overnight, and rinse clean with water. Dawn Dishwashing Liquid cuts through grease and cleans older tubs without harming the finish.

- **Easy-Off Oven Cleaner.** For really tough grease stains or mineral deposits, put on protective eyewear and rubber gloves and spray Easy-Off Oven Cleaner over the stubborn spots on your bathtub. Let set for thirty minutes, making sure the room is well ventilated. Scrub gently with an abrasive sponge and rinse clean with warm water.

- **Gillette Foamy.** To clean the bathtub and let your kids have a blast at the same time, give your kids a can of Gillette Foamy shaving cream to entertain themselves in the bathtub. They can use the shaving cream to draw on the tile walls, and when you wash the condensed soap off with water, the bathtub will be sparkling clean. Your kids will come out amazingly clean as well.

- **Heinz White Vinegar.** To make cleaning mineral deposits from hard water from your bathtub easier, fill the bathtub with hot water, pour in four cups Heinz White Vinegar, and let sit overnight. The acetic acid in the vinegar breaks up the mineral deposits, making them easier to scrub off with an abrasive sponge.

- **Jet-Dry.** To clean hard water stains from a bathtub, fill the bathtub with hot water, pour in four ounces Jet-Dry, and let soak for a few hours. This softens the hard-water buildup, making it easier to remove.

- **L'eggs Sheer Energy Panty Hose.** To scrub the bathtub and bathroom tiles, ball up a clean, used pair of L'eggs Sheer Energy Panty Hose. The nylon is a mild abrasive and doubles as a scouring pad. Or for more fun, wear the panty hose and roll around in the bathtub and against the tile walls.

- **McCormick Cream of Tartar** and **Hydrogen Peroxide.** To remove a stain from the bathtub, make a thick paste from McCormick Cream of Tartar and hydrogen peroxide, apply the paste to the stain, and let dry. Scrub with a brush and rinse thoroughly.

- **Skin So Soft Body Lotion.** To remove a ring from the bathtub, add three capfuls Skin So Soft Body Lotion under the faucet while filling the tub with hot water. Use a sponge to wipe the ring right off.

Decal Removal

- **Jif Peanut Butter.** Coat the decals in the bottom of the bathtub with Jif Peanut Butter and let sit for one hour. The peanut oil dissolves the glue between the decals and the tub. Then use a single-edge razor blade to carefully scrape the decals off the tub floor.

- **Shout.** To make decals easier to remove, spray the decals with Shout Stain Remover, let sit for five minutes, fill the tub with water, and let soak for one hour. Using a single-edge razor blade, carefully scrape the decals off the tub floor.

Drain Stopper

- **Wilson Tennis Balls.** If you lose the drain plug for your shower, sink, or bathtub, you can use a Wilson Tennis Ball to block the drain. The suction keeps the tennis ball in place.

Faucets

- **Cover Girl Continuous Color Classic Red.** To adjust the water in the bath effortlessly, turn on the bathtub faucet(s) to the temperature you prefer, then mark the faucet(s) and the wall with dots of Cover Girl Continuous Color Classic Red Nail Polish so they can be aligned immediately every time you bathe.

Leaks

- **DAP Caulk.** If a bathtub seems to be leaking, the cause may not be the tub itself. Water may be leaking into walls through the seams where the tub meets the tile wall, from around a soap dish, or from around the faucet or spout. Caulk around these areas.

Mildew

- **Parsons' Ammonia.** To remove mildew from walls, scrub with equal parts Parsons' Ammonia and water. Make sure the room is well ventilated and rinse clean with water.
- **Tidy Cats.** To prevent mildew in a bathtub when you leave your home for a long time, pour unused Tidy Cats cat box filler in a flat box and place it in your bathtub. (If you have

cats, be sure to keep the bathroom door closed so they don't use the cat box filler in the tub.)

Polishing

- **Turtle Wax.** After cleaning your bathtub, rub Turtle Wax into the tub, tiles, and faucets with a soft cloth, buffing as you go along. (Do not use Turtle Wax on the bathtub floor; otherwise you risk slipping.)

Rust Stains

- **Coca-Cola.** To clean rust stains from a bathtub, cover the stains with Coca-Cola, let sit for one hour, and rinse clean. The phosphoric acid in the Coke removes the rust.
- **20 Mule Team Borax** and **ReaLemon.** To clean rust stains from a bathtub, scrub with a paste made from 20 Mule Team Borax and ReaLemon lemon juice.

Whirlpool Baths

- **Cascade.** To clean pipes and tubes in a whirlpool bath, fill the bathtub with enough warm water to run the whirlpool. Add two cups Cascade dishwasher detergent and run the system for fifteen minutes, then drain the water. Refill with fresh water and run the system for one minute to rinse it clean.

Strange Facts

- President Franklin Pierce, the fourteenth president of the United States, ordered the first bathtub for the White House.
- President William Taft, the heaviest president in United States history, weighed 332 pounds. After getting stuck in the White

House bathtub, Taft installed an oversized bathtub (seven feet long and forty-one inches wide) in the White House. The tub could accommodate four average-sized men.

- On December 28, 1917, the *New York Evening Mail* published an article entitled "A Neglected Anniversary" by American journalist H. L. Mencken. In the article, written as a hoax, Mencken reported a phony history of the bathtub, insisting that the bathtub had not been introduced into the United States until 1842 and was initially opposed, until President Millard Fillmore had a bathtub installed in the White House in 1850. Mencken did not reveal that his article was a hoax until 1926.

- During Prohibition, Americans made "bathtub gin" by mixing grain alcohol and juniper berries in bathtubs and allowing the mixture to steep for several hours.

- On Labor Day, the city of Nome, Alaska, hosts an annual Great Bathtub Race. Four team members, wearing wide-brim hats and suspenders, push or pull a bathtub on wheels down Front Street with a fifth team member sitting in the tub filled with water and bubble bath and carrying a bath towel.

Books

Book Covers

- **Reynolds Freezer Paper.** Make a dust jacket to protect a book cover with a sheet of Reynolds Freezer Paper and then secure the cover in place by gently sealing the edges with a clothes iron set on warm.
- **Saran Wrap.** To protect a book cover, use a sheet of Saran Wrap to safeguard a dust jacket.
- **Scotch Packaging Tape.** To repair torn book covers, adhere the cover back to the binding with Scotch Packaging Tape.

Cleaning

- **Huggies Baby Wipes.** To clean spills on a book, wipe the book cover with a Huggies Baby Wipe.
- **Wonder Bread.** To remove grease stains from books, take a piece of bread from the center of a slice of Wonder Bread, cut off the crust, and rub the affected area.

Dampness

- **Bounty Paper Towels.** To prevent the wet pages of a book from wrinkling, place sheets of Bounty Paper Towels between every wet page, close the book, place a heavy book on top, and let sit overnight. The quicker picker-upper will absorb the dampness from the pages of the book.

Kingsford's Corn Starch. To prevent or kill mildew in damp books, sprinkle Kingsford's Corn Starch throughout the book to absorb the moisture from damp pages, wait several hours, and then brush clean. If the pages are mildewed, brush the corn-starch off outdoors to keep mildew spores out of the house.

Leather Bindings

- **Vaseline Petroleum Jelly.** Clean a leather binding on a book by rubbing in a dab of Vaseline Petroleum Jelly and buffing with a soft, clean cloth. Let sit for several hours and then repeat.

Mildew

- **Kingsford Charcoal Briquets.** Place an untreated Kingsford Charcoal Briquet in a closed bookcase to absorb moisture and prevent mildew.

Musty Odors

- **Arm & Hammer Baking Soda.** To remove musty odors from old books, place the books in an airtight Rubbermaid or Tupperware container, sprinkle some Arm & Hammer Baking Soda inside the tub, seal the container closed, and let sit for a week, turning the books over every few days to expose both sides to the baking soda equally.
- **Bounce** and **Ziploc Storage Bags.** To eliminate musty smells from an old book, place several sheets of Bounce throughout the pages of a book, seal it inside a large Ziploc Storage Bag, and let sit for two weeks.
- *USA Today.* To deodorize musty books, place the books inside a paper bag filled with crumpled up pages from *USA Today* and let sit for several days. The newsprint absorbs the musty smells. Repeat if necessary.

Strange Facts

- Before the advent of paper, most documents were written on parchment (made from the skin of sheep or goats) or vellum (made from the skin of calves). A three-hundred-page book would require the skins of an estimated eighteen sheep.
- Most people believe Marco Polo was the first European to visit China (despite the fact that his father and uncle had traveled to China five years before him), due to the popularity of Polo's 1298 book, *Description of the World* (known today as *The Travels of Marco Polo*), which became the most widely read book in Europe.

- In 1633, the Vatican summoned astronomer Galileo Galilei before the Inquisition and threatened to burn him at the stake for stating that the Earth revolves around the sun in his 1632 book, *Dialogue Concerning the Two Chief World Systems.* Instead, Galileo retracted his discoveries and spent the remaining eight years of his life under house arrest.

- In 1638, John Harvard, a young Puritan minister from Charlestown, Massachusetts, died of tuberculosis, leaving half of his estate and his collection of more than four hundred books to the two-year-old New School, a college in present-day Cambridge, Massachusetts, prompting the General Court of Massachusetts to rename the school Harvard College in his honor.

- In 1814, after British troops set fire to the Library of Congress (then housed in the Capitol building), former President Thomas Jefferson sold his personal library of 6,487 books—accumulated over more than fifty years and considered one of the finest collections in the United States—to Congress for $23,950.

- In L. Frank Baum's classic children's book, *The Wonderful Wizard of Oz,* Dorothy wears silver shoes. Hollywood screenwriter Noel Langley changed them to ruby slippers in the script for MGM's classic 1939 movie *The Wizard of Oz.* Also, in Baum's book, thousands of field mice pull the Cowardly Lion out of the Deadly Poppy Field. In the movie, Glinda—the Good Witch of the North—saves Dorothy, Toto, and the Lion by smothering the deadly scent of the poppies with snow.

- In 1978, Random House published *Woman's Day Crockery Cuisine,* a cookbook that included a recipe for "silky caramel slices." The recipe instructed readers to heat an unopened can of evaporated milk in a Crock-Pot, but accidentally neglected to tell readers to fill the pot with water. When Random House discovered that following the recipe could cause the can of evaporated milk to explode, it recalled ten thousand copies of the cookbook.

Box Springs and Mattresses

Bed-Wetting

- **Scotchgard.** Protect a mattress from a bed wetter by spraying the mattress with Scotchgard to resist moisture.

Deodorizing

- **Bounce.** To freshen a mattress, place a sheet of Bounce between the mattress and the box spring.

Dust Balls

- **L'eggs Sheer Energy Panty Hose.** To clean the dust from under a bed, cut off one leg from a clean, used pair of L'eggs Sheer Energy Panty Hose, place it over the end of a broomstick, and secure it in place with a rubber band. Slide the nylon-covered broomstick under the bed and move it back and forth. The panty hose leg will gather up the dust bunnies.

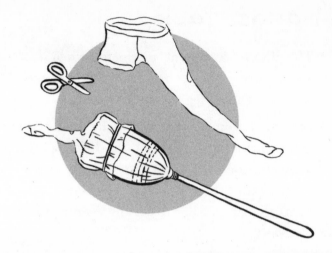

- **Scotch Packaging Tape.** To remove dust balls from under a bed, wrap Scotch Packaging Tape, adhesive side out, over the bristle end of a broomstick and slide it back and forth under the furniture.

Mattress Protectors

- **Arm & Hammer Baking Soda.** To clean plastic mattress protectors, sprinkle Arm & Hammer Baking Soda on a damp sponge, wipe clean, and dry with a clean, soft cloth.

Squeaks

- **WD-40.** To take squeaks out of a box spring, remove the fabric covering the bottom of the box spring (by simply removing the staples) and spray the springs with a light coat of WD-40. Staple the fabric covering back in place with a staple gun.

Urine Stains

- **20 Mule Team Borax.** To neutralize urine odors from mattresses and mattress covers, dampen the spot with water, rub in 20 Mule Team Borax, let dry, then vacuum or brush clean.

Strange Facts

- The phrase "sleep tight" originated when mattresses rested on top of ropes woven through the bed frame. A bed key was used to tighten sagging ropes.

- In the children's fairy tale "The Princess and the Pea," told by Hans Christian Andersen (1805–1875), a princess, sleeping on a tower made from twenty straw mattresses and twenty feather-erbeds with a single pea under the bottom mattress, tosses and turns all night, unable to get any sleep—proving that she really is royalty.

- One out of every seven children wets the bed.

- When asked how she wrote her memoirs, actress Mae West replied, "I do my best work in bed."

- Dr. William Scholl, founder of Dr. Scholl's foot care products, coined his own credo: "Early to bed, early to rise, work like hell, and advertise."

- When asked by reporters what she wore to bed, actress Marilyn Monroe smiled coyly and replied, "Chanel No. 5."

- Ozzie and Harriet were the only couple allowed a double bed on a television show—until *The Brady Bunch* premiered in 1969.

- After their wedding in 1969, John Lennon and Yoko Ono invited the press to join their seven-day "bed-in" in the Amsterdam Hilton to promote world peace. John and Yoko sat in bed for seven consecutive days in a suite decorated with posters that proclaimed "Bed Peace" and "Hair Peace."

Cabinets and Countertops

Burn Marks

- **Colgate Regular Flavor Toothpaste.** To remove a slight discoloration on a plastic laminate countertop, rub the area with Colgate Regular Flavor Toothpaste.

Candle Wax

- **Conair Pro Styler 1600.** To remove candle wax from a table or countertop, use a Conair Pro Styler 1600 hair dryer to blow warm air an inch above the drips, then wipe away the wax with a paper towel.

- **Coppertone.** To remove candle wax from a countertop, rub in a dollop of Coppertone sunscreen and wipe clean.

- **MasterCard** and **Bounty Paper Towels.** Use an old MasterCard to remove as much wax as possible. Then place a sheet of Bounty Paper Towels over the wax and press gently with a warm iron to absorb the remaining wax. The heat from the iron melts the wax, and the paper towel absorbs it.

- **Noxzema Deep Cleansing Cream.** To remove candle wax from a countertop, rub a dollop of Noxzema Deep Cleansing Cream into the wax and wipe clean.
- **Skin So Soft Body Lotion.** Rub a dollop of Skin So Soft Body Lotion to remove candle wax from a countertop.
- **Wish-Bone Thousand Island Dressing.** Rub in a dollop of Wish-Bone Thousand Island Dressing to remove candle wax from wood or Formica.

Cleaning

- **Arm & Hammer Clean Shower.** Spray Arm & Hammer Clean Shower on countertops, wait a few moments, and wipe clean.
- **Canada Dry Club Soda.** Pour Canada Dry Club Soda directly on the counter, wipe with a soft cloth, rinse with warm water, and wipe dry.
- **Colgate Regular Flavor Toothpaste.** To clean grease from a countertop, squeeze a dollop of Colgate Regular Flavor Toothpaste on a sponge and scrub gently. Wipe clean with a damp cloth. The toothpaste is a mild abrasive that cleans grease and grime easily and effortlessly.
- **Coppertone.** To clean grease and dirt from Formica surfaces, squeeze Coppertone sunscreen onto a soft cloth and polish.
- **Easy-Off Oven Cleaner.** To remove dried grease from wooden kitchen cabinets, spray with Easy-Off Oven Cleaner, let it set for a few minutes, and then wipe clean. Be sure to wear protective eyewear and rubber gloves, make certain the room is well ventilated, and test it in an inconspicuous spot first.
- **Gillette Foamy.** To clean a countertop, spray some Gillette Foamy shaving cream on the countertop and let kids rub it around and practice writing and drawing in the shaving cream.

The condensed soap easily cleans grease and grime from surfaces. Then wipe the countertop clean with a soft cloth dampened with water.

- **Huggies Baby Wipes.** Clean a sticky mess from cabinets or
  countertops with a Huggies Baby Wipe.

- **Jet-Dry.** To clean glass, Plexiglas, Formica, or wooden tabletops, fill a clean, empty sixteen-ounce trigger-spray bottle
  with water, add one tablespoon Jet-Dry, and shake well. Spray
  the surfaces with this cleanser and sponge clean.

- **Purell Instant Hand Sanitizer.** To get a Formica countertop
  squeaky clean, squirt Purell Instant Hand Sanitizer on a clean,
  soft cloth and wipe down the countertop. The antibacterial
  gel cleans the fine film of grime from the surface like magic.

- **Skin So Soft Body Lotion.** A dab of Skin So Soft Body Lotion
  on a soft cloth will remove grease stains from Formica countertops.

- **Wonder Bread.** If you don't have a sponge to wipe down the
  kitchen counter, use a slice of Wonder Bread. The doughy
  bread works like an eraser on grime and absorbs grease.

Formica

- **Crayola Crayons.** To hide unsightly scratches on a Formica
  surface, choose a Crayola Crayon that matches the color of the
  Formica and rub the crayon into the nick.

- **Turtle Wax.** A coat of Turtle Wax rejuvenates dulled Formica
  countertops and plastic tabletops.

Lubrication

- **Alberto VO5 Conditioning Hairdressing.** To prevent sliding
  doors on a medicine cabinet from sticking, rub a little Alberto
  VO5 Conditioning Hairdressing onto the tracks.

- **Vaseline Petroleum Jelly.** Rub a dab of Vaseline Petroleum Jelly into the ridges of a medicine cabinet so the doors glide smoothly over the lubricated runner.
- **WD-40.** A quick spritz of WD-40 along the tracks of a medicine cabinet door will help the doors slide easier.

Marble

- **Crayola Chalk.** Clean a marble countertop by pulverizing a few sticks of white Crayola Chalk with a mortal and pestle until it is a fine powder. Dip a soft cloth in the powder, wipe the marble, then rinse with clear water and dry thoroughly.
- **Downy Fabric Softener.** Mix two cups Downy Fabric Softener in a gallon of water and sponge down a marble countertop with the solution.

Polishing

- **Reynolds Cut-Rite Wax Paper.** Buff countertops with a sheet of Reynolds Cut-Rite Wax Paper.
- **Turtle Wax.** A coat of Turtle Wax rejuvenates dulled Formica counters and plastic tabletops.

Shutting

- **Velcro.** To secure cabinet doors closed, placed adhesive-backed Velcro tabs on the inside corner of each door and the corresponding frame.

Strange Facts

- Tradition holds that Joseph, the husband of Mary in the New Testament, was a cabinetmaker.

- The Cabinet is a group of advisors to the President of the United States, composed of the heads of executive and administrative departments of the government. The Constitution of the United States does not mention a Cabinet.

- President Andrew Jackson did not have a formal Cabinet. Instead, he conferred with personal advisors who became known as the "kitchen cabinet."

- From 1829 to 1971, the Postmaster General of the United States was a member of the President's Cabinet.

- In 1917, Italian immigrant Antonio Pasin, unable to find work as a cabinetmaker like his father and grandfather before him, began building coaster wagons for children, ultimately founding the Liberty Coaster Company and eventually producing steel wagons, creating the Radio Flyer line of red wagons.

- Edward Hopper's famous 1942 painting *Nighthawks* portrays three people sitting at a counter in a city diner late at night. One of the most recognizable paintings in American art, *Nighthawks* has been seen in the 1986 movie *Ferris Bueller's Day Off* and has been re-created in scenes in the 1973 movie *The Sting*, the 1981 movie *Pennies From Heaven*, and the animated television series *The Simpsons*.

- In February 1960, four black college students broke the segregation barrier by taking seats at F. W. Woolworth's downtown lunch counter in Greensboro, North Carolina. The peaceful civil disobedience sit-in against the Jim Crow custom spread nationwide and became a movement to end legal segregation. Today, the Smithsonian Institution features the four original chrome-and-vinyl stools from the Woolworth's lunch counter.

- In the groundbreaking 1919 German silent horror movie *The Cabinet of Doctor Caligari*, an evil hypnotist orders a sleepwalker to murder people.

Candle Wax

- **Bounty Paper Towels.** You can remove candle wax from carpet with Bounty, the quicker picker-upper. Cover the wax stain with a sheet of the paper towel and then carefully iron the paper towel. The heat from the iron melts the wax, and the paper towel absorbs it.

Cleaning

- **Clairol Herbal Essences Shampoo.** Use a capful of any scent Clairol Herbal Essences Shampoo in your carpet shampooer to clean carpet, simultaneously scenting your home.

Deodorizing

- **Arm & Hammer Baking Soda.** To deodorize carpet, sprinkle Arm & Hammer Baking Soda lightly over the dry carpet, let sit for fifteen minutes, and then vacuum up. The baking soda neutralizes odors.

- **Bounce.** To get rid of a stale smell in your home, place a sheet of Bounce in your vacuum cleaner bag before vacuuming the carpet.

- **Downy Fabric Softener.** To help your carpet stay clean, smell more fragrant, and feel softer, add two ounces Downy Fabric Softener and fourteen ounces water in a sixteen-ounce trigger-spray bottle and spray a fine mist of the solution over your carpet after vacuuming. The antistatic elements in the Downy Fabric Softener make vacuuming up pet hair and lint effortless.

- **Gain Powder Laundry Detergent.** To refresh carpets, lightly sprinkle Gain Powder Laundry Detergent on the carpet and then vacuum up the powder. The fragrance in the laundry detergent leaves the carpet smelling fresh.

- **Heinz White Vinegar.** To deodorize carpets, add one cup Heinz White Vinegar to your carpet cleaner when shampooing your carpets. The carpet will smell like vinegar for an hour or two after cleaning, but once the smell fades, any other odors in the carpet will be gone too.

- **Kingsford's Corn Starch.** Deodorize carpets by sprinkling one-quarter to one-half cup Kingsford's Corn Starch on the carpet. Let sit for thirty minutes and then vacuum clean. The cornstarch absorbs odors.

Gum

- **Jif Peanut Butter.** To remove chewing gum from carpet, rub a dab of Jif Peanut Butter over the spot, let sit for a few minutes, and then work out the gum with a fork or comb. The oils in the peanut butter dissolve the gums in the chewing gum.

- **Noxzema Deep Cleansing Cream.** Rub a dollop of Noxzema Deep Cleansing Cream into chewing gum stuck in a carpet, let sit for a few minutes, and then work out the gum with a fork or comb. The cold cream dissolves the gums in the chewing gum.

- **Skin So Soft Body Lotion.** A drop of Skin So Soft Body Lotion, rubbed into chewing gum, dissolves the gum, enabling you to remove it from carpet easily with a fork or comb.

- **WD-40** and **Dawn Dishwashing Liquid.** To get chewing gum out of carpeting, spray WD-40 on the spot, wait a few minutes, and wipe clean. The petroleum distillates in the WD-40 dissolve the gums in the chewing gum. To remove the resulting oil stain from your carpet, scrub gently with a soapy solution made from a few drops of Dawn Dishwashing Liquid in one cup of water and blot well.

Hair Dye

- **Bounty Paper Towels, Kingsford's Corn Starch, Gillette Foamy,** and **Parsons' Ammonia.** If you spill hair dye on your carpet, don't let it dry; otherwise, you've permanently dyed your carpet. First, blot up as much of the stain as possible with Bounty Paper Towels. Then cover the stain with a mountain of Kingsford's Corn Starch. Let it sit for about fifteen minutes and then sweep it up. The cornstarch will absorb much of the excess dye. Then spray a dab of Gillette Foamy shaving cream on the spot and add a little water. Work it into the carpet with your fingers. Blot well with either a paper towel or soft cloth. Repeat as many times as necessary. If the hair dye is still in the carpet, mix one tablespoon Parsons' Ammonia in one-half cup water, wet the stain with the solution, then blot well. If that doesn't work, you can always buy a dozen boxes of Clairol Nice 'n Easy and dye the entire carpet to match (an excellent way to add years to gray carpeting).

Ink Stains

- **Alberto VO5 Hair Spray.** To remove ink spots from carpet, spray Alberto VO5 Hair Spray on the affected area and blot with a paper towel or soft cloth until the stain comes up. The acetone in Alberto VO5 Hair Spray removes indelible marker and ballpoint pen marks from carpet.

- **Huggies Baby Wipes.** Use a Huggies Baby Wipe to gently rub an ink stain on carpeting and remove the spot (unless the stain is indelible ink).

- **Purell Instant Hand Sanitizer.** Saturate an ink stain on carpeting with Purell Instant Hand Sanitizer and blot with a paper towel or soft cloth. Repeat as many times as necessary until the ink stain vanishes.

- **Smirnoff Vodka.** Saturate a soft cloth with Smirnoff Vodka and dab the stain carefully and repeatedly until you blot up all the ink. The alcohol in the vodka doubles as a solvent for ink.

Nail Polish

- **Cutex Nail Polish Remover.** This may sound obvious, but to remove nail polish from a carpet, simply dab the area with a cotton ball soaked in Cutex Nail Polish Remover and blot well. Just be sure to test an inconspicuous spot on the carpet first to make sure the nail polish remover doesn't discolor the fabric. To remove the nail polish remover from the carpet, apply a drop of Ivory Dishwashing Liquid and some water and blot dry with a few sheets of Bounty Paper Towel.

- **Gillette Foamy** and **Oral-B Toothbrush.** To get nail polish out of a carpet, squirt a little bit of Gillette Foamy shaving cream on the spot, use a clean, used Oral-B Toothbrush to gently scrub the spot with a little water, then blot with a paper towel.

- **Kingsford's Corn Starch.** If you spill a lot of nail polish on your carpet, start by blotting up as much of the nail polish by covering the stain with a mountain of Kingsford's Corn Starch. Let it sit for about ten minutes and then sweep it up. The cornstarch will absorb most of the liquid from the carpet. Then use one of solvents listed above or below.

- **Shout.** Spray Shout Stain Remover on the wet nail polish stain, let sit for three minutes, and then blot with a wet cloth. Repeat as many times as necessary.

- **WD-40.** Spray WD-40 over the nail polish stain and blot it up with a paper towel or a soft cloth. Repeat if necessary. The petroleum distillates in the WD-40 work as a solvent on the nail polish. To remove the resulting oil stain from your carpet, scrub gently with a soapy solution made from a few drops of Dawn Dishwashing Liquid in one cup of water and blot well.

- **Windex.** Spray Windex on the wet nail polish stain and then blot up the stain with a paper towel or a soft cloth. Repeat if needed.

Padding

- *USA Today.* In a pinch, you can place a few copies of *USA Today* under rugs and carpets to create padding.

Pet Stains

- **Canada Dry Club Soda** and **Arm & Hammer Baking Soda.** After blotting up as much of the pet stain as possible from the carpet, pour a small amount of Canada Dry Club Soda onto the stain, rub gently with a sponge, and then blot up with a paper towel. Let dry thoroughly, sprinkle on Arm & Hammer Baking Soda, let it sit for fifteen minutes, and then vacuum up. The baking soda neutralizes the odor. (For more ways to clean pet stains from carpeting, see page 64.)

- **Heinz White Vinegar.** To get rid of pet stains in carpet, you don't have to re-carpet or put the house up for sale. Mix one part Heinz White Vinegar with one part water in a sixteen-ounce trigger-spray bottle. Or use it full strength. Just saturate the spot on the carpet. Your house is going to smell like urine and vinegar for about three days (so you may want to take a quick trip to Hawaii), but once it dries, the vinegar completely deodorizes the stain—effectively and inexpensively. The vinegar also discourages your pet from returning to that spot.
- **20 Mule Team Borax.** Dampen the spot, rub in 20 Mule Team Borax, let dry, then vacuum or brush clean. Borax absorbs the nasty odors. (Before treating, test an inconspicuous spot on the carpeting with a paste made from 20 Mule Team Borax and water to make sure the borax does not remove any color from the carpet.)

Play-Doh

- **Canada Dry Club Soda** and **Oral-B Toothbrush.** To remove Play-Doh from carpeting, pour a little Canada Dry Club Soda over the dried Play-Doh. The liquid will soften the caked-on Play-Doh, and the effervescent action of the sodium bicarbonate will help loosen it from the carpet. If you can't peel the Play-Doh up with your fingers, use a clean, used Oral-B Toothbrush and then blot the wet spot with paper towel.

Silly Putty

- **WD-40** and **Dawn Dishwashing Liquid.** It may sound silly, but the way to get Silly Putty out of carpeting is by spraying the Silly Putty with WD-40. Let sit for a little bit then scrape with a fork or a clean, used Oral-B Toothbrush. The Silly Putty comes right out. To remove the grease stain from the WD-40 from the carpeting, use a few drops of Dawn Dishwashing Liquid and some water, scrub lightly, and then blot up with a paper towel.

Stains

- **Arm & Hammer Clean Shower.** To clean spots from carpet, spray Arm & Hammer Clean Shower on the stain, rub with a wet sponge, and let dry.

- **Canada Dry Club Soda.** Pour a small amount of Canada Dry Club Soda onto the stain, rub gently with a sponge, and then blot up with paper towels.

- **Gillette Foamy.** To remove stains from carpet, spray some Gillette Foamy shaving cream on the spot, scrub with a wet scrub brush, and then blot with a wet cloth to remove the extra foam.

- **Gunk Brake Cleaner.** To clean stubborn oil stains from carpet, spray the stained area thoroughly with Gunk Brake Cleaner, rub it in with a sponge, let it dry, and then vacuum. As the brake cleaner dries, it absorbs all moisture, allowing you to vacuum up the resulting powder with ease.

- **Huggies Baby Wipes.** To lift minor stains out of the carpet, gently rub the stain with a Huggies Baby Wipe.

- **Kingsford's Corn Starch.** To clean spills from the carpet, sprinkle Kingsford's Corn Starch over the spot, wait thirty minutes, and then vacuum clean.

- **Lestoil.** To clean lipstick stains from carpet, dampen a clean cloth with a few drops of Lestoil and gently dab the lipstick stain until it disappears.

- **Murphy Oil Soap.** To clean stains from carpet, mix one-quarter cup Murphy Oil Soap in one gallon of water. Using a clean sponge, dampen the spot with the solution and then blot with a clean cloth.

- **Pampers.** To blot up spills from carpet, place a Pampers disposable diaper facedown over the stain and place a few heavy books on top of the diaper to hold it in place for ten to fifteen minutes. The super-absorbent polymer flakes in Pampers absorb messy spills quickly.

- **Parsons' Ammonia.** To clean stubborn stains from carpet, mix two cups Parsons' Ammonia in one gallon of warm water, dampen a sponge with the solution, rub it into the stain gently, and then blot up with paper towels.

- **Shout.** Spray Shout Stain Remover on the stain, let sit for five minutes, and then wipe clean with a clean, wet cloth. The fragrance in Shout also freshens the carpet, and the stain remover prepares the stained area for the next time you have the carpet steam cleaned.

- **Smirnoff Vodka.** Spray Smirnoff Vodka on the stain, scrub gently with a brush, then blot up with a clean cloth or paper towel.

- **Spray 'n Wash.** Spray stains on the carpet with Spray 'n Wash, let sit for five minutes, and then wipe clean with a clean, wet cloth.

- **Tide.** Mix one cup liquid Tide with two cups water. Scrub the stain with this color-safe solution. Rinse with cool water, blot with a clean cloth or paper towel, and let dry.

- **20 Mule Team Borax.** Blot up the spill, sprinkle 20 Mule Team Borax to cover the area, let dry, and vacuum. (Before treating, test an inconspicuous spot on the carpeting with a paste made from 20 Mule Team Borax and water to make sure the borax does not remove any color from the carpet.)
- **WD-40.** To clean grease, tar, or oil-based paint from carpet, spray a clean cloth with WD-40 and scrub the spot. To remove the grease stain from the WD-40 from the carpeting, use a mixture of a few drops of Dawn Dishwashing Liquid and some water, scrub lightly, and then blot up with a paper towel.
- **Windex.** To clean food or juice stains from carpet, blot up as much of the stain as possible, spray the affected area with Windex, and then wipe clean with a cloth or paper towel. Windex has been known to clean cherry-flavored Kool-Aid from white carpeting.
- **Wonder Bread.** If you spill oil or grease on your carpet, rub a slice of Wonder Bread over the spot to absorb the oil or grease, then vacuum up the crumbs.

Static Electricity

- **Downy Fabric Softener.** To eliminate static electricity from carpets, pour one capful Downy Fabric Softener into a sixteen-ounce trigger-spray bottle, fill it the rest of the way with water, spray the carpets, and let dry. The antistatic elements in the fabric softener reduce the static electricity, preventing unexpected shocks.

Throw Rugs

- **Pink Pearl Erasers.** To prevent throw rugs from skidding across the floor, glue thin slices of a Pink Pearl Eraser to the bottom of the rug at the four corners.

Vomit

- **Arm & Hammer Baking Soda.** To neutralize vomit odor, sprinkle Arm & Hammer Baking Soda generously on the stained area, let sit for an hour, and then vacuum up.

Wine Stains

- **Canada Dry Club Soda.** To clean a wine stain from carpet, pour Canada Dry Club Soda over the stain, rub it in with a sponge, wait a few minutes, and blot it up with a clean cloth or paper towel.
- **Morton Salt.** Pour a mountain of Morton Salt over the wine stain to cover it completely, wait a few minutes for the salt to absorb the wine from the carpet, and then sweep up the salt. Repeat if necessary.
- **20 Mule Team Borax.** Blot up the spill, dissolve one cup 20 Mule Team Borax in one quart of water. Sponge in the solution, wait thirty minutes, shampoo the spotted area, let dry, and vacuum. (Before treating, test an inconspicuous spot on the carpeting with a paste made from 20 Mule Team Borax and water to make sure the borax does not remove any color from the carpet.)

Strange Facts

- The Pazyryk rug, the earliest known rug woven with pile, was discovered in a tomb in Siberia and dates back to 425 BCE.
- The Magic Carpet, a mythological flying rug, appears in the story "Aladdin," which was incorporated into *The Book of a Thousand and One Nights* in 1710 by its French translator, Antoine Galland, who heard the story from a Syrian storyteller named Youhenna Diab.

- The custom of rolling out the red carpet to welcome dignitaries and celebrities to formal events most likely originated with the New York Central Railroad, which rolled out crimson carpets to welcome passengers aboard its chic Twentieth Century Limited, known to railroad buffs as the world's greatest train, which ran between New York City and Chicago from 1902 to 1967.

- The United States produces some one billion square yards of rugs and carpeting every year.

- Georgia produces roughly 60 percent of all the carpeting and rugs produced in the United States.

- The song "Magic Carpet Ride" by the rock group Steppenwolf was a Top Five hit and can be heard in the soundtrack to the movies *Candy*, *Legal Eagles*, *Mask*, and *Apollo 13*.

- Comedian Howie Mandel began his career as a salesman in a carpet store.

- Actor Rupert Everett titled his autobiography *Red Carpets and Other Banana Skins*.

Cars

Air Freshener

- **Bounce.** Freshen the air in your car by placing a sheet of Bounce under the front seat.
- **Mennen Speed Stick.** Remove the lid from a Mennen Speed Stick and place it under the front seat of your car.

Axle Grease

- **Jif Peanut Butter.** In a pinch, you can grease a car or truck axle with Jif Peanut Butter (creamy, not chunky). American scientist George Washington Carver developed axle grease from peanuts. The oil in the peanut butter lubricates the axle.

Baby Seats

- **Arm & Hammer Baking Soda.** To clean stains from baby car seats, sprinkle Arm & Hammer Baking Soda on a damp sponge, wipe clean, and air-dry. The baking soda also deodorizes the car seat.

Batteries

- **Bayer Aspirin.** To revive a dead car battery, open the cell covers, drop two Bayer Aspirin tablets into each battery cell, and reseal. Let sit for no more than one hour and then start the engine. The acetylsalicylic acid in the aspirin combines with the sulfuric acid in the battery to allow one more charge to start the engine.

- **Wilson Tennis Balls.** If you need to disconnect your car's negative battery cable to work on the engine, you must prevent the live end of the battery cable connector from touching the car frame or other metal. To do this, cut a slit in a Wilson Tennis Ball and carefully insert the negative battery connector into the rubber ball. Because the rubber tennis ball does not conduct electricity, you can safely place the encapsulated battery connector aside.

Battery Corrosion

- **Arm & Hammer Baking Soda.** To clean corrosion from car battery terminals, mix two teaspoons Arm & Hammer Baking Soda in one cup of water, pour it over the battery cable connections, and then use a brush to scrub the heavily corroded areas. After the baking soda bubbles away the corrosion, wash the terminals clean with water.

- **Canada Dry Club Soda.** Pour Canada Dry Club Soda over the corrosion on battery terminals to bubble away the decay.

- **ChapStick.** After cleaning corrosion from car battery terminals, smear any flavor of ChapStick on the clean terminals to prevent the terminals from corroding again.

- **Coca-Cola.** To clean corrosion from car battery terminals, pour Coca-Cola over the terminals. The carbonic acid in the soft drink fizzes away the corrosion.

- **Oral-B Toothbrush.** When using any of the methods listed here to clean corrosion from car battery terminals, you can also use a clean, used Oral-B Toothbrush to scrub encrusted battery terminals clean.
- **Vaseline Petroleum Jelly.** To prevent car battery terminals from corroding, coat the terminals with Vaseline Petroleum Jelly.

Brakes

- **Bon Ami.** To silence squeaky brakes, toss a handful of Bon Ami cleanser at the brake pads. The Bon Ami cleans the brake dust from the brake pads.
- **Dawn Dishwashing Liquid.** To clean brake dust from car wheels, mix a few drops of Dawn Dishwashing Liquid in a bucket of water, sponge down the wheels with the solution, and then rinse clean with water. The dishwashing detergent cuts through grease.
- **Pam Cooking Spray.** To prevent brake dust from sticking to car rims, spray Pam Cooking Spray on the inner side of the tires and rims of your car. The brake dust will wash right off with a shot of high-pressure water at your local car wash.

Bumper Stickers

- **Conair Pro Styler 1600.** To remove a bumper sticker from a car bumper, blow hot air at it with a Conair Pro Styler 1600 hair dryer for a few minutes. Let the hot air soften the adhesive and then peel off the bumper sticker.
- **Cutex Nail Polish Remover.** To remove a bumper sticker, saturate a clean cloth with Cutex Nail Polish Remover, place it on the bumper sticker, wait five minutes for the acetone in the nail polish remover to dissolve the adhesive backing on the bumper sticker, and then peel off the bumper sticker.

- **Heinz White Vinegar.** Soak a clean cloth in Heinz White Vinegar and cover the bumper sticker for several minutes until the vinegar soaks in. The acetic acid in the vinegar dissolves the glue, allowing you to peel off the bumper sticker easily.
- **Miracle Whip.** To remove a bumper sticker from a car bumper, rub Miracle Whip over the entire bumper sticker. Let it sit for fifteen minutes to allow the Miracle Whip to permeate the bumper sticker and dissolve the glue. Then peel off the bumper sticker with ease.
- **Smirnoff Vodka.** To remove the adhesive residue left behind by a bumper sticker, rub the remaining glue with a soft, clean cloth soaked with Smirnoff Vodka.
- **Turtle Wax.** To make bumper stickers easier to remove, apply a thin coat of Turtle Wax to the spot before applying the bumper sticker.

Bumpers

- **Alberto VO5 Conditioning Hairdressing.** To shine chrome bumpers, squeeze a dollop of Alberto VO5 Conditioning Hairdressing onto a soft, dry cloth and buff the bumper lightly.
- **Arm & Hammer Baking Soda.** To clean chrome bumpers, sprinkle Arm & Hammer Baking Soda on a damp sponge, gently scrub the bumper, and wipe clean with a dry cloth.
- **Coca-Cola** and **Reynolds Wrap.** To remove rust spots from a chrome bumper, crumple up a sheet of Reynolds Wrap aluminum foil, dip it in Coca-Cola, and scrub the bumper.
- **Johnson's Baby Oil.** To rejuvenate the color and luster of a rubber car bumper, apply a few drops of Johnson's Baby Oil to a rag and rub it into the bumper. The baby oil restores the discolored bumper, revitalizes the black coloring, and as a bonus helps prevent insects from sticking to it. The sheen lasts for weeks.

- **S.O.S Steel Wool Soap Pads.** To clean a chrome bumper, scrub it with a dampened S.O.S Steel Wool Soap Pad and rinse clean.

Carpet

- **Arm & Hammer Baking Soda.** To deodorize carpeting in a car, sprinkle Arm & Hammer Baking Soda on the carpet, let sit for fifteen minutes, and then vacuum up.

CB Antennas

- **Wilson Tennis Balls.** To prevent a CB antenna from whipping around while you're driving, cut a small slit in a Wilson Tennis Ball and place the ball over your CB antenna.

Club Lock

- **Pam Cooking Spray.** To lubricate a club locking device, spray the keyhole and moving parts with Pam Cooking Spray.

Coolant Reservoirs

- **Ziploc Freezer Bags.** To temporarily repair a leaking plastic coolant or windshield washer reservoir, insert a one-gallon Ziploc Freezer Bag inside the reservoir, leaving the top rim of the bag outside the mouth of the reservoir. Fill the bag with coolant or windshield washer fluid, replace the cap (screwing it into position over the plastic), and trim off any excess plastic.

Dashboards

- **Johnson's Baby Oil.** To restore the color and luster of a dashboard, apply a few drops of Johnson's Baby Oil onto a rag, rub into the dashboard, and then buff dry with a soft cloth. The baby oil revitalizes the coloring, and the sheen lasts for weeks.

Dead Insects

- **Arm & Hammer Baking Soda.** To clean dead insects from the hood and windshield of a car or truck, sprinkle Arm & Hammer Baking Soda on a damp sponge, wipe down the hood or windshield, and then wipe clean with a dry cloth. The baking soda is a mild abrasive that removes insects without harming the finish of the car.

- **Bounce.** To clean lovebugs from the hood and windshield of a car or truck, wet down the vehicle and then rub the dead insects with a wet sheet of Bounce. The antistatic elements in the mildly abrasive sheet of Bounce make cleaning off the splattered lovebugs effortless.

- **Coca-Cola.** To clean insects off a car windshield, pour a can or bottle of carbonated Coca-Cola over the windshield and squeegee clean. Because Coke can etch car paint, be sure to keep the soda off of the car's paint.

- **Jif Peanut Butter.** To clean dried, dead insects from the hood and grill of your car, apply Jif Peanut Butter (creamy, not chunky), let sit for five minutes, and then wash clean with soapy water. The oils in the peanut butter dissolve the stickiness of the splattered bug carcasses.

- **L'eggs Sheer Energy Panty Hose.** Ball up a pair of clean, used L'eggs Sheer Energy Panty Hose, dampen it with soapy water, and use it to gently scrub dead insects from the hood of the car. The nylon is a mild abrasive that cleans off the bugs without scratching the finish.

- **Pam Cooking Spray.** To prevent insects from sticking to the hood and grill of car, spray a thin coat of Pam Cooking Spray on the hood and grill before you set out on your journey. The cooking oil prevents dead insects from adhering to the finish and makes washing them off much simpler. After the car trip, simply hose off the hood and grill.

- **WD-40.** Spray WD-40 on the hood and grill of the car before going on a long road trip so you can wipe dead bugs off easily without harming the finish. The WD-40 prevents dead insects from adhering to the finish.

Decals

- **Heinz White Vinegar.** To remove decals from an automobile, soak a cloth in Heinz White Vinegar and cover the decals for several minutes until the vinegar soaks in. The acetic acid dissolves the glues in the decals, allowing you to peel of the decal swith ease.
- **Pam Cooking Spray.** Spray the decal with a liberal coat of Pam Cooking Spray, let sit for several minutes allowing the oil to permeate the decal, and then peel off the decal.
- **Wesson Corn Oil.** Saturate the decal with Wesson Corn Oil, let sit for several minutes, and then peel off the decal.

Deodorizing

- **Arm & Hammer Baking Soda.** To deodorize the inside of a car, sprinkle Arm & Hammer Baking Soda throughout the interior of the car, use a soft-bristled hand broom to brush the baking soda into the seats and carpet, let sit for one hour, and vacuum well. The baking soda neutralizes odors, leaving the inside of the car smelling fresh.
- **Maxwell House Coffee.** Pour one cup fresh, unused Maxwell House Coffee grounds into a small container or box without a lid or cover and place the container under the front seat or on the floor of the backseat. Coffee grounds absorb odors.

Doors and Locks

- **Conair Pro Styler 1600.** If the lock on a car door freezes, before calling a locksmith, aim a Conair Pro Styler 1600 hair dryer set on hot at the keyhole to gently thaw the frozen lock.

- **Glad Flexible Straws.** To defrost a frozen lock on a car, insert one end of a Glad Flexible Straw into the key slot and exhale a few times into the other end. The hot air should easily thaw the lock.
- **Pam Cooking Spray.** To lubricate a squeaky car door, spray Pam Cooking Spray on the hinges and wipe off any excess oil with a dry cloth or paper towel.
- **Pam Cooking Spray.** To prevent car doors from freezing shut in the winter, spray the rubber gaskets with Pam Cooking Spray. The vegetable oil seals out water without harming the gaskets.
- **Vaseline Petroleum Jelly.** If the car key doesn't open the car door, rub a little Vaseline Petroleum Jelly on the key before inserting it into the lock. The petroleum jelly will lubricate the tumblers.
- **WD-40.** To lubricate a squeaky car door, spray WD-40 on the hinges and wipe off any excess oil with a dry cloth or paper towel.
- **Wesson Corn Oil.** To prevent car doors from freezing shut in the winter, rub the gaskets with Wesson Corn Oil to seal out water without harming the gaskets.
- **Wilson Tennis Balls.** To keep your car door open without wasting the battery, wedge a Wilson Tennis Ball into the door-jamb to depress the interior light switch.

Emergency Reflectors

- **Maxwell House Coffee.** To make convenient emergency reflectors, wrap reflector tape around a couple of empty Maxwell House Coffee cans and store them in the trunk of your car for emergencies.

Engine Parts

- **Coca-Cola.** To clean grease and grime off car engine parts, soak the engine parts in Coca-Cola for thirty minutes and then rinse clean. The phosphoric acid in the Coke dissolves the grease and grime.

- **Easy-Off Oven Cleaner.** To clean stubborn grease and grime from engine parts (such as valve covers and cast-iron cylinder heads), spray the disconnected parts with Easy-Off Oven Cleaner, let the parts sit for ten minutes, and then hose clean. (Just be sure to do this in a well-ventilated place—or outdoors—and wear protective eyewear and rubber gloves. Do not use Easy-Off Oven Cleaner on aluminum parts.)

Fan Belts

- **L'eggs Sheer Energy Panty Hose.** If the fan belt breaks on your car while you're on the road and unable to get help, cut off one leg from a pair of clean, used L'eggs Sheer Energy Panty Hose and use it to temporarily replace the fan belt.

- **Vaseline Petroleum Jelly.** To lubricate a fan belt, put a small dab of Vaseline Petroleum Jelly on the inside edges of the belt, start the car, and let the engine idle for a couple of minutes. The Vaseline Petroleum Jelly renews the life of the belt, grips the pulleys better than the spray-on lubricants, and eliminates squeals and slippage.

Frozen Engine

- **Conair Pro Styler 1600.** To start a frozen car engine, carefully blow hot air with a Conair Pro Styler 1600 hair dryer onto the carburetor.

Gas Station Pumps

- **Wilson Tennis Balls.** When the little clamp is broken or missing from the handle of a gas station pump, wedge a Wilson Tennis Ball in the handle of the gas pump to hold it in place, so you don't have to hold the pump and inhale the gas fumes.

Gas Tanks

- **Wrigley's Spearmint Gum.** To repair a leaking gas tank temporarily, chew a piece of Wrigley's Spearmint Gum until all the sugar is gone and then use the gum to patch the hole.

Hoods

- **Wilson Tennis Balls.** To soften the blow to your head if you bump it on the latch under the hood, carefully cut a slot in a Wilson Tennis Ball and place it over the latch.

Hubcaps

- **Arm & Hammer Baking Soda.** To clean chrome hubcaps, sprinkle Arm & Hammer Baking Soda on a damp sponge, gently scrub the hubcaps, and wipe clean with a dry cloth.
- **Coca-Cola.** To remove a stubborn hubcap, take a bottle or can of Coca-Cola, uncap it or pop it open, shake it up while holding your thumb over the opening, and then spray the Coca-Cola around the hubcap. Let it sit for a few minutes to let the Real Thing soften any grease and grime, and then remove the hubcap with ease. Avoid getting the Coke on the car's paint.
- **Efferdent.** To clean chrome hubcaps, drop four Efferdent tablets into a sixteen-ounce trigger-spray bottle, fill the bottle with water, and let the tablets dissolve completely. Shake well and then spray the blue solution on the hubcaps. Let sit for ten minutes, then rinse clean with water.

Ice

- **Dannon Yogurt.** To scrape ice from a car windshield, use a clean, empty Dannon Yogurt cup as a scraper. The rim of the plastic cup is sharp and firm enough to chip away ice and frozen snow.

- **Glad Trash Bags.** To prevent ice from forming on a car windshield overnight, cut open a Glad Trash Bag, place it over the entire windshield, and close the car doors over the edges of the bag to hold it in place. When you're ready to drive, brush off any snow and peel off the plastic bag.

- **Heinz White Vinegar.** To avoid getting an icy car windshield overnight, mix twelve ounces Heinz White Vinegar and four ounces water in a sixteen-ounce trigger-spray bottle and spray the glass with the solution. The acetic acid helps prevent ice from forming on the glass.

- **MasterCard.** In a pinch, use a plastic credit card to scrape ice and frost off a car windshield. Just be careful not to scrape or damage the magnetic strip on the back of the card.

Ignition Keys

- **Pam Cooking Spray.** If the key doesn't slide easily into the ignition, spray the teeth of the key with Pam Cooking Spray and slide the key in and out of the lock repeatedly to lubricate the tumblers.

- **Vaseline Petroleum Jelly.** To get a key to work in the ignition, rub a little Vaseline Petroleum Jelly on your key before inserting it into the lock. The petroleum jelly will lubricate the tumblers so the ignition starts.

- **WD-40.** If a key fails to start the ignition, spray a small amount of WD-40 into the keyhole and insert the key several times to lubricate the tumblers.

Interiors

- **Huggies Baby Wipes.** To clean sticky messes from the cup holder, dashboard, and steering wheel, simply use Huggies Baby Wipes.
- **Johnson's Baby Oil.** To shine and rejuvenate the dashboard of a car, put a few drops of Johnson's Baby Oil on a clean, soft cloth and buff. The baby oil produces an inexpensive, long-lasting shine that outdoes Armor All.
- **Scrubbing Bubbles.** Spray Scrubbing Bubbles on dirty automobile upholstery, door panels, dashboard, and carpeting. Scrub gently with a soft brush and wipe clean with a damp cloth. The scrubbing bubbles do a magnificent job cleaning the dirt and grease.

Oil

- **Clorox Bleach.** To drain oil from a car with a drain plug angled toward the frame, cut off the bottom of a Clorox Bleach jug diagonally to make a funnel with one side taller than the other, so you can bank the flowing oil into the oil pan.
- **Glad Trash Bags.** To avoid a mess when changing the oil filter, loosen the filter, place a Glad Trash Bag around it, and then continue unscrewing the filter, allowing it to fall into the bag.

Paint

- **Comet.** To deoxidize dull paint on a car, sprinkle Comet cleanser lightly onto the car while washing, rinse well, and wax the car.
- **Crayola Crayons.** To repair a scratch on an automobile, find a matching color Crayola Crayon, warm the wax, and work it into the scratch.
- **Easy-Off Oven Cleaner.** To remove lettering painted on the side of a truck, spray the letters with Easy-Off Oven Cleaner, let sit for ten to fifteen minutes, and then spray with the highest pressure from the nozzle of a garden hose.

- **Liquid Paper.** To touch up a ding on a white car, use Liquid Paper as touch-up paint. (If the Liquid Paper is too thick, dilute it by mixing in a few drops of Cutex Nail Polish Remover.)
- **Maybelline Express Finish Nail Polish.** To touch up a ding in the side of your car, match the color with the appropriate non-sheer Maybelline Express Finish Nail Polish and paint the spot with a thin coat.

Parking

- **Wilson Tennis Balls.** To make parking a car in your garage easier and to avoid hitting the garage wall accidentally, drill a small hole in a Wilson Tennis Ball and insert an eye screw into the hole. Hang the ball with a string from the garage ceiling so the ball touches the windshield at the spot where you should stop your car.

Polishing

- **Colgate Regular Flavor Toothpaste.** To polish scratches out of a car's finish, squeeze a dollop of Colgate Regular Flavor Toothpaste onto a clean cloth, gently rub over the scratch marks, and then buff. The toothpaste is a mild abrasive that won't scratch the paint. After all, toothpaste is strong enough to clean your teeth without scratching the enamel.
- **L'eggs Sheer Energy Panty Hose.** Ball up a clean, used pair of L'eggs Sheer Energy Panty Hose dipped in soapy water to polish your car. The nylon is a mild abrasive that does a magnificent job cleaning dead bugs off the hood without scratching the finish. (If you'd really like to be the talk of the neighborhood, wear the panty hose and roll yourself all over the car, having a grand old time.)
- **Pledge.** To give your car a quick, long-lasting, protective, shiny wax job, spray Pledge furniture polish on the car and buff

with a clean, soft cloth. Pledge contains carnauba wax, the same ingredient found in many car waxes.

- **Skin So Soft Body Lotion.** To wax your clean car, squeeze Skin So Soft Body Lotion onto a clean, soft cloth and buff the car. Skin So Soft not only gives the car a terrific shine, but the body lotion also causes water and dirt to sheet off of the car.

Price-Tag Sheets

- **Pam Cooking Spray.** Spray the price-tag sheet with a generous coat of Pam Cooking Spray, let sit for several minutes so the oil can permeate the paper, and then scrape off the sheet.
- **Wesson Corn Oil.** To remove the price-tag sheet from an automobile, saturate the paper sheet with Wesson Corn Oil. Let it sit for ten minutes and then scrape away. The oil dissolves the gums in the glue.

Radiators

- **Cascade.** To fix a leaky radiator, put a pinch of Cascade dishwasher detergent in the radiator, fill with water, and drive away. The grains of dishwasher detergent get sucked into any small holes, blocking them.
- **McCormick Black Pepper.** To stop a small leak in a radiator, add one teaspoon McCormick Black Pepper to your radiator. The pepper sinks to the bottom, finds its way into small holes, and expands, filling them.
- **Wrigley's Spearmint Gum** and **Band-Aid Bandages.** To temporarily repair a small hole or crack in a radiator hose, chew a stick of Wrigley's Spearmint Gum until all the sugar is gone and then use the gum to patch the small hole. Secure the piece of gum in place by wrapping a Band-Aid Bandage around gum and hose.

Sparkplugs

- **WD-40.** To revive sparkplugs on a rainy or humid day, spray WD-40 on the sparkplug wires. WD-40 displaces water, keeping moisture away from your sparkplugs so they will work properly. WD-40 also prevents corrosion of sparkplug wires and removes carbon residue from the sparkplugs.

Spray Paint

- **Pledge.** If vandals graffiti your car with spray paint, spray Pledge furniture polish on the paint within twenty-four hours (before the polymers in the paint fully set), wipe clean with a soft cloth, and wash the car immediately.

Static Electricity

- **Downy Fabric Softener.** To eliminate static electricity inside a car, mix one teaspoon Downy Fabric Softener and two cups water in a sixteen-ounce trigger-spray bottle. Spray the fabric and carpeting inside the car and let dry. The antistatic elements in the fabric softener will prevent those annoying shocks from the static electricity.

Striping

- **Johnson's Baby Oil.** To rejuvenate dull chrome or black rubber striping along the sides of a car, put a few drops of Johnson's Baby Oil on a paper towel and rub the striping to give it a nice shine.

Taillights

- **Scotch Packaging Tape.** To repair a broken taillight temporarily, use clear Scotch Packaging Tape to hold the see-through red plastic together.

Tar

- **Coca-Cola.** To remove tar from a car without damaging the finish, saturate a clean cloth with Coca-Cola and use it to gently rub the spot. Wash clean with water.
- **Coppertone.** Pour a dollop of Coppertone sunscreen into a soft, clean cloth and rub the sunscreen into the tar stain until it glides off the car.
- **Noxzema Deep Cleansing Cream.** To remove tar spots from a car, apply Noxzema Deep Cleansing Cream to a cloth and rub the stain until it comes clean. The emollients in the cold cream dissolve the natural adhesives in the tar.
- **Shout.** To clean tar from the side of your car, spray the spot with Shout Stain Remover, wipe clean with a soft, clean cloth, wash off any residual Shout with soapy water, and rinse clean.
- **Skin So Soft Body Lotion.** Cover the tar stain with Skin So Soft Body Lotion, let sit for ten minutes, and then wipe off the tar with a soft cloth.
- **WD-40.** To clean tar from a car, spray WD-40 directly on the tar, immediately wipe the tar off, wash off any residual WD-40 with soapy water, and rinse clean.

Tires

- **Dawn Dishwashing Liquid.** To find a puncture in a tire, mix a few drops of Dawn Dishwashing Liquid with water and brush the soapy solution on a leaky tire. The bubbles will indicate the exact location of the puncture. Also, be sure to check around the tire valve.
- **Krazy Glue.** To temporarily patch a small hole in a flat tire, cover the puncture with Krazy Glue and let dry.
- **Play-Doh.** To temporarily stop a slow leak from a tire, squash some Play-Doh into the puncture. The heat from the pavement

and friction from the road will bake the Play-Doh into the hole and seal the puncture for the interim, giving you enough time to reach a safe location where you can change the tire.

Traction

- **Clorox Bleach.** To create traction for a car or truck stuck in snow or on ice, pour a little Clorox Bleach directly from the jug over the affected tire, wait one minute, and then try to move the car. The bleach chemically reacts with the rubber tire, making it stickier, increasing the traction.
- **Maxwell House Coffee.** Unused cat box filler, stored in empty Maxwell House Coffee cans, can be stored in the trunk of your car and used to create traction under the wheels of the car should it get stuck in snow or on ice.
- **Tidy Cats.** To create emergency traction for an automobile stuck in snow or on ice, keep a bag of unused Tidy Cats cat box filler in your car trunk to be poured under the tire in case such a situation arises.

Trailer Hitches

- **Wilson Tennis Balls.** Cut a hole in a Wilson Tennis Ball and put it over a trailer hitch to protect the metal coupler from rain and snow.

Tree Sap

- **Jif Peanut Butter.** To clean tree sap from the hood of a car, cover the pine pitch with Jif Peanut Butter, let sit for five to ten minutes, and then wipe clean with a soft cloth. The peanut oil dissolves the natural gum in the sap.
- **Miracle Whip.** To remove fresh pine tree sap from a car's finish, rub some Miracle Whip on the sap, let sit for ten minutes,

and then use a clean, soft cloth and some elbow grease to wipe the spot clean. Miracle Whip removes sap without stripping the car's finish.

- **Purell Instant Hand Sanitizer.** To clean pine pitch from a car or truck, cover the sticky tree sap with Purell Instant Hand Sanitizer and wipe clean with a soft cloth. Purell dissolves the natural adhesives in pine pitch from a car like magic, without harming the paint.

Upholstery

- **Budweiser.** To clean leather upholstery, wash the leather with stale Budweiser beer. Then wash the leather with saddle soap and water and buff dry with a soft cloth. Let the smell of beer air out of the car before driving anywhere. Otherwise, you may have some explaining to do if you're pulled over by the police.

- **Heinz White Vinegar.** Clean leather upholstery with a mixture of equal parts Heinz White Vinegar and water. Then wash the leather with saddle soap and water and buff dry with a soft cloth.

- **Ivory Dishwashing Liquid.** Mix two tablespoons Ivory Dishwashing Liquid and two quarts hot water and use the solution to scrub vinyl upholstery.

- **Noxzema Deep Cleansing Cream.** To clean vinyl car upholstery, apply Noxzema Deep Cleansing Cream to a soft cloth and wipe down the vinyl surfaces.

- **Scrubbing Bubbles.** To clean vinyl upholstery, spray with Scrubbing Bubbles, let foam, scrub, and then wipe clean with a clean, soft cloth.

- **Silly Putty.** To lift dirt from seats, mold Silly Putty into whatever shape will best fit into crevices and pat.

- **Skin So Soft Body Lotion.** To clean vinyl car upholstery, apply Skin So Soft Body Lotion to a soft cloth and wipe down the seats and other vinyl surfaces.

Washing

- **Clairol Herbal Essences Shampoo.** To wash your car, add two capfuls Clairol Herbal Essences Shampoo to a bucket of water and soap up your car with the biodegradable suds.
- **Dawn Dishwashing Liquid.** Mix one teaspoon Dawn Dishwashing Liquid and one gallon water and use the soapy solution to wash your car. Dawn cuts through grease. But it also removes some or all of the protective wax, so you'll have to re-wax the car.
- **Downy Fabric Softener.** Mix one-third cup Downy Fabric Softener and one gallon water, fill a trigger-spray bottle with the solution, spray a two-foot square section of the car or truck exterior, wait ten seconds, and buff dry with paper towels or a leather chamois cloth. Continue working in two-foot square sections, so the fabric softener solution doesn't dry on the car, until the entire vehicle is clean.
- **Murphy Oil Soap.** Squirt Murphy Oil Soap on a clean, soft cloth and wipe the exterior of the car clean. Murphy Oil Soap leaves a shine like car wax, and water will bead on the coating.

Waxing

- **Armor All.** To wax a car easily and effortlessly, spray Armor All on the exterior and buff it off with a soft rag. The Armor All gives the car a glimmering shine.
- **Jif Peanut Butter.** To remove white car wax from the black rubber trim and moldings of a car, wipe Jif Peanut Butter on the trim or molding and then wipe clean. The oils in the peanut

butter remove the wax, returning the rubber to its original rich, black color.

- **Kingsford's Corn Starch.** When waxing and buffing a car, sprinkle one tablespoon Kingsford's Corn Starch on the cloth you're using to buff. The cornstarch absorbs excess wax, giving your car a beautiful shine.

Whitewalls

- **Easy-Off Oven Cleaner.** To clean whitewalls on tires, spray Easy-Off Oven Cleaner on the whitewalls, wait two minutes, and then rinse off with a high pressure hose. The oven cleaner leaves the whitewalls looking like new. (When using oven cleaner, be sure to work in a well-ventilated place and wear protective eyewear and rubber gloves. Do not use Easy-Off Oven Cleaner on aluminum or chrome.)
- **Skin So Soft Body Lotion.** Apply a dollop of Skin So Soft Body Lotion to an abrasive sponge and scrub the whitewalls clean.
- **Soft Scrub.** Spray Soft Scrub cleanser on the whitewalls and scrub with an abrasive sponge. The ingredients in Soft Scrub—bleach, soft grit, and soap—brighten whitewalls and do not damage or dull chrome.
- **Tide.** Mix one-quarter cup liquid Tide and one gallon water, dip a scrub brush in the solution, and scour whitewall tires clean.
- **WD-40.** Spray dirty whitewalls with WD-40, wait ten seconds, and wipe off the dirt and grime with paper towels or an abrasive sponge. Rinse clean with water.

Windows

- **Huggies Baby Wipes.** To clean car windows, simply wipe the glass with Huggies Baby Wipes. (For more ways to clean car windows, see "Windshields" on the next page.)

Windshields

- **Canada Dry Club Soda.** To remove grease and grime from a car windshield, keep a trigger-spray bottle filled with Canada Dry Club Soda in the trunk of your car. Spray the glass with the carbonated soft drink and wipe clean.

- **Coca-Cola.** To clean road film from a car windshield, open a can or bottle of Coca-Cola, pour the Real Thing over the grease and grime on the windshield, being careful not to let the Coca-Cola come in contact with the paint. Then rinse clean with water.

- **Gillette Foamy.** To prevent your windshield from fogging up, rub a dab of Gillette Foamy shaving cream inside your car windshield and wipe off with a clean cloth.

- **Listerine.** To clean the inside of a car windshield, saturate a clean, soft cloth with Listerine antiseptic mouthwash and wipe clean.

- **Maybelline Express Finish Clear Nail Polish.** To fix a small chip in a car windshield, fill the hole with a few drops of Maybelline Express Finish Clear Nail Polish, let the nail polish dry, and then add a few more drops until the chip has been appropriately filled.

- **McCormick Cream of Tartar.** Sprinkle McCormick Cream of Tartar on the windshield and scrub with a damp sponge to clean off grease and grime. Rinse clean with water.

- **Parsons' Ammonia.** Mix one-half cup Parsons' Ammonia and one gallon water and dampen a sponge in the solution to clean grime or road film from a windshield.

- **Stayfree Maxi Pads.** To wipe a windshield clean, peel the adhesive strip from the back of a Stayfree Maxi Pad, adhere the pad to the palm of your hand, and use it to wipe down the windshield.

Windshield Wiper Fluid

- **Smirnoff Vodka** and **Ivory Dishwashing Liquid.** To make your own windshield wiper fluid, mix three cups Smirnoff Vodka, one quart water, and two teaspoons Ivory Dishwashing Liquid.

Windshield Wipers

- **Heinz White Vinegar.** To prolong the life of automobile wiper blades, use a sponge saturated with Heinz White Vinegar to clean the wiper blades. The vinegar dissolves any residue and keeps the rubber healthy.

Wires

- **Wrigley's Spearmint Gum** and **Reynolds Wrap.** To temporarily reattach a loose wire under the hood, chew a stick of Wrigley's Spearmint Gum until the sugar is gone, stick the well-chewed wad of gum on the connections and then wrap a piece of Reynolds Wrap (as if it were a piece of tape) around the gum to hold it in place.

Strange Facts

- In September 1957, after years of research and millions of dollars in investment costs, the Ford Motor Company introduced a new line of mid-size automobiles—the Edsel, named after the only son of company founder Henry Ford. Unfortunately, at least half of the Edsels purchased were lemons, with problems including malfunctioning doors, faulty brakes and power steering, poor paint jobs, frozen transmissions, and push buttons that stuck in the steering wheel. After three years, Ford had sold only 110,000 Edsels, losing an estimated 350 million dollars.

- In the 1960s television sitcom *Get Smart*, Control agent Maxwell Smart drives a Red Sunbeam Tiger, a blue Kharman Ghia convertible, and a 1969 Opel GT sports car.

- Turtle Wax, Inc., is frequently offered supplies of turtles. Former company president Carl Schmid would refuse these offers politely and point out that the turtles in Turtle Wax are like the horses in horseradish.

- In the 1968 movie *Bullit*, Steve McQueen's Dodge Charger loses three hubcaps during the long car chase scene, but when he crashes at the end of the chase, three more hubcaps fly off the car.

- In 1973, former General Motors executive John De Lorean, creator of the Pontiac GTO, left his $650,000 job, raised some $175 million in financing, and in 1974 formed the De Lorean Motor Co., building his car factory in Northern Ireland. In 1982, De Lorean was videotaped in a government sting operation attempting to broker a $24 million cocaine deal to rescue his financially troubled company. (In the 1985 movie *Back to the Future*, starring Michael J. Fox, a De Lorean car was used as the time machine.)

- In 1977, car manufacturers made 9.3 million cars. That same year, car manufacturers recalled 10.4 million cars.

Cats and Dogs

Bathing

- **Johnson's Baby Shampoo.** To shampoo your dog or cat, use Johnson's Baby Shampoo and then rinse clean. The fragrant baby shampoo leaves your pet smelling fresh, and it won't hurt your pet's eyes.
- **Kingsford's Corn Starch.** To give your pet a dry shampoo, rub Kingsford's Corn Starch into your dog or cat's fur, then brush out.
- **Murphy Oil Soap.** Add a few drops of Murphy Oil Soap in your dog's or cat's bath water to moisturize and soften its skin and coat. Murphy Oil Soap is pure vegetable oil soap and will not harm animals.
- **S.O.S Steel Wool Soap Pads.** To avoid clogging the bathtub or sink drain when bathing a dog or cat, ball up an S.O.S Steel Wool Soap Pad and shove it in the drain opening to catch stray pet hairs.

Catnip Balls

- **L'eggs Sheer Energy Panty Hose.** To make a catnip ball, cut off the foot of a clean, used pair of L'eggs Sheer Energy Panty hose, stuff it with catnip, and knot it closed.

Fleas

- **Alberto VO5 Conditioner.** To kill fleas on dogs or cats, bathe the animal, pour Alberto VO5 Conditioner on its coat, rub in thoroughly, and rinse clean. The hair conditioner kills fleas and gives your pet's coat a wonderful shine as well. (For ways to rid your home of fleas, see page 174.)

- **Dawn Dishwashing Liquid.** To kill fleas on a dog, lather up the dog with Dawn Dishwashing Liquid and some water, rub in thoroughly, and wait five minutes. Then rinse well. The dishwashing liquid destroys the fleas' exoskeletons, killing them.

- **Miracle Whip.** To repel fleas from a cat, cover the cat with a thick coat of Miracle Whip, rub it into your pet's skin and fur, and then wipe the animal clean with a damp towel. The cat will continue the bathing process by licking itself and the Miracle Whip clean, resulting in a clean coat that repels fleas.

- **Skin So Soft Bath Oil.** To prevent fleas on a dog, mix two ounces Skin So Soft Bath Oil in one gallon of water, pour the solution into a trigger-spray bottle, and spray the mixture on the dog. Skin So Soft repels fleas for at least one week and also leaves the animal's coat shiny.

Food Bowls

- **McCormick Ground Cinnamon.** To keep ants out of pet food left in a dog or cat's food bowl, sprinkle McCormick Ground Cinnamon around the pet's food. Cinnamon repels ants.

- **Vaseline Petroleum Jelly.** To repel ants from a pet's food bowl, rub a small dab of Vaseline Petroleum Jelly around the bottom rim of the bowl.

Furniture

- **Bounce.** To keep a cat from walking along the tops of chairs or sofas, rub the spot with a clean, used sheet of Bounce. The fragrance in Bounce repels cats.
- **Reynolds Wrap.** To prevent a cat from walking across your sofa or other furniture, place a sheet of Reynolds Wrap aluminum foil across the item. When your cat tries to walk on the aluminum foil, the metallic rustling sound will quickly frighten your pet away.
- **Tabasco Pepper Sauce.** To stop a dog from chewing wooden furniture around the house, put a few drops of Tabasco Pepper Sauce on a clean cloth and rub the tangy sauce into the wooden furniture. When the Tabasco Pepper Sauce dries, you won't smell it at all, but your dog, with its keen sense of smell, will stay away from the furniture.

Garbage Cans

- **McCormick Black Pepper.** To keep dogs and cats out of your garbage cans, sprinkle McCormick Black Pepper around the cans. The animals, with their keen sense of smell, catch a whiff of the pepper and take off for someone else's garbage cans.
- **Parsons' Ammonia.** To stop neighborhood dogs and cats from invading your garbage cans, sprinkle a few drops of Parsons' Ammonia around garbage cans. The foul, pungent fumes repel animals.
- **WD-40.** To keep dogs out of trash cans, give the trash cans a thin coat of WD-40. The unique fragrance of WD-40 repels animals.

Houseplants

- **Maxwell House Coffee.** To prevent a cat from having a love affair with your houseplants, add used Maxwell House Coffee grounds to the top of the potting soil. Kitty will be turned off by the scent of coffee. The coffee grounds, filled with nutrients, also fertilize the plants.

Lawns and Gardens

- **Arm & Hammer Baking Soda.** Is a neighborhood dog urinating on your lawn and causing yellow burn spots? In a watering can, mix one cup Arm & Hammer Baking Soda in one gallon of water and water the urine spots with the mixture every three days, saturating the area. The baking soda deodorizes the urine so the offending dog will no longer recognize the "marked territory," and the sodium bicarbonate neutralizes the acidity of the urine so the grass can regain its color.

- **Bounce.** To keep cats out of your yard, hang fresh sheets of Bounce on your fence posts, shrubs, or trees. The fragrance of oleander in Bounce is a natural cat repellent. Mist the Bounce sheets every few days with water from a trigger-spray bottle to reawaken the powerful scent.

- **French's Mustard, Gold Medal Flour,** and **McCormick Ground (Cayenne) Red Pepper.** To repel cats from your yard with a harmless, all-natural solution, mix two tablespoons French's Mustard, two tablespoons Gold Medal Flour, one tablespoon McCormick Ground (Cayenne) Red Pepper, and two cups water in a sixteen-ounce trigger-spray bottle. Shake vigorously and spray the spicy solution around flowerbeds, vegetable gardens, or the perimeter of your yard.

- **Heinz White Vinegar.** To repel cats naturally, fill a trigger-spray bottle with Heinz White Vinegar and spray around the border of the garden or the perimeter of your yard.

- **Maxwell House Coffee.** To repel cats from your garden and prevent them from digging up the soil, fertilize the plants around your garden with used Maxwell House Coffee grounds. Coffee grounds are packed with nutrients that your plants love, but cats are turned off by the scent of coffee. And yes, decaf works equally well.
- **Tabasco Pepper Sauce, McCormick Garlic Powder,** and **Dawn Dishwashing Liquid.** To repel cats and dogs from your yard, mix two tablespoons Tabasco Pepper Sauce, two tablespoons McCormick Garlic Powder, a few drops Dawn Dishwashing Liquid, and two cups water in a sixteen-ounce trigger-spray bottle. Spray the spicy solution around the perimeter of your yard to keep cats and dogs away.

Litter Boxes

- **Arm & Hammer Baking Soda.** To deodorize a cat litter box, cover the bottom of the litter box with a one-quarter-inch layer of Arm & Hammer Baking Soda and then add the litter on top.
- **Glad Trash Bags.** If you're tired of cleaning the cat litter box or you've run out of cat box liners, place the cat litter box inside a Glad Trash Bag and pour the cat box filler on top of the plastic covering the open side of the box. To clean, lift out the bag, turn it inside out, and discard.
- **20 Mule Team Borax.** To control the odors created in a cat litter box, mix one and a half cups 20 Mule Team Borax to every five pounds of cat box filler.

Pet Dishes

- **Frisbee.** When camping, hiking, or traveling, a Frisbee can double as a food or water dish for your dog or cat.

Pet Hair

- **Alberto VO5 Hair Spray** and **Kleenex Tissues.** To remove pet hair from furniture, spray a Kleenex Tissue with Alberto VO5 Hair Spray and pat the furniture with the sticky tissue to pick up the shed hairs.

- **Bounce.** To pick up shed pet hair, rub the area with a clean, used sheet of Bounce, which magnetically attracts all the loose hairs.

- **Scotch Packaging Tape.** To clean pet hair from upholstered furniture, take a strip of Scotch Packaging Tape, wrap it around your hand sticky-side out, and pat the upholstery.

- **Silly Putty.** Make a ball of Silly Putty, flatten it into a pancake, and gently pat the upholstery. You'll have furry Silly Putty, but a clean couch.

Pooper Scoopers

- **Clorox Bleach.** To make a pooper scooper, cut an empty, clean Clorox Bleach jug in half and use the half with the handle to scoop up whatever mess your pet makes.

- **Ziploc Storage Bags.** To scoop up presents left behind by your cat or dog, turn a Ziploc Storage Bag inside out, put your hand inside the bag like a glove, pick up the mess, pulling the bag right-side out again, seal shut, and discard.

Skunk

- **Arm & Hammer Baking Soda, Hydrogen Peroxide,** and **Dawn Dishwashing Liquid.** To remove the smell of skunk from a dog, mix one-quarter cup Arm & Hammer Baking Soda, one quart hydrogen peroxide, and two tablespoons Dawn Dishwashing Liquid in a large bowl. Immediately wash the dog with the foaming mixture.

- **Campbell's Tomato Juice.** If a skunk sprays your pet, pour Campbell's Tomato Juice over your pet and rub it in. Sponge the tomato juice over the animal's face. Rinse and repeat. The acids from the tomatoes neutralize skunk odor.
- **Listerine.** To remove the smell of skunk from a dog, apply Listerine antiseptic mouthwash full-strength to the affected areas, making sure to avoid getting Listerine in the animal's eyes or ears. Then wash the dog with soap and water and rinse clean. The antiseptic in Listerine neutralizes skunk odor.
- **Massengill Disposable Douche.** To deodorize a dog sprayed by a skunk, wash the animal with Massengill Disposable Medicated Douche to neutralize the pungent odor and then rinse well.
- **Playtex Living Gloves.** If you're attempting to wash skunk odor from a cat or dog, wear Playtex Living Gloves to avoid getting the skunk smell all over yourself.
- **ReaLemon.** Wash down your pet with several bottles of ReaLemon lemon juice. The acids in lemon juice eliminate skunk odor.

Stains

- **Canada Dry Club Soda** and **Arm & Hammer Baking Soda.** After blotting up as much of the pet stain as possible from the carpet, pour a small amount of Canada Dry Club Soda onto the stain, rub gently with a sponge, and then blot up with a paper towel. Let dry thoroughly, sprinkle on Arm & Hammer Baking Soda, let sit for fifteen minutes, and then vacuum up. The baking soda neutralizes the odor.
- **Heinz White Vinegar.** If your pet stains your carpet, you don't have to re-carpet or put the house up for sale. Mix one part Heinz White Vinegar to one part water in a sixteen-ounce trigger-spray bottle. Or use the vinegar full strength. Just satu-

rate the spot on the carpet. Your house is going to smell like urine and vinegar for about three days (so you may want to take a quick trip to Hawaii), but once the vinegar dries, it completely deodorizes the stain—effectively and inexpensively. The vinegar also discourages your pet from returning to that spot.

- **Huggies Baby Wipes.** To clean pet urine from carpet, use a Huggies Baby Wipe to blot up the liquid.

- **Lysol All Purpose Cleaner** and **Parsons' Ammonia.** Mix one-half cup Lysol All Purpose Cleaner, one teaspoon Parsons' Ammonia, and one quart water. Use a sponge dipped in this solution to clean a pet accident from the carpet. This mixture also deodorizes the stain.

- **Pampers** and **Heinz White Vinegar.** Open a Pampers disposable diaper, place it facedown over the stain, and put some heavy books on top of the diaper. Let it sit for one hour. After the superabsorbent polymer flakes in the diaper soak up most of the urine, clean the remaining stain with Heinz White Vinegar. (See opposite page.)

- **Parsons' Ammonia.** After cleaning cat urine from carpet using Heinz White Vinegar (see opposite page), rub the spot with a cloth dampened in Parsons' Ammonia, both deodorizing the spot and discouraging the cat from urinating in that spot again.

- **20 Mule Team Borax.** Dampen the spot, rub in 20 Mule Team Borax, let dry, then vacuum or brush clean. Borax absorbs the nasty odors.

Strange Facts

- Scientists believe that the ancient Egyptians first domesticated cats as early as 3500 BCE to kill mice, rats, and snakes on farms and in grain storehouses.

- The ancient Egyptian goddess Bast had the head of a cat and the body of a woman. The Egyptians worshipped Bast as the goddess of love and fertility.

- Archeologists discovered an ancient cat cemetery in Egypt that contains more than 300,000 cat mummies.

- During the Middle Ages, Europeans considered cats evil and associated them with witchcraft and the devil. They killed hundreds of thousands of cats, which may have led to the huge increase in the rat population in Europe and the resulting spread of bubonic plague that killed a quarter of the European people in the fourteenth century.

- The dogs survived the sinking of the *Titanic*: a Pomeranian belonging to Miss Margaret Hays (in lifeboat 7) and a Pekingese belonging to Henry Sleeper Harper (in lifeboat 3).

- The first living creature to orbit the Earth was a dog named Laika. The Soviet Union sent Laika on a one-way journey into space aboard Sputnik 2 in 1957. Laika died in space just a few hours after launch.

- On the night of November 12, 1974, Mrs. Hollis Sharpe of Los Angeles, California, walked her miniature poodle and cleaned up after him with a piece of newspaper and a plastic bag. A mugger came up from behind, grabbed the bag, pushed Mrs. Sharpe to the ground, hopped in a car, and drove off.

- The song "Who Let the Dogs Out?" originally written and recorded by Anslem Douglas for Trinidad and Tobago's 1998 Carnival season, became a hit in the United States after the band Baha Men recorded the song for the movie *Rugrats in Paris* and a sports marketing company persuaded sports stadiums to use the song to introduce sporting events.

- The Dog Museum in St. Louis, Missouri, exhibits paintings, sculptures, and other works featuring dogs.

Ceilings and Roofs

Cleaning

- **Arm & Hammer Clean Shower.** To clean ceilings, spray Arm & Hammer Clean Shower on the ceiling, wait fifteen minutes, then wipe off with a damp sponge.

- **Bounce.** To clean cobwebs and dust from ceilings, place a clean sock over one end of a stick or long PVC pipe, wrap several used sheets of Bounce over the sock, and secure the Bounce sheets in place with a rubber band. Hold up the stick and use the Bounce-covered sock to wipe dusty corners and ceilings.

- **Liquid Paper.** To cover up a stray mark on a white ceiling tile, paint the spot with Liquid Paper.

- **Scrubbing Bubbles.** To clean ceiling tiles with a thin plastic coating, spray Scrubbing Bubbles on the plastic coating and then rinse clean. (Be sure to avoid getting the insulation wet.)

- **Wilson Tennis Balls.** To remove cobwebs from unreachable corners of the ceiling, wrap a Wilson Tennis Ball inside a dust cloth secured with a few rubber bands, then gently toss it at the distant cobwebs.

Drilling

- **Maxwell House Coffee.** To prevent dust from falling all over the floor or into your eyes when drilling a hole in the ceiling, drill a hole through the center of the plastic lid from a can of Maxwell House Coffee. With the lid on the drill bit, hold the lid up to the ceiling and drill into the plaster, allowing the coffee lid to catch all the dust.

Gutters

- **Slinky.** To keep leaves out of your rain gutters, place a Slinky in your rain gutter and stretch if from one end to the next, keeping it in place by simply clipping the Slinky to each end.

Installing

- **Kingsford's Corn Starch.** To avoid getting smudges on ceiling tiles while installing them, dip your fingertips in Kingsford's Corn Starch before handling each tile. The cornstarch creates a protective barrier to prevent oil from your fingers from blemishing the tiles.

Wooden Shingles

- **Arm & Hammer Baking Soda.** To age new wooden shingles so they don't stand out from old ones on a shingle roof, mix one pound Arm & Hammer Baking Soda and two quarts water. Brush the solution onto the new wooden shingles and let sit for several hours until the new wood turns gray to match the older shingles.

Strange Facts

- Commissioned by Pope Julius II, Michelangelo spent four years painting the ceiling of the Sistine Chapel in the Vatican, between 1508 and 1512. The ceiling includes the image of the hand of God giving life to Adam.

- French philosopher and mathematician René Descartes invented coordinate geometry while lying in bed watching a fly walk across the ceiling.

- In the 1951 movie *Royal Wedding*, Fred Astaire, energized by his love for Sarah Churchill, dances in a hotel room—not just on the floor, but sideways on the walls and upside-down on the ceiling.

- The 1955 Pulitzer Prizewinning play *Cat on a Hot Tin Roof* by Tennessee Williams takes place at a birthday party for the family patriarch, "Big Daddy" Pollitt, at his Mississippi estate. The 1958 movie version of the play starred Paul Newman, Elizabeth Taylor, and Burl Ives.

- The title of the 1964 Broadway musical *Fiddler on the Roof*, based on the short stories of Russian Jewish author Sholom Aleichem, was inspired by a painting by Marc Chagall that depicts a Jewish violinist playing while balancing precariously on a rooftop.

- The Allied Roofing and Siding Company of Grand Rapids, Michigan, cleaned snow from roofs to prevent them from collapsing from the weight of the snow. In 1979, the company's roof collapsed from the weight of snow.

- In the music video made to promote Lionel Richie's 1986 hit song "Dancing on the Ceiling," the title song from his third album, Richie pays homage to Fred Astaire by dancing on the ceiling.

Cleaning

- **Colgate Regular Flavor Toothpaste.** To clean the gunk from the bottom of a steam iron, squeeze a dollop of Colgate Regular Flavor Toothpaste on a dry, soft cloth and scrub the bottom of your cool, unplugged steam iron. Wipe clean with a damp cloth.

- **Heinz White Vinegar.** To clean mineral deposits from a steam iron, fill the water tank with Heinz White Vinegar. Turn the iron to the steam setting and iron a soft, clean rag to scrub the steam ports. Repeat the process with water, then, with the iron unplugged and cooled down, thoroughly rinse out the water tank.

- **Morton Salt,** *USA Today,* **and Bounty Paper Towels.** To clean the gunk from the bottom plate of an iron (without a nonstick coating), mix two tablespoons Morton Salt with enough water to make a paste and rub the abrasive paste on the bottom plate of the unplugged iron with a crumpled-up sheet of *USA Today.* Wipe clean with a sheet of Bounty Paper Towel.

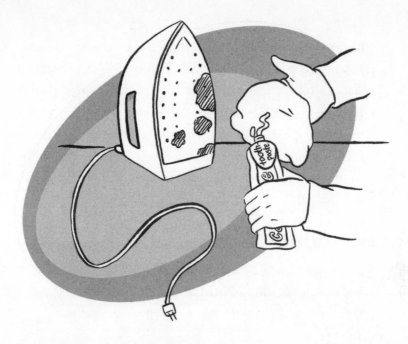

- **Reynolds Wrap.** To clean starch off the bottom of an iron, run the warm iron over a sheet of Reynolds Wrap. The starch will adhere to the aluminum foil. To make this tip even more effective, crumple up the sheet of Reynolds Wrap, uncrumple it again, and then iron the abrasive aluminum surface.

Quickening

- **Reynolds Wrap.** To speed up your ironing, place a sheet of Reynolds Wrap aluminum foil under the ironing board cover to reflect the heat from the iron back toward the underside of the garment being ironed.

Spray Starch

- **Downy Fabric Softener.** To make a substitute for spray starch for ironing, mix one tablespoon Downy Fabric Softener and two cups water in a trigger-spray bottle. The mixtures works like spray starch and also leaves clothes smelling springtime fresh.

- **Heinz White Vinegar.** To make a permanent crease in slacks, fill a trigger-spray bottle with Heinz White Vinegar, spray the slacks, fold where you'd like the crease to be, and iron.
- **Kingsford's Corn Starch.** To make your own spray starch, mix one tablespoon Kingsford's Corn Starch and two cups cold water in a sixteen-ounce trigger-spray bottle. Shake well to dissolve the cornstarch completely. Shake vigorously before each use.

White Shirts

- **Johnson's Baby Powder.** To prevent white shirts from absorbing oil and grime, lightly sprinkle Johnson's Baby Powder on the shirts before and after ironing.

Strange Facts

- In the fourth century BCE, ancient Greeks used a heated cylinder called a "goffering iron" like a rolling pin to smooth wrinkled linen robes and create pleats. Two hundred years later, Roman slaves used a flat metal mallet called a "mangle" to hammer out creases and press wrinkled garments.

- In the tenth century, Norse Vikings used an iron shaped like an upside-down mushroom to press wrinkles out of garments. Pleats in clothing distinguished the upper class from lower class because they could be achieved solely through time-consuming work, requiring slaves or servants.

- In the fifteenth century, upper-class Europeans owned irons with compartments that held heated coals. The lower classes used flat irons heated over fires.

- In the nineteenth century, inventors created gas-heated irons, but the devices, connected to gas lines, frequently leaked, exploded, and ignited fires.

- In 1882, Henry W. Weely invented the first electric iron. When plugged into its stand, the iron heated up. While being used, the iron cooled down rapidly, requiring the user to continually reheat the iron.

- At the turn of the twentieth century, manufacturers produced a variety of electric irons—all weighing more than ten pounds. Unfortunately, most consumers could use this laborsaving device only at night. At the time, most electric companies only ran their generators between sunset and sunrise.

- In 1905, Earl Richardson, a meter reader for an electric company in Ontario, California, devised a homemade lightweight iron and persuaded the power company to generate electricity all day on Tuesdays, the day most homemakers on his route ironed clothes. As housewives used more electricity, the power plant began generating electricity for longer hours. The following year, Richardson began manufacturing irons, which he named "Hot Point," after the fact that his original irons distributed the heat unevenly along the iron's flat plate, concentrating most of the heat at one spot.

- By the time the first electric steam irons were introduced in 1926, Americans were buying more than three million electric irons a year.

- Steam irons did not catch on until the 1940s when clothing makers introduced synthetic fabrics that scorched easily under hot irons. To sell more irons, steam iron manufacturers began increasing the number of steam holes as a competitive marketing gimmick. The number of holes in the bottom of a steam iron slowly escalated from eight large holes to seventy small holes—in what industry insiders called a "holey war."

Clothing

Baseball Caps

- **Velcro.** To fix a broken plastic strap on the back of a baseball cap, replace it with strips of Velcro.

Belts

- **Maybelline Express Finish Clear Nail Polish.** To keep belt buckles shiny, paint Maybelline Express Finish Clear Nail Polish on the buckle, let dry, and repeat several times.

Bras

- **Krazy Glue** and **Velcro.** To prevent bra pads from slipping, use Krazy Glue to attach Velcro to the inside cups of the bra and the outside of the pads.
- **Scotch Packaging Tape.** Instead of wearing an expensive adhesive strapless bra, use Scotch Packaging Tape to hold yourself together.

- **Velcro.** To prevent bra straps from showing when wearing a wide neckline, sew small strips of Velcro on the top of each bra strap and on the inside of each shoulder seam of the dress.

Buttons

- **Elmer's Glue-All.** To reinforce buttons on shirts, rub a drop of Elmer's Glue-All on the thread around each button and let dry. The glue helps stop the thread from unraveling and the buttons from falling off.

- **Maybelline Express Finish Clear Nail Polish.** To prevent buttons from popping off a shirt, paint the center of each button with a dab of Maybelline Express Finish Clear Nail Polish to coat the threads, strengthening them.
- **Oral-B Dental Floss.** Use Oral-B Dental Floss as a strong, durable substitute for thread to sew on buttons on coats and children's clothes.

Control-Top Underwear

- **L'eggs Sheer Energy Panty Hose.** To make an inexpensive pair of control-top underwear, when your L'eggs Sheer Energy Panty Hose get a run in one of the legs, cut off both nylon legs and wear the remaining panty hose as a girdle.

Dust Covers

- **Glad Trash Bags.** To make dust covers for clothes, cut a small hole in the center of the bottom of a Glad Trash Bag and slip the bag over the top of a suit or dress on a hanger.

Dyeing

- **Kool-Aid.** To dye a garment made from wool, mohair, or alpaca with Kool-Aid, wash the garment in mild soapy water and then rinse it clean. Dissolve the contents of a packet of Kool-Aid drink mix (the flavor of your choice) in one cup water and pour the mixture into a large pot. Place the garment in the pot and add enough water to cover it. Heat the water to nearly boiling, cover, remove pot from heat, and let sit for thirty minutes, stirring occasionally. The garment will absorb most of the dye. Let it cool. Rinse the garment thoroughly in lukewarm water, wash with mild soap, rinse clean, and hang to dry. Once the garment dries thoroughly, immerse it in full-strength Heinz White Vinegar to make it colorfast.

- **Lipton Tea Bags.** To dye fabric or a garment brown inexpensively, soak the item in hot, strongly brewed Lipton Tea, rinse the item in cold water, and let it dry. Repeat to achieve a darker color, if desired. Once the garment dries thoroughly, immerse it in full-strength Heinz White Vinegar to make it colorfast.

- **Maxwell House Coffee.** To dye fabric brown inexpensively, soak the fabric in a bucket of strongly brewed Maxwell House

Coffee for two minutes. No matter how strong the coffee is or how long you soak the garment, the fabric always comes out the color of coffee ice cream. Wring the excess coffee out of the garment and hang it up to dry. This technique is also an excellent way to cover up a permanent coffee stain on a white tablecloth. Once the garment dries thoroughly, immerse it in full-strength Heinz White Vinegar to make it colorfast.

- **Tang** and **Heinz White Vinegar.** To die a piece of clothing Tang-orange, mix one-half cup Tang powdered mix and one cup Heinz White Vinegar in a bowl until dissolved. Dip the garment into the orange solution. Wring the excess liquid out of the garment and hang it up to dry. Once the garment dries thoroughly, immerse it in full-strength Heinz White Vinegar to make it colorfast.

- **Welch's 100% Purple Grape Juice.** Pour one cup Welch's Grape Juice into a bowl and dip the garment into the grape juice. Wring the excess grape juice out of the garment and hang it up to dry. Once the garment dries thoroughly, immerse it in full-strength Heinz White Vinegar to make it colorfast.

Fraying

- **Maybelline Express Finish Clear Nail Polish.** To prevent cut fabric from fraying, paint a thin coat of Maybelline Express Finish Clear Nail Polish along the edges to stop the ends from unraveling.

Fuzz, Lint, and Pet Hair

- **Scotch Packaging Tape.** To remove fuzz, lint, or pet hair from clothing, wrap a strip of Scotch Packaging Tape around your hand, adhesive side out, and pat.

- **Silly Putty.** Make a ball of Silly Putty, flatten it into a pancake, and gently pat a garment covered with fuzz, lint, or pet hair to remove it.

Garment Bags

- **Arm & Hammer Baking Soda.** To deodorize garment storage bags, sprinkle a little Arm & Hammer Baking Soda into the bottom of the bag and zip closed. The baking soda neutralizes odors.

Gloves

- **Gold Medal Flour.** To clean white kid gloves, rub Gold Medal Flour into the leather and then brush clean.
- **Scotchgard.** To protect a clean pair of white gloves, spray them with Scotchgard and let dry.

Hangers

- **Pledge.** To make hangers glide easily over a wooden clothes rod in a closet, remove all clothes from the closet and saturate the wooden pole with Pledge furniture spray. Wipe off the excess furniture spay with a rag and repeat as many times as necessary until the pole feels waxy and you can glide a hanger over the pole. Hang the clothes back in the closet.
- **Reynolds Cut-Rite Wax Paper.** To make hangers glide easily along a wooden clothes rod, remove all clothes from the closet and rub a sheet of Reynolds Cut-Rite Wax Paper over the clothes rod, giving the wooden pole a thin coat of wax. Then hang the clothes back in the closet.
- **WD-40.** To make hangers glide along a clothes rod, remove all clothes from the closet and spray WD-40 on the clothes rod. Wipe off the excess WD-40 with a rag and hang the clothes back in the closet.

Hats

- **Stayfree Maxi Pads.** To prevent perspiration stains on the inside of a hat headband, peel off the adhesive strip on the back of a Stayfree Maxi Pad and stick the maxi pad inside your hat along the headband that rests against your forehead. Replace the maxi pad when necessary.

Hems

- **Scotch Packaging Tape.** In an emergency, reattach a drooping hem temporarily with a small strip of Scotch Packaging Tape.
- **Wrigley's Spearmint Gum.** In a pinch, reattach a drooping hem temporarily with a small wad of well-chewed Wrigley's Spearmint Gum.

Jeans

- **Downy Fabric Softener.** To soften a new pair of jeans, fill a bucket with water, add one capful Downy Fabric Softener, and soak the jeans in the solution overnight. In the morning, pour the contents of the bucket into your washing machine, run it through the regular cycle, and dry the jeans.
- **Jet-Dry.** To soften a new pair of jeans, fill your washing machine with water, add four ounces Jet-Dry, soak the jeans overnight, then run through the rinse cycle and dry. The Jet-Dry does double duty in the washing machine, simultaneously cleaning soap scum from the tubes and pipes in the washing machine.
- **Morton Salt.** To soften a new pair of jeans, toss the jeans in your washing machine, add one-half cup Morton Salt and your regular detergent, and wash the jeans. The sodium in the salt will soften the jeans.

Leather

- **Alberto VO5 Conditioning Hairdressing.** To condition a leather garment, handbag, or boots, if you're all out of mink oil, rub a dab of Alberto VO5 Conditioning Hairdressing into the leather with a soft, clean cloth.

- **Huggies Baby Wipes.** To clean and moisturize leather boots, handbags, or coats, wipe the item with Huggies Baby Wipes.
- **Jif Peanut Butter.** To clean a leather purse or shoe, smear a thin coat of Jif Peanut Butter (creamy) on the item, wait one minute, and wipe clean and buff with a soft cloth.

Lingerie

- **Maybelline Express Finish Clear Nail Polish.** To prevent the knots of small ribbons on lingerie from coming untied, dab the knots with Maybelline Express Finish Clear Nail Polish, securing the knots in place.

Organizing

- **Ziploc Storage Bags.** To separate lingerie, scarves, gloves, hosiery, and handkerchiefs in your dresser drawers, organize your smaller garments in Ziploc Storage Bags.

Panty Hose

- **Alberto VO5 Hair Spray.** To prevent runs in panty hose, spray a light coat of Alberto VO5 Hair Spray on the legs of your nylon panty hose.
- **Conair Pro Styler 1600.** To dry panty hose, hang the wet panty hose on a shower rod and gently blow them dry with a Conair Pro Styler 1600 hair dryer.
- **Liquid Paper.** To stop a run in panty hose, paint the edges of the snag with a generous coat of Liquid Paper and let dry.
- **Maybelline Express Finish Clear Nail Polish.** To stop a run in panty hose, paint the edges of the snag immediately with Maybelline Express Finish Clear Nail Polish.

- **Scotch Transparent Tape.** In a pinch, place a piece of Scotch Transparent Tape over the snag in the panty hose to prevent the run from getting bigger.

Raincoats

- **Glad Trash Bags.** To make a raincoat in a pinch, cut slits in a Glad Trash Bag for your head and arms and wear it.

Stains

- **Johnson's Baby Powder.** To hide a minor stain on a white suit, rub Johnson's Baby Powder into the stain.

Static Cling

- **Bounce.** To eliminate static electricity in socks, panty hose, or a slip, don the garment and rub a sheet of Bounce over it. The antistatic elements in Bounce impede the static electricity.
- **Lubriderm.** To eliminate static electricity in socks, panty hose, or a slip, put on the garment, rub a dab of Lubriderm into the palms of your hands until it disappears, then rub your palms over your panty hose or slip. The moisturizer prevents static electricity from building up.

Tassels

- **Krazy Glue.** To reattach loose tassels on shoes, a dress, or a jacket, use a few drops of Krazy Glue and hold the tassels in place until secure.

Ties

- **Scotchgard.** To protect neckties from getting stained from food spills, spray each tie with a thin coat of Scotchgard so spills bead off without being absorbed into the fabric.

Umbrellas

- **Scotchgard.** To waterproof an umbrella, spray the fabric with Scotchgard so water runs off with a quick shake, allowing the umbrella to dry faster.

White Suede

- **Crayola Chalk.** To cover minor spots or scuffs on white suede, rub the stain with a piece of white Crayola Chalk. The chalk absorbs grease and also hides the stain.

Windbreakers

- **Glad Trash Bags.** To improvise a windbreaker, cut holes in a Glad Trash Bag for your head and arms and wear the plastic trash bag under your coat (so it doesn't flap in the wind).

Zippers

- **Alberto VO5 Conditioning Hairdressing.** To lubricate a zipper, rub a dab of Alberto VO5 Conditioning Hairdressing into the teeth of the zipper.
- **ChapStick.** To make a zipper zip smoothly, rub ChapStick along the teeth of the zipper on trousers, jackets, backpacks, tents, or sleeping bags.
- **Ivory Soap.** Rubbing a bar of Ivory Soap over the teeth of a zipper lubricates the zipper, making it zip smoothly.
- **Reynolds Cut-Rite Wax Paper.** To make a metal zipper work with ease, run a sheet of Reynolds Cut-Rite Wax Paper up and down the teeth.
- **Vaseline Petroleum Jelly.** To make a zipper glide effortlessly, apply a dab of Vaseline Petroleum Jelly to the teeth.

Strange Facts

- A 1560 version of the Bible, published in Geneva, Italy, translated Genesis 3:7 to read that Adam and Eve "sewed fig leaves together and made themselves breeches." Breeches are knee-length trousers that did not exist in biblical times.

- In the 1719 novel *Robinson Crusoe* by Daniel Defoe, Crusoe takes off his clothes, swims to a wrecked ship, finds some biscuits there, and then, we are told, puts them in his pockets.

- After 1851, most people in small-town America made their own clothes from spun fabrics, using an invention developed by Elias Howe and Isaac Singer—the lockstitch sewing machine.

- In the 1850s, manufacturers began making inexpensive "ready-made" clothing. Still, most Americans continued making clothes by hand, aided by the paper dress pattern, invented and patented in 1864 by Ebenezer Butterick of Stering, Massachusetts.

- In the late 1800s, improved manufacturing methods helped lower the cost of "ready-made" clothing, so more and more people began wearing mass-produced clothes.

- In the 1933 film *The Invisible Man*, Claude Rains becomes invisible, except for his clothes. At the end of the film, he strips naked to escape from the police, but the cops follow after his footprints in the snow—footprints made by shoes that the invisible man was not wearing.

- In April 1970, radical Abbie Hoffman appeared on *The Merv Griffin Show* wearing a shirt designed with an American flag motif. CBS network officials had the shirt masked out by a blue square, bringing even greater media attention to Hoffman. More than 88,000 viewers called CBS to protest the censoring, protests took place in front of CBS offices in three cities, and Merv Griffin publicly apologized. Prior to Hoffman's appearance, Ricky Nelson, Raquel Welch, Roy Rogers, and Ryan O'Neal had worn similar shirts on television.

- In 1974, ABC-TV refused to allow the character Fonzie on the television sitcom *Happy Days* to wear a black leather jacket because it made him look like a hoodlum. In the first few episodes, Fonzie (played by Henry Winkler) wears a light-gray windbreaker. Producer Garry Marshall convinced the network to let Fonzie wear a black leather jacket and boots whenever he was near his motorcycle. Marshall then instructed his staff to make sure Fonzie was with his motorcycle in every scene. Fonzie became one of the most popular characters on television, and in 1980, Fonzie's black leather jacket was enshrined in the Smithsonian Institution.

- When Pope John Paul II visited Miami, Florida, in 1987, a local T-shirt maker translated the phrase "I saw the Pope" into Spanish by incorrectly using the feminine *la papa* instead of the masculine *el pape*, which made the T-shirts read: "I saw the potato."

- In June 1999, Columba Bush, wife of Florida Governor Jeb Bush, returned to the United States from a trip to Paris and told customs officials at Atlanta's International Airport that she had nothing to claim. Customs officials inspected her luggage and discovered $19,000 worth of designer clothing and accessories that Mrs. Bush was apparently attempting to smuggle into the country to avoid paying taxes. She claimed that she had lied on her customs form because she didn't want her husband to find out how much money she had spent in Paris.

Cooling and Heating

Air Conditioners

- **Glad Trash Bags.** To reduce cold drafts and keep the condenser coil and fan on a room air conditioner clean during the winter, slice open the sides of a Glad Trash Bag to make a long sheet and cover the exterior of the window air conditioner with the plastic, securing it in place with Scotch Packaging Tape. Be sure to remove the plastic before using the air conditioner in the spring.

Ceiling Fans

- **Scotch Transparent Tape** and **Krazy Glue.** To balance a wobbly or vibrating ceiling fan, balance the blades by using Scotch Transparent Tape to attach coins as weights to the tops of the unbalanced blades. Once you've balanced the blades, glue the coins in place with Krazy Glue.

Furnaces

- **Johnson's Baby Oil.** To make the filter in your furnace more efficient at trapping small dust particles, pour one-quarter cup Johnson's Baby Oil in a small trigger-spray bottle and spray a light coat of the oil over the filter. The oil helps trap small dust particles and simultaneously adds a welcome fragrance to your home.

Radiators

- **Heinz White Vinegar.** If the automatic air vent on your radiator isn't working properly, let the unit cool, close the valve to the radiator, and unscrew the air vent. Soak the air vent in Heinz White Vinegar for thirty minutes to loosen any debris stuck inside and then blow through the vent holding it upright and then again upside-down.

- **Reynolds Wrap.** To make a radiator more efficient, cover one side of a sheet of corrugated cardboard with Reynolds Wrap and place the board behind the radiator with the aluminum foil facing it. The radiator will send heat toward the wall, but the shiny board will act like a mirror, reflecting the heat back into the room.

Thermostats

- **Cover Girl Continuous Color Classic Red.** To readjust your thermostat quickly, paint a dot of Cover Girl Continuous Color Classic Red Nail Polish to mark the temperature at which you usually set your thermostat.

- **Q-Tips Cotton Swabs** and **Heinz White Vinegar.** To clean the contacts on an old-fashioned thermostat, turn off the electrical power at the fuse box, remove the cover, and wipe the contacts with a Q-Tips Cotton Swab dampened with a solution made from equal parts Heinz White Vinegar and water.

Strange Facts

- In the first century CE, the Romans invented central heating by embedding tubes made from terra cotta in the walls of homes to carry smoke generated by wood or coal fires in the basements.

- Around 1500, Italian Renaissance artist Leonardo da Vinci invented the first mechanical fan, powered by water.

- Around 1880, Americans began using coal furnaces in their basements to heat water tanks to send steam through pipes and hot water to radiators in each room of their houses.

- In July 1881, while President James Garfield, wounded by an assassin, lay in bed in a hot and humid White House, a corps of naval engineers who specialized in ventilating mine shafts designed a large iron box filled with ice, salt, water, and a series of terry-cloth filters. A fan blew air over the cloths saturated with melted ice water, cooling the president's room down to 81 degrees Fahrenheit.

- In 1892, British inventors R. E. Crompton and J. H. Dowsing patented the first electric room heater.

- In 1902, William Carrier, who had graduated from the engineering college at Cornell University the year before, invented the first air conditioner—by modifying a steam heater to accept cold water and circulate cool, filtered, dehumidified air.

- During the lifetime of an air conditioner, the owner spends three times the original price of the air conditioner to pay for the energy to run it.

Dishwashers

Deodorizing

- **Arm & Hammer Baking Soda.** If your dishwasher is creating a stink, sprinkle one-half cup Arm & Hammer Baking Soda on the bottom of the dishwasher and let sit overnight. Run the baking soda through the machine with your next load of dishes, which also helps clean both the inside of the machine and the dishes.

Dishwashing Soap

- **20 Mule Team Borax** and **Arm & Hammer Super Washing Soda.** To make your own automatic dishwashing soap, mix equal parts 20 Mule Team Borax and Arm & Hammer Super Washing Soda to create an old-fashioned cleanser made from borax and sodium carbonate. (When working with washing soda, wear rubber gloves to protect your hands from the caustic pH 11.)

Excess Suds

- **Bounce.** If you use the wrong detergent or too much detergent in the dishwasher and it starts to overflow with suds, open the door and put in a sheet of Bounce to eliminate the excess suds. The antistatic elements in Bounce pop the bubbles.

Gasket

- **DAP Caulk.** You can repair a torn dishwasher gasket (the rubber lining around the inside of the door) by simply filling the tear with DAP Caulk and allowing it to dry.

Glassware

- **Heinz White Vinegar.** To prevent soapy film on glassware, place one cup Heinz White Vinegar on the bottom rack of your dishwasher, run for five minutes, then run though the full cycle. A cup of white vinegar run through the entire cycle once a month will also reduce soap scum on the inner workings.

Indicator

- **Post-it Notes.** For an easy way to tell if dishes in the dishwasher are clean, stick a Post-it Note on the front of the dishwasher after turning it on. When the dishwasher stops, the Post-it Note will alert others that the dishes inside are clean.

Lime Deposits

- **Clorox Bleach** and **Heinz White Vinegar.** Reduce lime build-up inside the dishwasher by pouring one cup Clorox Bleach into the empty dishwasher and running the machine through the first wash cycle. Let the machine drain, then add two cups Heinz White Vinegar and run the machine through the rinse cycle. Skip the dry cycle and instead run the dishwasher through an entire regular cycle using regular detergent.

Racks and Runners

- **Pam Cooking Spray.** If the racks in your dishwasher don't slide in and out easily, do not be tempted to lubricate them with WD-40, otherwise the petroleum-based ingredients in the water displacement formula can come into contact with kitchenware and eating utensils. Instead, spray the rollers with Pam Cooking Spray, a vegetable oil that lubricates the racks without any possible ill effects.

Soap Scum and Grime

- **Country Time Lemonade.** To clean the pipes and tubes inside your dishwasher, fill the detergent cup in the dishwasher with Country Time Lemonade powder and run the machine through its normal cycle (without any dishes inside). The citric acid in the Country Time Lemonade cleans soap scum and grunge from the inside of the dishwasher and leaves your dishwasher smelling lemon fresh. Plumbers will tell you all about this trick—after charging you sixty dollars for the house call.

- **Kool-Aid.** Clean soap scum from the tubes and pipes of a dishwasher by filling the detergent cup with Kool-Aid drink powder and running the dishwasher through its regular cycle. The citric acid in Kool-Aid cleans the soap scum and mineral and iron stains.

- **Tang.** The astronauts took Tang to the moon; now you can use it to clean your dishwasher. Clean soap scum from the tubes and pipes of a dishwasher by simply filling the detergent cups with Tang powder and running the dishwasher through its regular cycle (without any dishes inside). The citric acid in Tang cleans the soap scum and mineral and iron stains.

Water Spots

- **20 Mule Team Borax.** Reduce water spots on glasses and dishes by adding one tablespoon 20 Mule Team Borax to the dishwasher soap receptacle.

Strange Facts

- In the 1880s, wealthy socialite Josephine Cochrane decided to invent a dishwashing machine because she frequently hosted formal dinners and could no longer tolerate having her expensive china broken by irresponsible servants as they washed the dishes. Using her woodshed as a workshop, Cochrane attached a motorized sprinkler wheel on top of a large copper boiler, devised wire compartments to hold her china plates, saucers, and cups, and fastened the compartments in place around the sprinkler wheel. When she activated the motor, the sprinkler wheel spun, showering the dishes with hot soapy water from the boiler.

- In 1914, Josephine Cochrane's company introduced the first mass-produced dishwasher designed for use in homes, but the machines failed to sell because most homes did not have hot water tanks large enough to provide enough scalding water needed by the machine to clean a load of dishes.

- A poll taken in the early twentieth century revealed that most American housewives considered washing the dishes by hand to be a pleasant chore that helped them unwind at the end of the day.

- The average dishwasher uses between six and ten gallons of water to clean the same number of dishes that would require nine to twenty-four gallons of water if they were cleaned by hand in the sink.

- To save energy and money, open the dishwasher after it completes the wash cycle and let the dishes air dry.

- Before turning on your dishwasher, run the hot water in your kitchen sink for a minute to make sure the dishwasher fills with hot water during the first wash cycle.

Drains

Clogs

- **Alka-Seltzer** and **Heinz White Vinegar.** To unclog a drain, drop three Alka-Seltzer tablets down the drain, add one cup Heinz White Vinegar, and wait fifteen minutes to allow the reaction to fizz. The bubbling action can unclog your drain by breaking down grease and allowing the clog to wash down the pipe. Then pour a kettle of boiling water down the drain to flush it. Do not put Alka-Seltzer or vinegar down the drain if you have poured any commercial drain cleaner down the drain or into any standing water.

- **Arm & Hammer Baking Soda** and **Morton Salt.** Pour one-half cup Arm & Hammer Baking Soda and one-half cup Morton Salt down the clogged drain, followed by six cups boiling water. Let sit overnight. In the morning, flush with water. The boiling hot water should dissolve the clog, allowing the abrasive baking soda and salt to burst through the stoppage.

- **Arm & Hammer Clean Shower.** Pour Arm & Hammer Clean Shower down the clogged drain of a shower or sink, let sit for one hour, then flush with hot water. Arm & Hammer Clean Shower contains a natural enzyme that devours grease and food debris.

- **Cascade Gel.** Drain as much water as possible from the clogged sink, pour Cascade Gel dishwasher detergent into the drain, then carefully and slowly pour a kettle of boiling water down the drain. The boiling hot water softens the clog while the phosphates in the Cascade Gel devour the debris.

- **Clorox Bleach.** If your home's plumbing drains to a municipal sewage plant, pour two cups Clorox Bleach down the drain of your sinks, bathtub, and shower once a month. Let sit overnight. The bleach sitting in the trap saturates any partial clogs, softening biofilm and debris. The next day run the water for three minutes to flush the debris to the sewer. When pouring bleach down the drain of a stainless steel kitchen sink, do not let bleach drip or puddle on the stainless steel. Otherwise permanent stains in the stainless steel may result. Don't pour bleach down the drain if you have a septic tank system; the bleach will kill the bacteria that break down waste products.

- **Coca-Cola.** Once a week, pour a bottle of Coca-Cola down the kitchen drain and let sit overnight to dissolve grease build-up and prevent clogs.

- **Conair Pro Styler 1600.** To clear grease clogging a drain, use a Conair Pro Styler 1600 hair dryer set on high with the nozzle directed at the trap. The heat from the blow dryer will warm the pipe and melt the grease. Then run the hot water to flush the grease through the system.

- **Dawn Dishwashing Liquid.** To clear a clogged kitchen drain, boil three to four tablespoons Dawn Dishwashing Liquid in a pan full of water and carefully pour the heated mixture down the drain of the kitchen sink. The solution will dissolve most kitchen sink clogs because Dawn breaks down grease.

- **Efferdent.** Drop several Efferdent tablets into a clogged drain, fill with water, and let sit overnight. The denture cleansing tablets loosen caked grease and debris.

- **Jell-O** and **Heinz White Vinegar.** Vinegar dissolves most clogs, but, unfortunately, if you pour vinegar down a clogged drain, the acetic acid will seep down your pipes before it gets a chance to eat away the clog. Instead, dissolve one small package of Jell-O in one cup boiling water. Let cool. In a measuring cup, mix 1.5 ounces Heinz White Vinegar with 6.5 ounces water. Add the vinegar mixture to the Jell-O mixture. Let gel in the refrigerator until almost set, but liquid enough to flow slowly. Pour the mixture down the drain. Let sit overnight. The Jell-O will clog up the pipes, giving the acetic acid in the vinegar a chance to eat away the clog. Then flush the drain with water to wash away the Jell-O.

- **Nair.** Remove hair clogged in bathtub, shower, and sink drains by squeezing as much Nair lotion as you think necessary into the drain. Let sit for fifteen minutes, then flush with water.

Nair, a depilatory that breaks down hair, contains a high pH substance (usually sodium thioglycolate or calcium thioglycolate) that reacts with the protein structure of hair.

- **Super Soaker.** To unclog a drain clogged with food debris, fill a Super Soaker with water, pump the handle to increase the air pressure, then point the nozzle into the drain and fire. The high-pressure jet spray can break up the clog, sending the debris down the drain.

Insects

- **Wilson Tennis Balls.** To prevent insects from crawling up through drains in a basement or laundry room floor, unscrew the faceplate from the drain, place a clean, used Wilson Tennis Ball inside the drain to block the hole, and screw the faceplate back in place. When the drain fills with water, the tennis ball will float, allowing water to go down the pipe. Once the water is gone, the ball will automatically reseal the hole.

Plungers

- **Vaseline Petroleum Jelly.** When using a plunger, make sure the suction cup covers the drain opening, fill the clogged basin with enough water to cover the plunger cup, and then coat the rim of the suction cup with Vaseline Petroleum Jelly to seal the drain tightly. Plunge with ten strong strokes. Try several times before turning to other remedies.

Stoppers

- **Wilson Tennis Balls.** If you lose the drain plug for your shower, sink, or bathtub, use a Wilson Tennis Ball to block the drain. The suction from the drain will keep the ball in place.

- **Ziploc Storage Bags.** Missing the plug to the bathtub? Fill a Ziploc Storage Bag with water, seal it shut, and place it over the open drain. The bag of water conforms to the shape of the drain, and the weight of the water prevents the plastic bag from floating to the surface.

Strange Facts

- When using a plunger in a sink or bathtub, be sure to use a damp cloth to block the overflow opening in the sink or bathtub to create a vacuum. Otherwise, the plunger will merely suck air from the overflow opening, rather than dislodging the debris causing the clog.

- If you free the clog from your pipes but the drain still empties slowly, check the vent pipe on your roof. The vent pipe allows air to flow through your pipes, but if a bird or squirrel nest blocks the top of the vent pipe, the water won't drain properly. Now all you need to do is remove the nest.

- In his play *Alcestis*, ancient Greek playwright Euripides wrote: "Today's today. Tomorrow, we may be ourselves gone down the drain of Eternity."

- In Act I, Scene iii of William Shakespeare's play *Macbeth*, the first witch says: "I'll drain him dry as hay."

- Contrary to popular belief, James Watt did not invent the steam engine. In 1698, Thomas Savery patented the first practical steam engine, a pump to drain flooded mines in Cornwall, England. Steam entered a sealed vessel through a hand-operated valve, cold water was poured on the vessel to condense the steam inside and create a partial vacuum, then the valve was opened so the vacuum could suck water up a pipe and into the vessel.

- In his 1857 novel *Madame Bovary*, French novelist Gustave Flaubert wrote: "It never occurred to her that if the drainpipes of a house are clogged, the rain may collect in pools on the roof; and she suspected no danger until suddenly she discovered a crack in the wall."

- In Alfred Hitchcock's 1951 murder mystery movie *Strangers on a Train*, Bruno Anthony (played by actor Robert Walker) accidentally drops a cigarette lighter belonging to tennis pro Guy Haines (engraved with two crossed tennis rackets and the letters "A to G")—down a drain and struggles to retrieve it.

- In 1980, Texaco began drilling for oil from a new rig in the middle of Lake Peigneur in Louisiana. The water immediately drained from the 1,300-acre lake, sucking eight tugboats, nine barges, five houses, a mobile home, and two oil rigs into the abandoned salt mine beneath the lake.

- Mexico City is sinking at the rate of six to eight inches a year because the city is built on top of a natural underground water source that is being drained by wells for the fifteen million residents of the city.

- Musician Boz Scaggs's 1997 album *Come On Home* includes the song "It All Went Down the Drain."

ROCKET SCIENCE: THE SUPER SOAKER

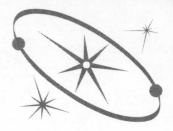

✳ ✳ ✳ ✳ ✳ ✳ ✳ ✳ ✳ ✳

In 1982, nuclear engineer Lonnie Johnson, who worked at NASA's Jet Propulsion Laboratory in Pasadena, California, on the Galileo and Mars Observer Projects and the Cassini Mission to Jupiter, was experimenting with a new type of refrigerator that used water instead of freon. He hooked a nozzle to a faucet in his bathroom, and when he turned on the water, pressurized air sent a stream of water shooting across the bathroom.

"Boy, this would really make the neatest water gun," thought Johnson, who decided to build a high-tech squirt gun engineered with an air pump that would enable a child to pump the gun up with very high pressure. Five years later, in his home workshop, Johnson used a lathe to build a prototype of his water gun from PVC pipe, Plexiglas, and an empty plastic Coke bottle. After letting his six-year-old daughter test the high-tech squirt gun on neighbors, Johnson named his invention the "Power Drencher" and took the prototype for his invention to Daisy Manufacturing, the maker of BB guns. After two years of discussions, Daisy Manufacturing passed on the idea.

In 1989, Johnson arranged a meeting at the Larami Corporation, where he opened his suitcase, took out his Power Drencher, and fired a gigantic stream of water across the room. Johnson renamed the toy the "Super Soaker" and launched a nationwide advertising campaign. While traditional squirt guns sold for twenty-nine cents, the Super Soaker, manufactured by Larami, was priced at ten dollars. When Johnny Carson used a Super Soaker to drench Ed McMahon on *The Tonight Show*, sales skyrocketed. Within a year, the Super Soaker became the most popular water gun in American retail history.

Electronic Equipment

Batteries

- **Reynolds Wrap.** If the batteries in a toy or appliance are loose as the result of a broken spring, wedge a small, crumpled-up piece of Reynolds Wrap between the battery and the spring to improve the connection.

Boom Box Speakers

- **Scotch Packaging Tape.** To attach loose speakers to a boom box, use a few strips of Scotch Packaging Tape.

Cables and Extension Cords

- **Scotch Packaging Tape.** To organize cables and extension cords, tape the cords together with a few small strips of Scotch Packaging Tape.

CDs and DVDs

- **ChapStick.** To clean a scuff mark from a CD or DVD, rub a little ChapStick lip balm over the mark and buff clean.

- **Colgate Regular Flavor Toothpaste.** To clean compact disks and fix skips, rub a dab of Colgate Regular Flavor Toothpaste over the shiny side of the disk and buff clean.

- **Jif Peanut Butter.** To clean a scuff mark from a CD or DVD, rub a dab of Jif Peanut Butter (creamy, not chunky) on the disk with a soft cloth and wipe clean. The oils in the peanut butter clean the disk.

- **Mr. Coffee Filters.** To buff a CD or DVD, use a Mr. Coffee Filter to wipe it clean, starting from the center and working out to the edge. Made from 100 percent virgin paper, Mr. Coffee Filters do a great job cleaning disks without leaving behind any lint.

- **Pledge.** To clean a scuff mark from a compact disc that skips, spray a small amount of lemon Pledge on the disk and buff clean.

- **Purell Instant Hand Sanitizer.** To clean compact disks and fix skips, put a few drops of Purell Instant Hand Sanitizer, the soapless, antibacterial hand sanitizer, on the disk and buff clean.

- **Turtle Wax.** To clean superficial scratches and put an end to skips from a compact disc, use a drop of Turtle Wax and buff clean.

Computer Printers

- **Bounce.** To prevent a laser printer from jamming, place a sheet of Bounce in the front of the paper trays on the printers. The Bounce eliminates the static cling that causes the printer to grab two or more sheets at a time, allowing the paper to feed into the printer with greater ease.

- **Mr. Coffee Filters**. To clean the rollers in a laser printer, use a Mr. Coffee Filter and denatured (not isopropyl) alcohol to clean ink dust from the rollers and passageways.

Computers

- **Bounce.** To clean dust from a computer screen (a cathode tube, not a plasma screen), wipe the glass screen with a clean, used sheet of Bounce. The antistatic elements in the dryer sheet prevent dust from resettling as quickly.
- **Clean & Clear Deep Cleaning Astringent.** To clean the oils left behind by your fingertips on your computer keyboard, wipe the keys with a cotton ball dampened with Clean & Clear Deep Cleaning Astringent. The astringent, formulated to clean oils from skin, also cleans them from computer keyboards.
- **Huggies Baby Wipes.** Wipe down your computer, screen (a cathode tube, not a plasma screen), keyboard, mouse, and mouse pad with Huggies Baby Wipes to keep the machines cleaner and germ-free.
- **Listerine.** To clean grime from a computer screen (a cathode tube, not a plasma screen), wipe the glass screen with a soft, clean cloth dampened with Listerine. The antiseptic also kills germs.
- **Scrubbing Bubbles.** To clean computer components (the monitor case, motherboard, speakers, and mouse), spray Scrubbing Bubbles on a clean, soft cloth and scrub gently. Then wipe clean with a cloth dampened with water and buff dry.
- **Sea Breeze Astringent.** To clean the oils left behind by your fingertips on your computer keyboard, wipe the keys with a cotton ball dampened with Sea Breeze Astringent. The astringent, formulated to clean oils from skin, also cleans them from computer keyboards.

- **Stridex Medicated Pads.** To clean the oils left behind by your fingertips on your computer keyboard, wipe the keys with Stridex Medicated Pads, which are made to clean oils from skin.

Remote Controls

- **Velcro.** To prevent a remote control from disappearing or being misplaced, adhere a hook-sided strip of Velcro to the back of the remote control and a fluffy strip of Velcro on the top of your television set or a nearby wall.

Stereo Speakers

- **Mr. Coffee Filters** and **Maybelline Express Finish Clear Nail Polish.** To repair a damaged stereo speaker cone, trim down a Mr. Coffee Filter to an appropriate size, place it over the hole or tear as a patch, and then coat it with clear nail polish. The patch will hold strong.
- **Wilson Tennis Balls.** Rather than purchasing expensive fabricated dampers for your speakers, carefully cut two Wilson Tennis Balls in half and set the speakers on top of four tennis ball halves. The tennis ball halves improve the speakers' sound performance, and if you place your speakers on the floor of an upstairs apartment, buffer the sound for your downstairs neighbors.

Storage

- **L'eggs Sheer Energy Panty Hose** and **Tidy Cats.** To absorb moisture and odors from inside a box of electronic equipment, cut off the leg from a clean, used pair of L'eggs Sheer Energy Panty Hose, fill the foot with unused Tidy Cats cat box filler, tie a knot in the open end, and place that in the box of electronic equipment.

Telephones

- **Purell Instant Hand Sanitizer.** To disinfect germs from a telephone receiver, squirt some Purell Instant Hand Sanitizer onto a paper towel and wipe down the telephone receiver with it.

Televisions

- **Armor All.** To clean a cathode-ray television screen and prevent dust from resettling on the screen, spray some Armor All on a soft, clean cloth and wipe the glass screen.
- **Bounce.** To eliminate static electricity from your cathode-ray television screen, wipe the glass screen with a clean, used sheet of Bounce. The antistatic elements in the Bounce help keep dust from resettling on the screen.
- **Huggies Baby Wipes.** Use Huggies Baby Wipes to wipe fingerprints off a television screen.
- **Slinky.** Extend a television antenna with a Slinky by simply attaching one end of the spring toy to the existing television antenna and stretching the Slinky across the room. During the Vietnam War, communications soldiers would toss a Slinky over a high tree branch as a makeshift radio antenna.

VCRs

- **Q-Tips Cotton Swabs.** To clean the heads on a VCR, dip a Q-Tips Cotton Swab in rubbing alcohol and gently wipe the metal heads.
- **Smirnoff Vodka.** If you don't have any rubbing alcohol to clean the metal heads of a VCR, use Smirnoff Vodka.

Strange Facts

- In 1880, Emperor Menelik II of Abyssinia (now Ethiopia) ordered three electric chairs to be shipped from New York to his country, not realizing that the electric chairs required an outside electrical source. At the time, Abyssinia did not have any electrical power. Instead, Emperor Menelik II used one of the electric chairs as his throne.

- On the animated television series *The Flintstones*, Fred and Wilma own a hi-fi composed of a turntable and a bird with a long beak to serve as a needle.

- In 1970, actor Mickey Rooney turned down the role of Archie Bunker on *All in the Family*, convinced that Norman Lear's new television show was too harsh for television audiences. Lear cast Carroll O'Connor instead, and *All in the Family* became the number one show on television for five years.

- In 1986, Silo, a discount electronics store chain, ran a television commercial in Seattle, Washington, and El Paso, Texas, offering a stereo system for "299 bananas." Dozens of customers lined up outside the stores with bags of bananas, compelling Silo to honor the offer, losing $10,465.

- In 1989, convicted murderer Michael Anderson Godwin, having avoided the electric chair through legal appeals, accidentally electrocuted himself in his cell sitting on a steel toilet while trying to fix a pair of headphones.

- On January 15, 2000, George Crowley—the eighty-year-old inventor of the electric blanket—died of pneumonia.

Eyeglasses and Contact Lenses

Contact Lenses

- **Arm & Hammer Baking Soda.** To clean soft contact lenses, mix one-quarter teaspoon Arm & Hammer Baking Soda and your regular disinfectant solution to make a paste in the cupped palm your hand. Dip each contact lens in the paste and gently rub with your finger. Rinse thoroughly.

- **Close-Up Classic Red Gel Toothpaste.** To clean hard contact lenses, use a dab of Close-Up Classic Red Gel Toothpaste and rinse thoroughly. Close-Up does not contain any grit and works wonderfully.

- **Glad Flexible Straws, Johnson & Johnson Cotton Balls,** and **Scotch Transparent Tape.** To rescue a contact lens accidentally dropped down the drain of the sink, use Scotch Transparent Tape to make a long stick from two or three Glad Flexible Straws and attach a cotton ball at one end. Insert the end of the stick with the cotton ball down the drain and fish for the contact lens, which will stick to the cotton.

- **L'eggs Sheer Energy Panty Hose.** If you lose a contact lens in the carpeting, cut off the toe from a clean, used pair of L'eggs Sheer Energy Panty Hose, use it to cover the end of a vacuum cleaner hose attachment, and secure it in place with a few rubber bands. Vacuum an inch above the carpet, frequently checking the panty hose to see if you've sucked up the contact lens.

- **Lemon Joy.** In a pinch, you can use a drop of Lemon Joy and water to clean hard or gas permeable contact lenses.

Defogging

- **Bioré Facial Cleansing Cloths.** To prevent a pair of eyeglasses from fogging up, wipe both sides of the lenses clean with a Bioré Facial Cleansing Cloth.

- **Colgate Regular Flavor Toothpaste.** Polish both sides of the lenses of eyeglasses with a dab of Colgate Regular Flavor Toothpaste. Colgate Toothpaste prevents the lenses from fogging up.

- **Dawn Dishwashing Liquid.** Rub a small drop of Dawn Dishwashing Liquid on both sides of the eyeglass lenses and then wipe them clean. The thin film of soap left behind prevents the lenses from fogging up.

- **Gillette Foamy.** Keep eyeglasses from fogging up by rubbing a small dab of Gillette Foamy shaving cream over both sides of the eyeglass lenses and then wiping them clean. The residual film of condensed soap prevents the lenses from fogging up.

- **Pledge.** Spraying both sides of the eyeglass lenses with Pledge furniture polish and then wiping them clean prevents the lenses from fogging up.

- **SPAM.** To prevent a pair of eyeglasses from fogging up, wipe the lenses with a piece of SPAM luncheon meat and buff clean. The oils in the SPAM stop the glasses from fogging.

Glasses

- **Bounce.** To clean a pair of eyeglasses, wipe the lenses with a clean, used sheet of Bounce. The mildly abrasive dryer sheets clean the lenses without scratching.
- **Coca-Cola.** To clean grime from a pair of eyeglasses, pour Coca-Cola over the eyeglasses and rinse clean with water. The phosphoric acid cleans the grunge from the eyewear.
- **Colgate Regular Flavor Toothpaste.** Polish the lenses of eyeglasses with a dab of Colgate Regular Flavor Toothpaste. Colgate Toothpaste—a mild abrasive strong enough to clean teeth without harming the enamel—gently cleans glasses and removes scuff marks from the lenses.
- **Heinz White Vinegar.** Use a drop of Heinz White Vinegar to clean glass lenses on eyeglasses. (Do not use vinegar on plastic lenses because the acetic acid may etch into them.)
- **Huggies Baby Wipes.** To clean eyeglasses with plastic lenses, wipe clean with a Huggies Baby Wipe.
- **Lysol Disinfectant Bathroom Cleaner.** To clean stubborn grease and grime from a pair of eyeglasses, spray the eyewear with Lysol Disinfectant Bathroom Cleaner, wait five minutes, then rinse thoroughly with water.
- **Mr. Coffee Filters.** Mr. Coffee Filters, made from 100 percent virgin paper, do an excellent job cleaning eyeglass lenses without leaving behind any lint.
- **Pledge.** To clean eyeglasses, spray Pledge on a soft, clean cloth and wipe clean. The Pledge also prevents the glasses from fogging up.

- **Purell Instant Hand Sanitizer.** Put a dab of Purell Instant Hand Sanitizer on a tissue and polish the lenses of your eyeglasses, simultaneously cleaning them and sanitizing them.
- **Smirnoff Vodka.** To clean a pair of eyeglasses, put a drop of Smirnoff Vodka on each lens and wipe clean with a soft cloth.
- **Stayfree Maxi Pads.** In a pinch, you can wipe the lenses of a pair of eyeglasses clean with an unused Stayfree Maxi Pad.
- **Tampax Tampons.** To clean grime from the lenses of a pair of eyeglasses, rub the glass with an unused Tampax Tampon. The cotton absorbs the grease, without leaving behind any lint.

Repairing

- **Band-Aid Bandages.** If your eyeglasses break, use a Band-Aid Bandage to adhere them back together temporarily.
- **Forster Toothpicks.** To temporarily replace the lost screw from the hinge of your eyeglasses, slip a Forster Toothpick through the screw hole until you can get the glasses fixed properly.
- **Maybelline Express Finish Clear Nail Polish.** To prevent the screws in eyeglasses from loosening, apply a small drop of Maybelline Express Finish Clear Nail Polish to the threads of the screws before tightening them.
- **Oral-B Dental Floss.** If the screw from the hinge of your eyeglasses is lost, tie a piece of Oral-B Dental Floss through the screw holes for a temporary repair until you can get the glasses fixed properly.

- **Scotch Transparent Tape.** To temporarily hold a cracked lens in place, use a small piece of Scotch Transparent Tape.
- **Wrigley's Spearmint Gum.** If a lens in your eyeglasses is loose, use a small piece of Wrigley's Spearmint Gum (well-chewed so all the sugar is gone) in the corner of the lens to hold it in place. In a pinch, you can also use a well-chewed piece of Wrigley's Spearmint Gum to hold together a pair of eyeglasses broken at the nose bridge.

Scratches

- **ChapStick.** To clean a scuff mark from an eyeglass lens, rub a little ChapStick lip balm over the mark and buff clean.
- **Colgate Regular Flavor Toothpaste.** To clean a scuff mark from the lenses of eyeglasses, rub a dab of Colgate Regular Flavor Toothpaste over the mark and buff well.
- **Jif Peanut Butter.** To clean a scuff mark from eyeglasses, rub a dab of Jif Peanut Butter (creamy, not chunky) on the lens and wipe clean. The oils in the peanut butter clean any stray marks.
- **Pledge.** To clean a scuff mark from eyeglasses, spray a small amount of Pledge furniture polish on the lens and buff clean.
- **Purell Instant Hand Sanitizer.** To clean a scuff mark from eyeglasses, put a few drops of Purell Instant Hand Sanitizer, the soapless, antibacterial hand sanitizer, on the lens and buff clean.

Strange Facts

- No one knows who invented eyeglasses or when. Legend holds that the Chinese wore glasses as early as 500 BCE. Italian explorer Marco Polo reported that he saw many people wearing glasses in China around 1275.

- In the sixteenth century, Italian Renaissance artist Leonardo da Vinci first proposed the idea of contact lenses. He suggested that a short tube filled with water and covered at one end with a flat lens be placed directly against the eyeball. Today, soft contact lenses—made from porous, liquid-absorbing plastic— contain a high percentage of water.

- In 1784, American statesman Benjamin Franklin invented bifocals—glasses with lenses that have one part for reading and one part for seeing distance.

- Eyeglasses with very thick lenses are called "Coke bottle glasses."

- To prevent anyone from suspecting that he is really Superman, Clark Kent wears glasses.

- Platinum blonde sex symbol Marilyn Monroe was a natural brunette who wore eyeglasses.

- The granny glasses worn and popularized by Beatle John Lennon starting in 1966 were Windsor glasses, wire-frame spectacles issued by the National Health. Lennon first wore the glasses to star as Private Gripweed in the movie *How I Won the War.* Windsor glasses have also been worn by Ernest Hemingway, Groucho Marx, Theodore Roosevelt, and Mahatma Gandhi.

Bricks

- **Clorox Bleach.** Remove any soot that has settled or hardened on the fireplace glass or external decorative bricking with a solution of three-quarters cup Clorox Bleach and one gallon water.

- **Dawn Dishwashing Liquid** and **Morton Salt.** Mix equal parts Dawn Dishwashing Liquid and Morton Salt and add enough water to make a cream. Rub the mixture into the brick surface with a cloth. Let dry for ten minutes and then scrub with a stiff brush. Wipe clean with water and a sponge. The salt cleans off the soap.

- **Easy-Off Oven Cleaner.** To clean a brick fireplace, make sure the room is well ventilated and don rubber gloves and protective eyewear and spray the bricks with Easy-Off Oven Cleaner. Wait fifteen minutes and wash off with soapy water.

Deodorizing

- **Arm & Hammer Baking Soda.** To eliminate the lingering smell of smoke from a fireplace, empty four to five large boxes of Arm & Hammer Baking Soda into the shelf behind the damper. Simply open the damper, reach up above it, and pour the baking soda behind it. Sodium bicarbonate absorbs smoke odor.

Fire Screens

- **Heinz White Vinegar** and **Parsons' Ammonia.** To clean a painted fire screen, mix one-half cup Heinz White Vinegar, one teaspoon Parsons' Ammonia, and one gallon warm water. Dampen a clean cloth with the solution and wipe down both sides of the screen. Rinse the screen clean with a cloth dipped in warm water.

Flames

- **NoSalt.** To make the flames in a wood fireplace glow pink for a romantic occasion, sprinkle NoSalt on the wood logs before lighting. NoSalt, a salt substitute made from potassium chloride (rather than sodium chloride), makes the flame burn pink.

Glass Doors

- **Easy-Off Oven Cleaner** and **Heinz White Vinegar.** To clean stubborn smoke stains from glass fireplace doors, wearing gloves and protective eyewear, spray Easy-Off Oven Cleaner on the doors, let sit for ten minutes, making sure the room is well ventilated, then wipe clean. Rinse the doors well with a solution made from equal parts Heinz White Vinegar and water and buff dry.

Soot

- **Arm & Hammer Baking Soda.** To absorb the smell of soot, fill a shallow pan with Arm & Hammer Baking Soda and place it on the floor inside your fireplace.

- **Morton Salt.** To reduce the amount of soot in your wood fireplace, toss a handful of Morton Salt on the fireplace logs every few weeks.

Squirrels

- **Old Spice After Shave Lotion.** To repel pesky squirrels from your chimney, spray the area with Old Spice After Shave Lotion. The brisk, fragrant aroma of the after shave naturally repels squirrels.

Strange Facts

- American statesman and scientist Benjamin Franklin did not invent the Franklin stove. In 1742, Franklin invented the Pennsylvania Fireplace, a stove he thought would be more efficient by drawing smoke from the bottom rather than the top. The smoke, however, refused to defy the laws of heat convection (namely that hot air rises), making the stove inoperable. In the 1790s, David R. Rittenhouse redesigned the cast-iron stove, adding an L-shaped exhaust pipe to vent out the smoke. Although he properly renamed the device the Rittenhouse stove, it is incorrectly known today as the Franklin stove.

- In 1822, Dr. Clement C. Moore, a professor at the General Theological Seminary in New York, wrote a poem entitled "A

Visit from St. Nicholas" to entertain his family on Christmas Eve. A friend mailed a copy to the *Troy Sentinel*, which printed the poem anonymously on December 23, 1823. Moore's poem added some key elements to Santa Claus folklore, including the idea that Santa Claus enters homes by climbing down the chimneys.

- Between 1933 and 1944, President Franklin D. Roosevelt gave a series of thirty-one radio addresses known as fireside chats, broadcast at 10 p.m. to reach as many Americans as possible and written in basic English to make the speeches understandable to a wide audience. The fireside chats became more popular than many radio shows and helped unite the American people during the Depression and World War II.

- In the 1964 movie *Mary Poppins*, Dick Van Dyke plays a chimney sweep who does an elaborate dance number with his fellow chimney sweeps on London rooftops.

- When Apollo 11 astronauts Neil Armstrong and Buzz Aldrin took off their space helmets inside the lunar module after their first walk on the moon on July 21, 1969, they noticed a strong odor of moon dust. Armstrong described the smell as "wet ashes in a fireplace."

- Around 1 a.m. on Christmas morning 2003, a naked man got stuck in the chimney of a bookstore in Minneapolis, Minnesota. At 9 a.m., a passerby heard screams coming from inside the store and called the police. Firefighters rescued the thirty-four-year-old man by breaking the chimney with sledgehammers. Police suspected that the nude man was drunk when he climbed onto the roof of the one-story building and took off his clothes in the hopes of squeezing through the chimney. Police charged the naked man with attempted burglary.

Floors

Chairs

- **Wilson Tennis Balls.** To prevent chair legs from screeching across the floor, carefully cut Xs in four Wilson Tennis Balls and place one ball over the bottom of each chair leg to silence any skids.

Dance Floors

- **Coca-Cola.** To give a freshly waxed dance floor more traction, mop the floor with Coca-Cola and let it dry to add a sticky coating to the floor that prevents the dancers from sliding across a slippery dance floor.

Dents

- **Maybelline Express Finish Clear Nail Polish.** To repair a small dent in a wooden floor, fill the hole with a few drops of Maybelline Express Finish Clear Nail Polish, let dry, then add a few more drops until full.

Eggs

- **Morton Salt.** To clean a broken egg from the floor, pour a mountain of Morton Salt over the gooey albumen and yolk, wait one minute for the salt to absorb the mess, and then brush up the salt and wipe the floor clean.

Grout

- **Coca-Cola.** To clean stained grout, pour Coca-Cola over the affected area, let sit for five minutes, and wipe clean. The phosphoric acid in the Coke cleans the grout.
- **Heinz White Vinegar** and **Oral-B Toothbrush.** To clean grout, fill a sixteen-ounce trigger-spray bottle with Heinz White Vinegar, spray the grout with the vinegar, wait five minutes, then scrub with a clean, used Oral-B Toothbrush.
- **Listerine.** To clean mold and mildew in grout, fill a sixteen-ounce trigger-spray bottle with Listerine, spray the grout with the mouthwash, wait two minutes, and wipe clean. The antiseptic kills mold and mildew.

Hardwood Floors

- **Downy Fabric Softener.** To clean a wooden floor, mix one capful Downy Fabric Softener in a plastic bucket filled with hot water and mop the floor. Aside from giving the floor a fresh fragrance, Downy helps the mop lift dirt and dust.
- **Heinz White Vinegar.** To give wooden floors a magnificent shine, mix two parts Heinz White Vinegar to one part water in a bucket, dampen a soft, clean cloth with the solution, and wipe down the floor.
- **Jet-Dry.** To clean hardwood floors, mix four ounces Jet-Dry to four cups water in a plastic bucket. Dip a soft cloth into the solution, wring it out so the cloth is damp, and wipe the floors clean.

- **L'eggs Sheer Energy Panty Hose.** Cut off one leg from a clean, used pair of L'eggs Sheer Energy Panty Hose, insert a folded bath towel into the leg, and use it to buff the floor by hand.
- **Lipton Tea Bags.** Steep two Lipton Tea Bags in a quart of boiling water, let cool, and pour into a plastic bucket. Dip a soft cloth into the tea, wring it out so the cloth is damp, and wipe the floors clean. The tea helps give the wood a beautiful luster.
- **Nestea.** Dissolve eight tablespoons unsweetened Nestea in one quart of cool water in a plastic bucket. Dip a soft cloth into the tea, wring it out so the cloth is damp, and wipe the floors clean. The tea revitalizes the wood, giving it a lovely shine.
- **Reynolds Cut-Rite Wax Paper.** To clean and shine a floor between waxings, put a piece of Reynolds Cut-Rite Wax Paper under the mop head and give the floor a rubdown.

Knee Pads

- **Stayfree Maxi Pads.** To protect your knees when scrubbing floors, peel the adhesive strips from two Stayfree Maxi Pads and stick the pads to your knees for cushioned support that makes an interesting fashion statement.

Marble

- **Crayola Chalk.** To clean marble floors, pulverize a few sticks of white Crayola Chalk with a mortal and pestle until it is a fine powder. Dip a soft cloth in the powder, wipe the marble, then rinse with clear water and dry thoroughly.
- **Downy Fabric Softener.** Mix two capfuls Downy Fabric Softener in a gallon of water and mop the marble floor with a sponge mop. The surfactants in the Downy boost the cleaning power of the water.

Mops

- **Bounce.** For an inexpensive substitute for Swiffer sheets, attach a clean, used sheet of Bounce to the Swiffer mop and get the same results. The antistatic elements in Bounce attract dust and dirt.

Scratches

- **DAP Caulk.** To hide a nick in a vinyl floor, dab a little DAP Caulk in a matching color into the spot and wipe up the excess with a damp cloth.
- **Maxwell House Instant Coffee.** To hide scratches in hardwood floors, mix one teaspoon Maxwell House Instant Coffee with enough warm water to make a thick paste. Then dip a cloth in the coffee paste and wipe it into the scratches in the floor to color the scratches until they seem to disappear. Repeat until you achieve the desired hue.

Scuff Marks

- **Colgate Regular Flavor Toothpaste** and **Oral-B Toothbrush.** Squeeze some Colgate Regular Flavor Toothpaste on a clean, used Oral-B Toothbrush and scrub scuff marks off the floor with ease.
- **Cutex Nail Polish Remover.** Gently rub a scuff mark on a tile floor with a cotton ball saturated with Cutex Nail Polish Remover, then wipe any residue clean with soapy water.
- **Kiwi Scuff Remover.** To clean black scuff marks from a vinyl floor, rub Kiwi Scuff Remover (for shoes) on the mark and then wipe clean with a paper towel or a soft, clean cloth.
- **Miracle Whip.** Use a dab of Miracle Whip to clean black scuff marks from a tile or vinyl floor.

- **Pam Cooking Spray.** To remove scuff marks from the floor, spray the marks with Pam Cooking Spray and wipe clean with a soft cloth.
- **Pink Pearl Erasers.** Use a Pink Pearl Eraser to erase scuff marks from the floor.
- **Skin So Soft Body Lotion.** Use a drop of Avon Skin So Soft Body Lotion on a soft, clean cloth to wipe scuff marks from a tile or vinyl floor.
- **Vaseline Petroleum Jelly.** Rub a dab of Vaseline Petroleum Jelly on scuff marks on vinyl or tile floors and buff with a soft, clean cloth.
- **WD-40.** To clean stubborn black scuff marks from vinyl floors, spritz the spots with a little WD-40 and rub clean with a paper towel. The petroleum distillates in WD-40 help dissolve the blotch.
- **Wesson Corn Oil.** Put a few drops of Wesson Oil on a soft, clean cloth or a sheet of paper towel and gently rub the scuff mark away.
- **Wilson Tennis Balls.** Carefully cut an X in a Wilson Tennis Ball, insert a broomstick into the tennis ball, and then use the tennis ball on a stick as if it were a giant pencil eraser to erase the scuff marks. The janitorial staffs of large buildings use this handy trick.

Squeaks

- **Johnson's Baby Powder.** To stop a floorboard from squeaking every time someone steps on a certain spot, sprinkle Johnson's Baby Powder into the crevices of the floorboard, along the edges. The baby powder lubricates the joints, alleviating the friction.

Tile Floors

- **Bounce.** Place a sheet of Bounce on the bottom of a dry sponge mop and dust the tile floor with it. The Bounce will cling to the dry sponge mop without having to be attached to the sponge mop.

- **Cascade.** To clean tile floors, mix one-quarter cup Cascade dishwasher detergent in a bucket of hot water. Scrub the tiles with a scrub brush dipped in the solution and then rinse clean with a mop and water.

- **Downy Fabric Softener.** To eliminate the stickiness on your floors left by typical cleansers, add one-half capful Downy Fabric Softener to the sudsy mop water. The surfactants in Downy boost the cleaning power of the water, and the fragrance in the fabric softener leaves behind a fresh scent.

- **Listerine.** To clean tile floors and kill germs, mix one cup Listerine antiseptic mouthwash in one gallon of water and mop the tile floor with this antiseptic cleanser.

Vinyl Floors

- **Arm & Hammer Baking Soda.** To clean a vinyl floor, sprinkle Arm & Hammer Baking Soda on a damp sponge, wipe clean, and dry.

- **Arm & Hammer Clean Shower.** Mop the vinyl floor with water, spray the floor with Arm & Hammer Clean Shower, and then mop it up.

- **Coca-Cola.** To clean a grease stain from a vinyl floor, pour Coca-Cola over the stain, let sit for two hours, and mop it up. The phosphoric acid in Coke helps dissolve the grease stain.

- **Downy Fabric Softener.** To clean a vinyl floor, pour one cap Downy Fabric Softener into a plastic bucket filled with hot water and mop the floor. Aside from giving the floor a fresh fragrance, Downy helps the mop lift dirt and dust.
- **Huggies Baby Wipes.** Use Huggies Baby Wipes to mop up sticky messes, tempera paint, or crayon marks from a vinyl floor.
- **Procter-Silex Iron.** To remove a vinyl floor tile, place a cloth over the tile and iron it with medium heat. The heat from the iron will soften the tile and the adhesive under it, making it easy to pry the tile from the floor with a putty knife.
- **Reynolds Wrap.** To re-adhere a loose vinyl floor tile, place a sheet of Reynolds Wrap aluminum foil on top of the tile and run a hot iron over it several times to melt the glue underneath the tile. Place several books on top of the tile to hold it securely in place until the glue dries completely.
- **20 Mule Team Borax, Dawn Dishwashing Liquid,** and **Parsons' Ammonia.** Add one-half cup 20 Mule Team Borax, one-half teaspoon Dawn Dishwashing Liquid, and one teaspoon Parsons' Ammonia to two gallons warm water. Mop the floor with the solution.
- **Westley's Whitewall Tire Cleaner.** To clean a discolored vinyl floor tile, spray Westley's Whitewall Tire Cleaner on the tile, scrub with a scrub brush, and rinse clean.

Wax

- **Easy-Off Oven Cleaner.** To remove stubborn wax buildup on flooring, spray Easy-Off Oven Cleaner (while wearing protective eyewear, rubber gloves, boots, and rain gear) on the floor in a well-ventilated room, let sit for ten minutes, and mop clean with soapy water followed by water alone. (Be sure to test an inconspicuous spot of the flooring first, to make certain the harsh chemicals in the oven cleaner do not ruin the flooring.)

- **Parsons' Ammonia.** To remove wax from a vinyl or tile floor, mix one cup Parsons' Ammonia in one gallon water. Make sure the room is well ventilated, mop the floor, wait a few minutes, then wipe clean with clean rags. Only clean small areas at a time to prevent the mixture from drying on the floor.

Strange Facts

- The ancient Greeks had marble floors in their temples and buildings.

- The ancient Romans invented cement and made floors from it.

- In the 1500s, the Venetians developed terrazzo floors by mixing granulated marble with cement.

- The log cabins of early American pioneers had dirt floors.

- Around 1860, Frederick Walton of England invented linoleum, a smooth-surfaced floor covering made from linseed oil. Walton mixed purified linseed oil with oxygen to produce a rubbery substance, adding heat and gums to strengthen it.

- After performing with the Beatles in nightclubs in Hamburg, Germany, Paul McCartney returned to Liverpool in 1960 and got a job sweeping the yard of Massey and Coggins, a coil-winding factory. Fellow Beatles John Lennon and George Harrison convinced McCartney to quit the job, and the Beatles began playing at the Cavern Club in Liverpool, soon becoming the most influential rock and roll band in music history.

- In 1973, singer/songwriter Paul Simon released his solo album *There Goes Rhymin' Simon*, which includes the song "One Man's Ceiling Is Another Man's Floor."

Flowers and Vases

Arranging

- **Glad Flexible Straws.** To lengthen flower stems that have been cut too short for a vase, insert each stem into a Glad Flexible Straw cut to the desired length.

- **L'eggs Sheer Energy Panty Hose.** To prevent the stems of flowers from bending over in a vase, use a pair of scissors to cut off the toes from the feet of a pair of clean, used L'eggs Sheer Energy Panty Hose, and then cut one-inch strips from the legs, creating circular loops of panty hose. Use the loops to gently tie the stems together, just below the flowers.

- **Scotch Transparent Tape.** To keep flowers standing upright in a vase, crisscross pieces of Scotch Transparent Tape across the mouth of the vase and then insert the stems. The flowers cover up the tape, so no one will know it's there.

Artificial Flowers

- **Bounce.** To clean dust off artificial flowers, wipe the petals and leaves with a clean, used sheet of Bounce. The antistatic elements in Bounce also prevent dust from resetting as quickly.
- **Conair Pro Styler 1600.** Use a Conair Pro Styler 1600 hair dryer to blow cool air to blow dust off artificial flowers.
- **Huggies Baby Wipes.** Use a Huggies Baby Wipe to clean dust off artificial flowers.
- **L'eggs Sheer Energy Panty Hose.** To dust artificial flowers, wipe the flowers with a balled-up pair of clean, used L'eggs Sheer Energy Panty Hose.
- **Morton Salt.** To brush dust off silk flowers, place the flowers in a large paper bag, pour in two cups Morton salt, close the bag, and shake. The flying grains of salt knock the dust off the flowers. Remove the flowers from the bag and shake off the excess salt.
- **Oral-B Toothbrush.** To clean artificial flowers, brush the petals with a clean, used Oral-B Toothbrush dipped in soapy water.

Coloring

- **McCormick Food Coloring.** To color freshly cut white carnations or white roses, mix any color McCormick Food Coloring in warm water and place the flower stems in the solution overnight. The stems will absorb the color by morning, carrying the color to the petals, revealing lively designs.
- **Mrs. Stewart's Liquid Bluing.** Color freshly cut white carnations by placing the flowers in a vase of water tinted with a high content of Mrs. Stewart's Liquid Bluing. Osmosis quickly sends the vibrant blue color into the tips of the petals.

Preserving

- **Alberto VO5 Hair Spray.** To preserve floral arrangements, spray Alberto VO5 Hair Spray on baby's breath, bromegrass, and cattails. Hair spray works like a fixative, holding delicate buds and flowers in place.

- **20 Mule Team Borax, Albers Corn Meal,** and **Tupperware.** To preserve flowers, mix one part 20 Mule Team Borax and two parts Albers Corn Meal. Fill the bottom one inch of an empty, airtight Tupperware canister with the powdered mixture. Place the flowers on top of the layer of mixture and gently cover the flowers with more mixture, being careful not to crush the flowers or distort the petals. (For flowers with a lot of overlapping petals, such as roses and carnations, sprinkle the mixture directly into the blossom before placing it into the canister.) Seal the canister and store at room temperature in a dry place for seven to ten days. When the flowers are dried, pour off the mixture and dust the flowers with a soft artist's brush. Borax absorbs the moisture from blossoms and leaves, preventing the wilting that would normally result.

Prolonging

- **Alka-Seltzer.** To prolong the life of cut flowers in a vase, drop in two Alka-Seltzer tablets for every quart of water.

- **Arm & Hammer Baking Soda.** Cut flowers last longer if you add one teaspoon Arm & Hammer Baking Soda for every quart of water in the vase.

- **Bayer Aspirin.** To sustain the life of cut flowers in a vase, drop in two Bayer Aspirin tablets per quart of water.

- **Clorox Bleach.** Flowers in vases stay alive longer if you add one-quarter teaspoon Clorox Bleach to each quart of water. The sodium hypochlorite kills the harmful bacteria in the water.

- **Heinz White Vinegar** and **C&H Sugar.** To prolong the life of cut flowers, dissolve two tablespoons Heinz White Vinegar and three tablespoons C&H Sugar per quart of warm water in a vase, making certain that the water level in the vase covers the bottom three to four inches of the stems. The acetic acid in the vinegar inhibits bacterial growth in the water, and the sugar feeds the plants.
- **Hydrogen Peroxide.** To extend the life of cut flowers in a vase, add a capful hydrogen peroxide for every quart of water in the vase. Hydrogen peroxide kills bacteria that would otherwise clog the stems and cause the flowers to wilt.
- **Johnson & Johnson Cotton Balls.** To keep freshly cut amaryllis, daffodils, and delphiniums alive longer, cut off two inches from the end of the stems and place the flowers in a bucket of cold water in a cool spot away from direct sunlight for a few hours. Having conditioned the flowers, turn them upside down, fill each hollow, tubular stem with water, plug with a Johnson & Johnson Cotton Ball, and place the stems in a water-filled vase.
- **Kingsford Charcoal Briquets.** To prevent mold in an opaque vase filled with freshly cut flowers, place an untreated Kingsford Charcoal Briquet in the water. The charcoal deodorizes the water.
- **Listerine.** To sustain cut flowers, add one-half teaspoon Listerine (original or Cool Mint) per quart of water in a vase. The antiseptic inhibits the growth of harmful bacteria.
- **Morton Salt.** Another simple way to prolong the life of freshly cut flowers is to add a pinch of Morton Salt to the water in the vase. Salt slows the growth of harmful bacteria that would otherwise cause the flowers to wilt prematurely.
- **7-UP.** To make cut flowers last longer and look more vibrant, fill the vase with one part 7-UP to two parts water. The high sugar content in 7-UP nourishes the plants.

- **Smirnoff Vodka.** To extend the life of cut tulips specifically, add a few drops Smirnoff Vodka to the water. The alcohol kills harmful bacteria.

Sealing

- **Crayola Crayons.** To seal the stem of a cut flower, carefully melt a green Crayola Crayon, dip the cut end of the stem into the hot wax, and let dry. The green wax seals the stem so it retains moisture, keeping the flower alive longer.

Transporting

- *USA Today.* To transport freshly cut flowers in a car, dampen a section of *USA Today* with water, wrap the bouquet in the wet newsprint, and place it in the trunk or in a dark space to shelter the flowers from the heat of direct sunlight.

Vases

- **Alka-Seltzer.** To clean gunk from the bottom of a glass vase, fill the vase with water, drop in two Alka-Seltzer tablets, wait ten minutes, and then rinse clean. The effervescent action of sodium bicarbonate cleans the vase.
- **Cascade.** To clean the inside of a filthy vase, fill the vase with warm water, add one teaspoon Cascade dishwasher detergent, and let sit overnight. The next morning, rinse clean. The phosphates in Cascade will loosen all the grime from the vase.
- **Clorox Bleach.** Deodorize and sanitize a dirty vase by washing it with a solution made from three-quarters cup Clorox Bleach and one gallon water.
- **Conair Pro Styler 1600.** After cleaning a crystal vase, prevent water spots from forming on the glass by using a Conair Pro Styler 1600 hair dryer to blow warm air into the vase.

- **Crayola Crayons.** To fix a crack in a leaking ceramic vase, choose a Crayola Crayon that matches the color of the vase, carefully hold a lit match under the pointed end of the crayon, and let the melted wax drip into the crack. Let the wax cool and gently scrape away the excess.

- **Efferdent.** To clean gunk from inside a vase, fill with water, drop in two Efferdent tablets, wait ten minutes, then rinse thoroughly. The nontoxic denture cleanser leaves the vase sparkling clean.

- **Gatorade.** To make a vase, peel off the label from a clean, empty Gatorade bottle, fill the bottle one-quarter of the way with marbles (to weight it down), fill halfway with water, and fill with flowers.

- **Heinz White Vinegar.** To clean hard water stains from inside a crystal vase, fill the vase with Heinz White Vinegar, wait thirty minutes, and rinse clean. The acetic acid in vinegar dissolves lime deposits.

- **Morton Salt.** To clean gunk from inside a vase, fill the bottom of the vase with Morton Salt, fill the vase with ice cubes, and then swivel the vase for several minutes so the ice cubes and salt swirl around the vase, cleaning it. The salt works as a gentle but effective abrasive.

- **Parsons' Ammonia.** To keep a crystal vase shining, fill a sink with warm water, add one-quarter cup Parsons' Ammonia, and wash the vase in the solution. Then rinse thoroughly.

- **Uncle Ben's Converted Brand Rice.** To clean grime from inside a vase, pour one tablespoon uncooked Uncle Ben's Converted Brand Rice into the vase and add one cup warm water. Cup your hand over the opening, shake vigorously, and then rinse clean. Repeat if necessary. The rice works as a mild abrasive, scouring the vase clean.

Watering

- **Pampers.** To prevent water from evaporating rapidly from a vase, use a pair of scissors to carefully cut open a Pampers disposable diaper. Pour the superabsorbent polymer flakes from the diaper into the vase and add water. The polymer flakes absorb three hundred times their weight in water and also give the vase a decorative look. Then add the flowers to the vase.

Wilting

- **Bounty Paper Towels.** To revitalize wilted flowers in a vase, add a few ice cubes to the water and cover the flowers with a sheet of Bounty Paper Towel dampened with cold water.

Strange Facts

- The custom of placing flowers on a loved one's grave began more than 50,000 years ago.

- The Japanese tradition of flower arranging began as early as the sixth century CE, when Japanese Buddhists began making floral arrangements to decorate their temple altars.

- The Parade of Roses, held every year on January 1st in Pasadena, California, features floats decorated with hundreds of thousands of roses.

- Flowers contain the reproductive organs of the plant: the stamens and the pistils. The stamens produce pollen; the pistils bear seeds.

- In the language of flowers (used in poetry and flower giving), roses symbolize love, daffodils symbolize unrequited love, chrysanthemums symbolize truth, and magnolias symbolize perseverance.

- In 1965, Beat poet Allen Ginsberg coined the phrase "flower power" to describe the nonviolent ideology embraced by hippies, who wore flowers in their hair, gave flowers to authority figures, and inserted flowers into the barrels of guns.

Furniture

Brass

- **Alberto VO5 Hair Spray.** To prevent tarnish from forming on freshly polished brass, spray Alberto VO5 Hair Spray on the brass object to add a protective coating.
- **Bounce.** Polish brass items with a clean, used sheet of Bounce. The antistatic elements in Bounce help clean tarnish from brass.
- **French's Mustard.** Cover the bronze object with French's Mustard, wait ten minutes, then rinse clean with water. The vinegar in mustard helps clean the tarnish from brass.
- **Gold Medal Flour, Morton Salt,** and **Heinz White Vinegar.** Mix equal parts Gold Medal Flour and Morton Salt and add one teaspoon Heinz White Vinegar to make a thick paste. Spread a thick layer of the salty flour on the brass object and let dry. Rinse and wipe off paste. The acetic acid in the vinegar dissolves the tarnish, and the salt works as a mild abrasive.

- **Heinz Ketchup.** Cover the brass object with Heinz Ketchup, let sit for ten minutes, then rinse clean. The acids from the tomatoes and the acetic acid from the vinegar clean brass.
- **Kool-Aid.** Mix the contents of one packet of any flavor Kool-Aid with two quarts water and soak your brass in the fruit-flavored drink. The citric acid cleans brass. (Be sure to discard the Kool-Aid afterward so nobody accidentally drinks it.)
- **Lea & Perrins Worcestershire Sauce.** To clean tarnish from brass, apply Lea & Perrins Worcestershire Sauce with a damp cloth, rub gently, and then rinse clean.
- **Morton Salt** and **ReaLemon.** Make a paste from Morton Salt and ReaLemon lemon juice, scrub gently, and then rinse with water. The lemon juice chemically removes the tarnish, and the salt works as a mild abrasive.
- **Parsons' Ammonia.** Scrub brass lightly with a soft brush dampened with Parsons' Ammonia.

Burn Marks

- **Cutex Nail Polish Remover** and **Q-Tips Cotton Swabs.** To remove burn marks from wooden furniture, dip a Q-Tips Cotton Swab in Cutex Nail Polish remover and gently rub over the burn. The acetone helps clean the scortch.
- **Maybelline Express Finish Clear Nail Polish.** After cleaning a burn mark in furniture, fill the resulting hole by applying a thin coat of Maybelline Express Finish Clear Nail Polish. Let dry and repeat as many times as necessary. Sand with extra-fine sandpaper.

Dents

- **Procter-Silex Iron.** A dent in wooden furniture results when the moisture is pushed out of the wood. To fix those dents, use a fine pin to prick a few holes in the finish so that moisture can penetrate into the wood. Place a towel over the dent, dampen the towel with water in the spot over the dent, and run a hot steam iron over it for a few minutes, being careful not to scorch the table. The dent will disappear as it reabsorbs the moisture. If necessary, touch up the pinholes with varnish.

Desktops

- **Gillette Foamy.** To clean a desktop, spray some Gillette Foamy shaving cream on the desk and let kids rub it around and practice writing and drawing in the shaving cream. The condensed soap clean glue, pencil marks, and grime from surfaces. Then wipe clean with a soft cloth dampened with water.

Drawers

- **Alberto VO5 Conditioning Hairdressing.** To lubricate drawers in dressers or chests, rub a dab of Alberto VO5 Conditioning Hairdressing on the casters so they slide in and out easily.
- **ChapStick.** Rub ChapStick lip balm on the casters of drawers so they slide open and shut with ease.
- **Cover Girl Continuous Color Classic Red.** To avoid pulling drawers out too far and having them tumble onto the floor, paint lines on the top edges of the drawer with Cover Girl Continuous Color Classic Red nail polish to remind you how far the drawer can be pulled out safely.
- **Ivory Soap.** Rub Ivory Soap on the casters of drawers and windows so they slide open and shut easily.
- **Pam Cooking Spray.** To prevent dresser drawers from squeaking or getting stuck, spray the metal tracks generously with Pam Cooking Spray.

- **Pledge.** To lubricate the runners in drawers, spray them with Pledge furniture polish and wipe off the excess. The wax reduces the friction, enabling the drawers to slide freely.
- **Vaseline Petroleum Jelly.** To make drawers slide open and shut easily, coat the runners with a few dabs of Vaseline Petroleum Jelly.
- **WD-40.** To lubricate the runners of drawers, spray them with WD-40 and wipe off the excess. Now they'll slide open easily without any squeaks.

Dusting

- **Bounce.** To dust furniture, wipe the furniture clean with a used sheet of Bounce. The antistatic elements in Bounce lift the dust from furniture and prevent it from resetting as quickly.
- **Conair Pro Styler 1600.** Use a Conair Pro Styler 1600 hair dryer to blow cool air to clean dust off high shelves, pleated lampshades, carved furniture, and knickknacks.
- **Huggies Baby Wipes.** To wipe up dust from furniture, use a Huggies Baby Wipe.
- **L'eggs Sheer Energy Panty Hose.** To clean the dust from under a bed, sofa, or entertainment unit, cut off a leg from a clean, used pair of L'eggs Sheer Energy Panty Hose, place it over the end of a broomstick, and secure with a rubber band. Slide the nylon-covered broomstick under the furniture and move it back and forth. The dust bunnies will cling to the nylon.
- **Scotch Packaging Tape.** To remove dust balls from under any heavy furniture, wrap Scotch Packaging Tape, adhesive side out, to the end of a broomstick and slide it under the furniture. The dust will stick to the tape.

Fingerprints

- **Pink Pearl Eraser.** To erase fingerprints from wooden furniture, gently rub the spot with a Pink Pearl Eraser.

Formica

- **Crayola Crayons.** To hide unsightly scratches on a Formica surface, choose a Crayola Crayon that matches the color of the Formica and rub the crayon into the nick.

Glass Furniture

- **Downy Fabric Softener.** To give your glass tabletops or shelving a long-lasting shine, add a few drops Downy Fabric Softener to your glass cleaner to reduce static cling and prevent dust from settling.

Glue

- **Coca-Cola.** To remove Krazy Glue from furniture, pour Coca-Cola over the glue, wait five minutes, and then wipe up the glue and soda. The acids in the Real Thing dissolve the ethyl cyanoacrylate.
- **Jif Peanut Butter.** To remove airplane glue or cement glue from furniture, cover the spot with Jif Peanut Butter (creamy, not chunky), let sit for five minutes, and then wipe clean. The oils in the peanut butter dissolve the adhesives in the glue.
- **Wesson Corn Oil.** To remove airplane glue or cement glue from furniture, apply a few drops of Wesson Corn Oil and rub with a soft, clean cloth. The oil dissolves the gum in the glue.

Grease

- **Heinz White Vinegar.** To cut through the thin layer of greasy buildup on a kitchen or dining room table, do what restaurants do: Mix equal parts Heinz White Vinegar and water in a trigger-spray bottle, spray the table, and wipe it down. The vinegar also deodorizes the table.

Ink Stains

- **Alberto VO5 Hair Spray.** The acetone in hair spray removes permanent marker from laminated surfaces. Spray the ink mark with Alberto VO5 Hair Spray and wipe clean. (Be sure to test the hair spray on an inconspicuous spot on the furniture first to make sure the acetone doesn't remove the paint or finish.)
- **Arm & Hammer Baking Soda.** To clean indelible ink from a wooden or plastic surface, sprinkle some Arm & Hammer Baking Soda over the spot and wipe with a damp cloth or paper towel.
- **Crisco All-Vegetable Shortening.** Rub a dab of Crisco All-Vegetable Shortening on the ink marks, wait a few minutes, and wipe clean. Repeat if necessary.
- **Lysol Disinfectant.** Spray an indelible ink mark with Lysol Disinfectant and wipe clean with a soft cloth.
- **Murphy Oil Soap.** Murphy Oil Soap removes permanent marker from varnished wooden furniture.
- **Pond's Cold Cream.** To remove indelible ink from furniture, smear Pond's Cold Cream on the ink spot and wipe off.
- **Smirnoff Vodka.** To clean indelible ink from any hard surface, saturate a cotton ball with Smirnoff Vodka and wipe clean.

Knickknacks

- **Alberto VO5 Conditioning Hairdressing.** To clean wooden knickknacks and other wooden objects, lightly coat the wood with Alberto VO5 Conditioning Hairdressing, then buff.

- **Conair Pro Styler 1600.** Use a Conair Pro Styler 1600 hair dryer to blow cool air to gently dust off knickknacks.
- **Pam Cooking Spray.** To polish wooden knickknacks, spray a soft, clean cloth with a little Pam Cooking Spray and wipe down the knickknacks to give them a natural sheen.
- **Scotch Transparent Tape.** To prevent knickknacks from scratching highly polished tabletops, line the bottoms of the objects with strips of Scotch Transparent Tape to create an unnoticeable cushion.

Knobs

- **Elmer's Glue-All** and **Forster Toothpicks.** To reattach a loose knob on a drawer or cabinet, dip the end of a Forster Toothpick in Elmer's Glue-All, insert the toothpick into the screw hole (making the hole narrower), carefully use a single-edge razor blade to slice the exposed end of the toothpick flush with the side of the furniture, and reattach the knob.
- **Maybelline Express Finish Clear Nail Polish.** To tighten a loose dresser drawer knob, unscrew the knob, paint the end of the screw with a thick coat of Maybelline Express Finish Clear Nail Polish, and replace the knob in the hole to dry snugly in place.

Leather

- **Huggies Baby Wipes.** To clean stains from leather furniture, wipe the area with a Huggies Baby Wipe, simultaneously moisturizing the leather.
- **Jif Peanut Butter.** To clean leather furniture, smear a thin coat of Jif Peanut Butter (creamy, not crunchy) over the affected area, wait a minute, and then wipe off. Buff with a soft, clean cloth. (Test an inconspicuous spot first, to make sure the peanut butter does not stain the leather.)

Nail Polish

- **MasterCard.** To remove nail polish spilled on wooden furniture, avoid the temptation to wipe it up, otherwise the solvents in the nail polish may remove the finish from the furniture. Instead, allow the nail polish to dry and use the side of an old credit card to carefully and gently scrape it off. Then wax the surface, buffing well.

Pianos

- **Colgate Regular Flavor Toothpaste.** To clean piano keys, squeeze Colgate Regular Flavor Toothpaste on a damp cloth, rub the keys, wipe dry, and buff with a soft, dry cloth.
- **Miracle Whip.** Use a dab of Miracle Whip on a clean, soft cloth to clean piano keys.
- **Pink Pearl Erasers.** To clean marks from piano keys, rub gently with a Pink Pearl Eraser.

Polishing

- **Alberto VO5 Conditioning Hairdressing.** To polish furniture, squeeze a dollop of Alberto VO5 Conditioning Hairdressing on a soft, clean cloth, rub the furniture gently, and buff well.

- **Armor All.** To revitalize varnished furniture, pump some Armor All on a soft, clean cloth and polish the furniture.

- **Bounce.** Polish your furniture with a clean, used sheet of Bounce fabric softener for a beautiful shine.

- **Colgate Regular Flavor Toothpaste.** To remove excess polish from furniture, squeeze some Colgate Regular Flavor Toothpaste on a damp, clean, soft cloth and wipe down the furniture. A mild abrasive, toothpaste gently but effectively removes the layer of built-up furniture polish.

- **Coppertone.** To polish furniture, squeeze a dollop of Coppertone sunscreen onto a soft cloth and polish the natural wood. The emollients in the sunscreen shine the wood.

- **Kingsford's Corn Starch.** After polishing furniture, sprinkle on a little Kingsford's Corn Starch and rub wood with a soft cloth. The cornstarch absorbs any excess furniture polish.

- **L'eggs Sheer Energy Panty Hose.** Nylon is a mild abrasive that does an excellent job polishing furniture without scratching the surface. Simply ball-up a pair of clean, used L'eggs Sheer Energy Panty Hose and use them to polish the furniture. (To make the housecleaning more exciting, wear the panty hose and roll around on the furniture.)

- **Lipton Tea Bags.** Brew a cup of strong tea with one Lipton Tea Bag, let the tea cool down, and use a soft, clean cloth dampened in the tea to polish wooden furniture.

- **Nestea.** Make a glass of Nestea according to the directions on the label, without adding any ice. Dampen a cloth with the tea and polish varnished wooden furniture. The tea makes an excellent cleaning agent for wood.

- **Parsons' Ammonia.** To revitalize stained furniture, dampen a soft, clean cloth with full-strength Parsons' Ammonia and, wearing rubber gloves, rub down the furniture outside or in a well-ventilated room.

- **Skin So Soft Body Lotion.** Use a drop of Skin So Soft Body Lotion as furniture polish and buff with a soft, clean cloth.

- **SPAM.** In 1994, the *New York Times Sunday Magazine* first reported that SPAM can be used to polish furniture. The first person to discover this was probably eating SPAM at the dining room table, made a mess, and when he wiped it up realized the SPAM was polishing the furniture. Suppose you've got company coming over, the furniture desperately needs polishing, you don't have any Lemon Pledge, and you've just had some SPAM for lunch. Well, don't throw out the leftover luncheon meat. Rub it into your wooden furniture and buff with a balled-up pair of L'eggs Sheer Energy Panty Hose. The animal oils in SPAM give wood a nice luster. Oddly, the furniture won't smell. The side benefit? Pets will love it. They'll keep licking that coffee table so it stays shiny.

- **Star Olive Oil** and **ReaLemon.** To make your own furniture polish, mix two parts Star Olive Oil and one part ReaLemon lemon juice in a trigger-spray bottle.

- **Turtle Wax.** A coat of Turtle Wax rejuvenates dulled plastic tabletops and Formica countertops.

- **WD-40.** In a pinch, you can spray WD-40 on a soft, clean cloth and use the petroleum distillate to polish furniture. WD-40 contains similar ingredients found in furniture polish, but it leaves behind a more industrial fragrance.

- **Wesson Corn Oil** and **Heinz White Vinegar.** To make your own furniture polish, mix two-thirds cup Wesson Corn Oil and one-third cup Heinz White Vinegar in a trigger-spray bottle.

Repairing

- **Heinz White Vinegar.** Before gluing pieces of furniture back together, remove the old glue from the joints by brushing hot Heinz White Vinegar on the spots and waiting a few minutes. Wipe the vinegar off with a clean cloth.
- **L'eggs Sheer Energy Panty Hose and Elmer's Glue-All.** To glue a slightly loose tenon of a support beam into the hole in the chair leg, coat the tenon with Elmer's Glue-All, wrap strips of L'eggs Sheer Energy Panty Hose around it, and let dry. Then glue the tenon into the mortise.
- **Oral-B Dental Floss** and **Elmer's Glue-All.** To glue a slightly loose tenon of a support beam into the hole in the chair leg, coat the tenon with Elmer's Glue-All, wrap Oral-B Dental Floss tightly around it, and let dry. Then glue the tenon into the mortise.

Scratches

- **A1 Steak Sauce.** To repair scratches on wooden furniture, use a cotton ball to dab A1 Steak Sauce on the mark until it attains the appropriate hue of brown.
- **Alberto VO5 Conditioning Hairdressing.** Put a dab of Alberto VO5 Conditioning Hairdressing on a clean, soft cloth and buff the scratch until it fades away.
- **Crayola Crayons.** Choose a Crayola Crayon in the shade of brown that matches the color of the furniture. Warm the crayon to make the wax more pliable, work the colored wax into the scratch, and gently scrape away any excess.
- **Crisco All-Vegetable Shortening.** To conceal a fine scratch on wooden furniture, rub a dab of Crisco All-Vegetable Shortening into the scratch and buff with a clean, soft cloth.

- **Forster Toothpicks.** Dip a Forster Toothpick in the appropriate color paint to retouch fine scratches in wooden furniture.
- **Heinz White Vinegar, Iodine,** and **Q-Tips Cotton Swabs.** Mix a few drops of Heinz White Vinegar with a few drops of iodine to match the color of mahogany or cherry wood furniture and use a Q-Tips Cotton Swab dipped in the solution to touch up a scratch in furniture.
- **Jif Peanut Butter.** To conceal a fine scratch on wooden furniture, rub the spot with a little dab of Jif Peanut Butter and wipe clean. The oil in the peanut butter will color and hide the scratch.
- **Kikkoman Soy Sauce.** Use a cotton ball to dab Kikkoman Soy Sauce on the scratch until achieving the right tone of brown.
- **Kiwi Shoe Polish.** To hide scratches on wooden furniture, apply a dab of the appropriate color Kiwi Shoe Polish, wait one minute, and buff with a clean, soft cloth. Repeat until you achieve the desired color tone.
- **Lea & Perrins Worcestershire Sauce.** Use a cotton ball to apply a few drops of Lea & Perrins Worcestershire Sauce to the scratch to make it vanish.
- **Maxwell House Instant Coffee** and **Wesson Corn Oil.** Mix one tablespoon Maxwell House Instant Coffee and one tablespoon Wesson Corn Oil and use this all-natural paint to touch-up scratches on wooden furniture (Do not use this formula on a shellac or varnish finish because it might take off the finish.)
- **Miracle Whip.** Apply a dab of Miracle Whip to the scratch, let sit for few minutes, and then buff with a clean, soft cloth.
- **Pam Cooking Spray.** To obscure a fine scratch on wooden furniture, spray a little Pam Cooking Spray into the scratch and buff with a soft, clean cloth.

- **Star Olive Oil.** To cover up a fine scratch on wooden furniture, rub a drop of Star Olive Oil into the scratch and buff with a soft, clean cloth.
- **Wesson Corn Oil.** To conceal a fine scratch on wooden furniture, rub a drop of Wesson Corn Oil into the scratch and wipe clean.

Stains

- **Huggies Baby Wipes.** To clean spills and washable marker from furniture, use a Huggies Baby Wipe.

Table Leafs

- **Alberto VO5 Conditioning Hairdressing.** Having trouble pulling apart your leafed dining room table to insert another leaf? Lubricate the metal runners under the table with Alberto VO5 Conditioning Hairdressing so the table halves slide apart easily.
- **ChapStick.** Rub ChapStick lip balm along the metal runners under the leafed table to lubricate the sliding parts.
- **Crisco All-Vegetable Shortening.** To make a leafed dining room table slide apart with greater ease, lubricate the metal runners under the table with a few dabs of Crisco All-Vegetable Shortening.
- **Ivory Soap.** Rub Ivory Soap along the metal runners under the leafed table so the table halves slide open and shut readily.
- **Pam Cooking Spray.** Spray Pam Cooking Spray along the metal runners under a leafed table so the table slides apart easily.
- **Pledge.** To lubricate the metal runners under a leafed table, spray them with Pledge furniture polish and wipe off the excess.
- **Vaseline Petroleum Jelly.** To make a leafed table slide open and shut easily, coat the metal runners under the table with a few dabs of Vaseline Petroleum Jelly.

- **WD-40.** To lubricate the metal runners under a leafed table, spray them with WD-40 and wipe off the excess.
- **Wesson Corn Oil.** Lubricate the metal runners under a leafed table with a few drops of Wesson Corn Oil on a paper towel.

Teak

- **Wesson Corn Oil.** Oil teak or unfinished furniture with Wesson Corn Oil to revitalize it.

Upholstery

- **Crisco All-Vegetable Shortening.** To clean ink stains from vinyl, apply a dab of Crisco All-Vegetable Shortening to the stain and wipe clean.
- **Gillette Foamy.** To clean cotton upholstery, apply a quick squirt of Gillette Foamy shaving cream to the stain and rub gently with a damp cloth. The condensed soap lifts out stains.
- **Heinz White Vinegar.** To remove stubborn stains from furniture upholstery, apply Heinz White Vinegar directly to the stain and then wash clean as directed by the manufacturer's instructions.
- **Pink Pearl Eraser.** To clean minor marks on cotton upholstery, rub lightly with a Pink Pearl Eraser.
- **Skin So Soft Body Lotion.** To clean ink from vinyl surfaces, apply Skin So Soft Body Lotion and wipe clean.
- **20 Mule Team Borax.** To remove stubborn stains from furniture upholstery, blot up the spill, sprinkle 20 Mule Team Borax to cover the area, let dry, and vacuum. (Before treating, make sure the fabric dye is colorfast by testing an unexposed area with a paste of 20 Mule Team Borax and water.) For wine and alcohol stains, dissolve one cup 20 Mule Team Borax in one quart water. Sponge in the solution, wait thirty minutes,

shampoo the spotted area with the hose attachment of a steam cleaner, let dry, and vacuum.

- **WD-40.** To remove chewing gum, crayon, tar, and Silly Putty from most surfaces, spray on WD-40, wait, and wipe.

Veneer

- **Glad Flexible Straws.** To glue veneer back into position, flatten the long end of a Glad Flexible Straw, fill the short end of the straw with carpenter's glue (one drop at a time), slide the flattened end of the straw under the veneer, and slowly blow the end of the straw, sending the glue into position. Wipe off any excess glue and place heavy books on top of the veneer to hold it in place overnight.

Water Rings

- **Colgate Regular Flavor Toothpaste.** To remove water rings from wooden furniture, rub the affected area with Colgate Regular Flavor Toothpaste and buff clean with a soft cloth.
- **Conair Pro Styler 1600.** After wiping up a water ring and allowing it to dry, if the ring persists, set a Conair Pro Styler 1600 hair dryer on low heat, direct the nozzle at the ring, and move back and forth over it about six inches above the spot, allowing the wood to get warm but not hot.
- **Johnson's Baby Oil.** Gently rubbing Johnson's Baby Oil into the wood may remove stubborn spots and white rings from furniture.
- **Land O Lakes Butter.** Mix two tablespoons Land O Lakes Butter with ashes from the fireplace and, using a soft cloth, rub the paste into the whitened water ring in a circular motion until the discoloration vanishes.
- **Miracle Whip.** Spread Miracle Whip on the white ring, wait one hour, wipe off, and polish the furniture.

- **Star Olive Oil.** Warm one teaspoon Star Olive Oil in a microwave oven, let cool, and rub it over the water ring. Buff with a soft, clean cloth, and then wipe clean.
- **Turtle Wax.** Apply a dab of Turtle Wax to a discolored water ring with your finger and buff clean.
- **Vaseline Petroleum Jelly.** Cover the water ring with a thick coat of Vaseline Petroleum Jelly and let sit for twenty-four hours. With a clean, soft cloth, rub the petroleum jelly into the wood, wipe away the excess, and polish the furniture as usual.
- **Wesson Corn Oil.** Saturate a small section of a soft, clean cloth with Wesson Corn Oil and rub the corn oil into the water ring with the grain until the spot disappears. Wipe clean and buff.

Wobbly Tables

- **Pink Pearl Eraser.** To fix a wobbly table, cut a Pink Pearl Eraser to fit the bottoms of the table legs and affix with nails or glue.
- **Silly Putty.** Place a piece of Silly Putty under the short leg to balance the table (unless the table is sitting on carpet).

Strange Facts

- F. Scott Fitzgerald's wife, Zelda, celebrated the success of his first novel, *This Side of Paradise*, published in 1920, by dancing on the dinner table at parties.
- Under the pen name Patrick LaBrutto, comedian Stan Laurel wrote a short story parodying Sherlock Holmes called "The Little Problem of the Grosvenor Square Furniture Van." He and Oliver Hardy adapted the story as the basis for their 1932 movie *The Music Box*, the only Laurel and Hardy film to win an Academy Award.

- Johnson Wax introduced Pledge furniture polish in the Netherlands, unaware that the American brand name means "urine" in Dutch.

- After being arrested for treason in 1956, Nelson Mandela returned home from prison on bail to find himself abandoned by his first wife, Evelyn, who took his two children and all their possessions, including the furniture and curtains.

- According to historian Doris Kearns Goodwin, President Lyndon B. Johnson's passion for the grapefruit-flavored soda Fresca prompted him to have a soda fountain installed in the Oval Office that he could operate by pushing a button on his desk chair.

- The song "Consider Yourself," from the hit 1968 movie musical *Oliver!*, includes a lyric that urges listeners to consider themselves on par with the furniture.

- The song "I'd Like to Teach the World to Sing (in Perfect Harmony)," sung by a large group of young people standing on a hill in a renowned 1971 television commercial for Coca-Cola, includes a lyric that expresses a desire to "furnish" the world with love.

- Movie director Guy Ritchie was fired from his job as a furniture mover after he tied an antique table to the roof of his van and inadvertently drove through a low tunnel.

Garages and Driveways

Bumper Guards

- **Goodyear Tires.** To avoid scuffing up your car should you accidentally hit the garage wall, cut wide strips of rubber from a used Goodyear Tire and nail them to the inside of your garage wall to align with your car's bumper.

Garage Doors

- **Pam Cooking Spray.** To lubricate the hinges and chain on a squeaky garage door, spray it with Pam Cooking Spray.
- **WD-40.** Lubricate the hinges and chain on a garage door with WD-40, the product originally developed in 1953 for the aerospace industry to displace water from electrical circuitry. Engineers working at the Rocket Chemical Company began taking WD-40 home to use on squeaky garage doors, inspiring the company to make WD-40 available to the public.

149

Oil Spots

- **Arm & Hammer Baking Soda.** To clean fresh oil spots or grease stains from a driveway or garage floor, cover the stains with Arm & Hammer Baking Soda and let sit overnight. In the morning, sweep up the baking soda, and the oil spots will be gone. Baking soda absorbs oil and grease from floors.

- **Cascade.** To clean oil spots from a driveway or garage floor, sprinkle Cascade dishwasher detergent on the oil stains, wait a few minutes, and then carefully pour boiling water over the stain. Scrub with a stiff brush and then rinse clean with water.

- **Coca-Cola.** To clean oil spots from a driveway or garage floor, just pour a can of Coca-Cola on the oil stain, let sit overnight, and hose clean. Coca-Cola works as a nontoxic degreaser. If the oil stain has been there for twenty years, you may have to use a six-pack—one can of Coca-Cola at a time.

- **Easy-Off Oven Cleaner.** To clean an oil spill from a concrete driveway (never asphalt), spray Easy-Off Oven Cleaner on the spot (while wearing protective eyewear, rubber gloves, boots, and rain gear), let sit for a few minutes, and then rinse clean with the highest pressure from the nozzle of a garden hose.

- **OxiClean.** To scrub away oil stains on a driveway, use Oxi-Clean, water, and a big broom or scrub brush.

- **Tide.** Cover the grease stain with liquid Tide, scrub with a wet scrub brush, then hose down the driveway. Tide cuts through grease stains.

- **Tidy Cats.** To clean oil drips from a driveway or garage floor, cover the puddle with a thick layer of unused Tidy Cats cat box filler, let it sit for twenty-four hours, and sweep it up with a broom. The absorbent cat box filler soaks up all sorts of oil stains from cement floors. Scrub clean with hot soapy water.

- **WD-40.** To clean oil stains from your garage floor, spray WD-40 on the oil spot and blot clean with a paper towel. The petroleum distillates in WD-40 work as a solvent.

Parking

- **Wilson Tennis Balls.** To make parking cars in your garage easier, hang a Wilson Tennis Ball on a string from the garage ceiling so it will hit the windshield at the spot where you should stop your car.

Snow

- **Crisco All-Vegetable Shortening.** To prevent snow from sticking to a snow shovel, lubricate the shovel with Crisco All-Vegetable Shortening before you start shoveling snow from the driveway.
- **Pam Cooking Spray.** Spray Pam Cooking Spray on the snow shovel before shoveling the driveway so snow slides right off.
- **Tidy Cats.** To provide traction for your car on a snow-covered driveway, sprinkle the area with unused Tidy Cats cat box filler.
- **Turtle Wax.** To prevent snow from sticking to a snow shovel, cover the shovel with two thick coats of Turtle Wax.
- **Wesson Corn Oil.** To make snow slide right off a snow shovel, coat the shovel with Wesson Corn Oil before starting the job.

Urine Stains

- **Heinz White Vinegar.** If your pet saturates the concrete floor of your garage with urine, after blotting up the mess, scrub the floor with a solution made of equal parts Heinz White Vinegar and water, allowing the concrete to absorb the vinegar solution, just like it absorbed the urine. Let dry. The vinegar will neutralize the smell of urine.

Strange Facts

- Upon moving to California in 1923, Walt Disney used his uncle's garage at 4406 Kingswell Street in North Hollywood as his animation studio.

- In 1939, David Packard and William Hewlett launched Hewlett-Packard, now the world's second-largest computer maker and the biggest printer maker, in a garage at 367 Addison Avenue in Palo Alto, California. The garage belonged to the house rented by Hewlett, then a bachelor, and Packard and his wife, Lucile.

- From 1959 to 1972, songwriter Berry Gordy Jr. used the garage of the two-family house on West Grand Boulevard in Detroit, Michigan, as the recording studio of his Motown Recording Corporation and Hitsville USA. Diana Ross and the Supremes, Stevie Wonder, Smokey Robinson and the Miracles, the Temptations, the Four Tops, and Gladys Knight and the Pips recorded their hit songs in Gordy's garage.

- In 1976, Reed College dropout Steve Jobs and University of California, Berkeley, dropout Steve Wozniak developed a prototype for the Apple I, the first single-board computer with a built-in video interface and on-board ROM. Jobs sold his Volkswagen van and Wozniak sold his programmable calculator to raise $1,300 to start their company, Apple Computer Corp, in Jobs's parents' garage in Los Altos, California.

- In 1993, chemist Bob Black invented Clean Shower in his garage so he and his wife would never have to scrub the shower again.

- In 1998, two doctorate students at Stanford University, Larry Page and Sergey Brin, started their company, Google Inc., in a rented garage of a friend in Menlo Park, California. Google soon became the most widely used Internet search engine.

Garbage Cans

Animals

- **Clorox Bleach.** To keep raccoons, squirrels, dogs, or cats away from garbage cans, sprinkle Clorox Bleach over the garbage to mask the smell of decaying food.

- **McCormick Black Pepper.** McCormick Black Pepper does an excellent job keeping raccoons, squirrels, dogs, or cats away from garbage cans—without harming the animals. These creatures all share a highly sensitive sense of smell, and simply sprinkling the area around your garbage cans with pepper will keep them far away. Want proof this trick works? Whenever you go to a fancy restaurant and the waiter comes over to put pepper on your salad, you'll notice there are no raccoons or squirrels around.

- **Parsons' Ammonia.** Sprinkling Parsons' Ammonia around garbage cans fends off invading dogs, cats, raccoons, and squirrels. The pungent fumes repel animals.

- **WD-40.** To keep dogs out of garbage cans, coat the trash cans with a thin film of WD-40.

Cleaning

- **Clorox Bleach.** To disinfect a garbage can, wash the inside of the can with a solution made from three-quarter cup Clorox Bleach to one gallon of water. Let stand for five minutes, then rinse clean.

- **Parsons' Ammonia.** Wash the inside of a garbage can with a solution made from one-half cup Parsons' Ammonia to one gallon of water. Let stand for five minutes, then rinse clean.

Deodorizing

- **Arm & Hammer Baking Soda.** To deodorize kitchen garbage, sprinkle a handful of Arm & Hammer Baking Soda in the garbage pail each time you add garbage.

- **Bounce.** To eliminate odors in wastebaskets or kitchen garbage pails, place a sheet of Bounce at the bottom of the wastebasket or pail.

- **Bounty Paper Towels.** To absorb moisture from the bottom of a kitchen garbage pail, place a sheet of Bounty Paper Towel on the bottom of the trash pail.

- **Clorox Bleach.** To deodorize a garbage can, wash the inside of the can with a solution made from three-quarter cup Clorox Bleach to one gallon water. Let stand for five minutes, then rinse clean.

- **Tidy Cats.** To absorb grease and moisture from the bottom of a garbage can, cover the bottom of the can with a one-inch layer of unused Tidy Cats. Be sure to keep the lid of the can sealed to prevent neighborhood cats from using the cat box filler.

- **20 Mule Team Borax.** To kill mold and bacteria that thrive in garbage cans, sprinkle one-half cup 20 Mule Team Borax onto the bottom of the can.

Securing

- **L'eggs Sheer Energy Panty Hose.** To secure the rim of a plastic garbage bag folded around the rim of a trash can, cut off the elastic waistband from a clean, used pair of L'eggs Sheer Energy Panty Hose and stretch the extra-large rubber band around the rim of the trash can to hold the plastic garbage bag in place.

Strange Facts

- In the 1950s, computer scientists came up with the aphorism "garbage in, garbage out."

- Garbology is the study of trash, a peculiar outgrowth of archeology.

- Yippie author A. J. Weberman wrote the 1980 book *My Life in Garbology*, revealing the results of his searches through the garbage cans left outside by Bob Dylan, Norman Mailer, Dustin Hoffman, and Spiro Agnew.

- In 1987, a barge called the *Mobro*, carrying 3,100 tons of garbage and pulled by a single tug boat, traveled six thousand miles down the Atlantic coast of the United States and around the Gulf of Mexico for nearly four months, in search of a place to dump its cargo. Six states and three countries turned the barge away. The garbage was ultimately incinerated in Brooklyn and buried in Islip, New York.

- On the children's television show *Sesame Street*, Oscar the Grouch lives in a garbage can and frequently sings the song, "I Love Trash."

- No one knows who came up with the saying "One man's trash is another man's treasure."

- The word for garbage in French is *ordures*.

Glue

Applicators

- **Forster Toothpicks.** To apply small drops of glue to an object, dip one end of a Forster Toothpick into the glue and use it as an applicator to reach small crevices.
- **Q-Tips Cotton Swabs.** A Q-Tips Cotton Swab doubles as an excellent brush for dabbing on glue.

Dispensers

- **French's Mustard.** A clean, empty French's Mustard plastic squeeze bottle makes an excellent glue dispenser. Be sure to relabel the bottle to prevent any unforeseen mishaps with hotdogs.
- **Heinz Ketchup.** For a handy glue dispenser, fill a clean, empty Heinz Ketchup plastic squeeze bottle with glue. Be sure to identify the bottle with an accurate label to prevent any sticky surprises.

- **SueBee Honey.** Fill a clean, empty SueBee Honey bear with glue. Be sure to label the bottle correctly so no one pours glue into a cup of hot tea.

Krazy Glue

- **Coca-Cola.** To remove Krazy Glue from any surface, pour the Real Thing over the dried glue, wait five minutes, and wipe up the glue and the puddle of cola.
- **Cutex Nail Polish Remover.** If you accidentally glue your fingers together with Krazy Glue, separate them with a few drops of Cutex Nail Polish Remover. The acetone in the nail polish remover works as a solvent to dissolve Krazy Glue.

Making

- **Gold Medal Flour.** To make glue, mix Gold Medal Flour and water and whisk to the consistency of pancake batter. Use the flour glue on paper, lightweight fabric, and cardboard.
- **Heinz White Vinegar** and **Arm & Hammer Baking Soda.** Make glue from milk by simply adding one-third cup Heinz White Vinegar to one cup milk in a wide-mouthed jar. When the milk separates into curds (coagulated milk) and whey (liquid), pour off the liquid and wash it away. Add one-quarter cup water and one tablespoon Arm & Hammer Baking Soda. When the bubbling stops, you've got glue.
- **Kingsford's Corn Starch** and **C&H Sugar.** Mix one-half cup Kingsford's Corn Starch, two tablespoons C&H Sugar, and one cup water in a saucepan, blending well until you achieve the consistency of paste. Cook the mixture over low heat, stirring well until the paste attains the consistency of pudding. Store in an airtight container or a Ziploc Storage Bag in the refrigerator.

- **Uncle Ben's Converted Brand Rice.** Mix one-half cup Uncle Ben's Converted Brand Rice with one-half cup water and stir together until the rice dissolves and you get glue.

Price Tags

- **Coppertone.** To remove dried glue and gum left by price tags and labels peeled from glass, metals, and most plastics, apply a few drops of Coppertone sunscreen and wipe clean.

- **Crisco All-Vegetable Shortening.** To clean the adhesive left by a price tag, coat the spot with a dab of Crisco All-Vegetable Shortening, let sit for ten minutes, then wipe clean.
- **Heinz White Vinegar.** To remove a price tag from a picture frame, glass, or metal, saturate the price tag with Heinz White Vinegar, wait a few minutes for the vinegar to dissolve the adhesives in the glue, and wipe clean.
- **Jif Peanut Butter.** To remove a price tag, cover the tag with a dab of Jif Peanut Butter (creamy, not chunky), wait two minutes for the peanut oil to penetrate the paper, and scrub clean. The oils in the peanut butter dissolve the adhesives in the glue.
- **Miracle Whip.** To remove the glue left behind by price stickers, cover the dried adhesive with a dab of Miracle Whip, wait

three minutes, and wipe clean. The Miracle Whip works as a solvent to dissolve the gums in the glue.

- **Pam Cooking Spray.** Spray a stubborn price tag sticker with Pam Cooking Spray and then rub with a cloth.

- **Ronsonol Lighter Fuel.** To remove a price tag from glass, wood, or metal, saturate a cotton ball with Ronsonol Lighter Fuel and scrub the price tag clean. The solvents in the lighter fluid dissolve the sticky residue.

- **Scotch Transparent Tape.** For a simple way to remove a price tag from glass, metal, or plastic, stick a piece of Scotch Transparent Tape on the price tag, burnish it well, and then pull off the strip of tape. The price tag will come off with the tape.

- **WD-40.** To remove a price tag from glass, metal, or plastic, spray the price sticker with WD-40, let soak for a minute, peel off the sticker, and wipe clean.

- **Wesson Corn Oil.** To remove a price tag, apply a few drops of Wesson Corn Oil to the sticker, wait two minutes for the corn oil to penetrate the paper, and scrape it away.

Removing

- **Cutex Nail Polish Remover.** To clean dried glue from any surface, rub the adhesive with a cotton ball saturated with Cutex Nail Polish Remover. Test it first on an inconspicuous place.

- **Jif Peanut Butter.** To clean glue from any surface or the adhesive left behind by a sticky label or price tag, cover the dried glue with a dab of Jif Peanut Butter (creamy, not chunky), wait two minutes, and wipe clean. The oils in the peanut butter dissolve the adhesives in the glue.

- **Miracle Whip.** To remove glue from any surface, cover the dried adhesive with a dab of Miracle Whip, wait three minutes, and wipe clean. The Miracle Whip works as a solvent to dissolve the gums in the glue.

- **Pam Cooking Spray.** Give dried glue on any surface a quick spritz of Pam Cooking Spray, then wipe clean. The oils in the cooking spray dissolve the adhesives in the glue.
- **Purell Instant Hand Sanitizer.** Cover the dried glue with a dollop of Purell Instant Hand Sanitizer, wait a few minutes, and wipe clean.
- **Skin So Soft Body Lotion.** To remove glue from any surface, pour Skin So Soft Body Lotion over the dried glue and wipe clean with a soft, dry cloth.
- **WD-40.** Clean dried glue from any hard surface by spraying the spot with WD-40, waiting thirty seconds, and wiping clean.
- **Wesson Corn Oil.** To clean glue or adhesive from any surface, add a few drops of Wesson Corn Oil to the spot and then wipe clean.

Storing

- **Scotch Packaging Tape.** To hang up a tube of glue, fold a piece of Scotch Packaging Tape about two inches long over the edge of the bottom end of the tube, punch a hole in the tape, and hang it on a peg in your workshop.
- **Vaseline Petroleum Jelly.** To prevent the cap on a tube or bottle of glue from getting glued shut, coat the tip with a dab of Vaseline Petroleum Jelly before sealing the cap securely closed.

Thinning

- **Heinz White Vinegar.** To thin glue, add a couple of drops of Heinz White Vinegar to the thickened glue and mix well.

Strange Facts

- In 1804, French chemist Armand Seguin erroneously concluded that the ingredient in the bark of the cinchona tree that cured malaria was gelatin. Seguin published his wrong findings, prompting physicians to treat their malaria patients with clarified glue.

- In 1929, the Borden Company purchased the Casein Company of America, the leading manufacturer of glues made from casein, a milk by-product. Borden introduced its first non-food consumer product, Casco Glue, in 1932.

- While promoted by a cartoon spokesbull and made by a milk company (Borden), Elmer's Glue-All is a synthetic resin glue that does not contain any casein (a milk byproduct frequently used to make glue).

- Cyanoacrylate (the adhesive substance sold as Krazy Glue or Super Glue) was invented by accident. In 1942, Dr. Harry Coover of Kodak Laboratories concocted cyanoacrylate glue while trying to make optically clear plastic for gun sights. Nine years later, while seeking a heat-resistant acrylate polymer for jet canopies with Coover, Dr. Fred Joyner spread a film of ethyl cyanoacrylate between two refractometer prisms and discovered that the prisms were glued together. Coover suddenly realized the potential uses for the adhesive, and Kodak began marketing the glue in 1958 as Eastman Compound #910.

- The first country to issue self-adhesive postage stamps was the African nation Sierre Leone in 1964.

Houseplants

Aphids and Other Insects

- **Dawn Dishwashing Liquid.** To repel insects from house-plants, put a drop of Dawn Dishwashing Liquid in a trigger-spray bottle, fill the rest of the bottle with water, shake well, and mist your household plants with the soapy water.

- **Listerine** and **Dawn Dishwashing Liquid.** To repel insects from houseplants, mix one teaspoon Listerine antiseptic mouthwash (regular flavor) and one teaspoon Dawn Dish-washing Liquid in a sixteen-ounce trigger-spray bottle, fill the rest of the bottle with water, shake well, and mist your house-plants with the solution once a week.

- **Tabasco Pepper Sauce, McCormick Garlic Powder,** and **Ivory Dishwashing Liquid.** To control spider mites, white-flies, aphids, and thrips on houseplants, mix two teaspoons Tabasco Pepper Sauce, two teaspoons McCormick Garlic Pow-der, one teaspoon Ivory Dishwashing Liquid, and two cups water in a sixteen-ounce trigger-spray bottle, shake well, and mist the leaves of the plants with the spicy solution.

- **Smirnoff Vodka.** To keep aphids off houseplants, wash the pests off the plants with tap water and then dab the leaves with a cotton ball dipped in Smirnoff Vodka. (Do not use alcohol on delicate plants such as African violets, however.)

Cats

- **Maxwell House Coffee.** To prevent a cat from having a love affair with your houseplants, add used Maxwell House Coffee grounds to the top of the potting soil. Aside from repelling cats, the coffee grounds, which are filled with nutrients, also fertilize the plants.

Light

- **Reynolds Wrap.** To give houseplants more natural light during the winter months, wrap a sturdy piece of cardboard with Reynolds Wrap. Place the plant between the homemade mirror and the window, with the aluminum foil facing the window to reflect the sunlight at the plant.

Planters

- **Bounce.** Before filling a planter with soil, place a used sheet of Bounce in the bottom of the planter to prevent the soil from leaking out. The porous dryer sheet lets water seep through—without rotting the sturdy fabric.
- **Bubble Wrap** and **Scotch Packaging Tape.** To protect plastic, wood, and fiberglass planters left outside during the winter months, wrap the planters with Bubble Wrap and secure in place with Scotch Packaging Tape. The Bubble Wrap helps insulate the plants from the elements. (Do not line the bottom of the planter to allow for drainage.)
- **Clorox Bleach.** To disinfect recycled plastic pots and planters, mix three-quarters cup Clorox Bleach per one gallon of water

in a bucket, let the planters soak in the sanitizing solution for one hour, then rinse and dry.

- **Depend.** If excess water leaks from a planter, place the pot inside a pair of Depend, creating a diaper for the plant. Conceal the adult diaper by placing the planter inside a second, larger pot.
- **L'eggs Sheer Energy Panty Hose.** Before filling a planter with soil, place a used, balled-up pair of L'eggs Sheer Energy Panty Hose in the bottom of the pot. The nylon screen prevents soil from leaking from the bottom of the planter, while allowing water to drain freely.
- **Lipton Tea Bags.** Before potting a plant, place several Lipton Tea Bags (new or used) on top of the drainage layer of pebbles, pottery shards, or panty hose (see L'eggs Sheer Energy Panty Hose above) at the bottom of the planter. The tea bags retain water and provide nutrients for the plant.

Potting Soil

- **Arm & Hammer Baking Soda.** To neutralize the acidity of potting soil, dissolve four tablespoons Arm & Hammer Baking Soda in one quart of water and water the soil once with the solution.
- **Glad Trash Bags.** Store leftover potting soil in a Glad Trash Bag for future use. Organic potting soil mix stays fresh for several months.

Rejuvenating

- **Aunt Jemima Original Syrup.** To rejuvenate a wilting houseplant, add two tablespoons Aunt Jemima Original Syrup at the trunk of the plant once a month.

- **Epsom Salt.** To revitalize a houseplant, sprinkle one teaspoon Epson Salt evenly around the base of the plant for every foot of a houseplant's height. Adding Epson Salt enriches the color of flowering plants and aids in disease resistance.
- **Geritol.** To restore a sickly houseplant to health, add two tablespoons Geritol to the soil twice a week for three months.
- **Heinz Apple Cider Vinegar.** To resuscitate a frail houseplant, mix one tablespoon Heinz Apple Cider Vinegar in one gallon of water and water the plant with the liquid. The vinegar neutralizes the pH of the water, so the plant can better absorb the vital nutrients in the water.
- **Maxwell House Coffee.** Maxwell House Coffee grounds are full of nutrients that plants love. Instead of throwing out the used coffee grounds after you make a pot of coffee, give them to your potted plants. Just work the grounds into the soil. Coffee grounds also repel cats, preventing them from digging up the soil of a houseplant.

- **Star Olive Oil.** To invigorate ferns or palm plants, add two tablespoons Star Olive Oil to the soil at the base of the plant once a month.

Shining

- **Alberto VO5 Conditioning Hairdressing.** To give the leaves of a houseplant a healthy shine, apply a small dab of Alberto VO5 Conditioning Hairdressing to the leaves with a soft cloth.
- **Miracle Whip.** Rub a dab of Miracle Whip on houseplant leaves to make them shine and to prevent dust from settling on them.
- **Star Olive Oil.** To shine the leaves of a houseplant, put a few drops of Star Olive Oil on a paper towel and gently rub each leaf, then wipe off the excess oil.

Vacations

- **Ivory Dishwashing Liquid.** If you place houseplants outside while away on vacation, before bringing the plant back inside the house, put a drop of Ivory Dishwashing Liquid in a trigger-spray bottle, fill the rest of the bottle with water, shake well, and mist the leaves and soil of the plant well to kill any insects.
- **Reynolds Wrap.** Before going on vacation for a few days, wrap clay pots with Reynolds Wrap to prevent the soil from drying out.
- ***USA Today.*** Before going on vacation longer than a week, cut a doughnut shape from a section of *USA Today*, water the plant well, dampen the newspaper ring with water, and place the dampened newspaper donut around the trunk of the plant on top of the soil in the pot. The wet newspaper will keep the plant moist during your absence.

Watering

- **Canada Dry Club Soda.** Water your potted plants with flat Canada Dry Club Soda. The minerals in club soda benefit green plants.

- **Jell-O.** Work a few teaspoons of powdered Jell-O into the soil of potted plants to absorb water, reduce how often you need to water the plants, and prevent water from leaking out of the bottom of the pot. The nitrogen in Jell-O enhances plant growth and hastens sprouting, and the sugar feeds the microbes in the soil, producing more nutrients for the plant.

- **Pampers.** Use a pair of scissors to carefully cut open a Pampers disposable diaper and pot a houseplant by alternating potting soil with the superabsorbent polymer flakes from the diaper. The polymer flakes absorb three hundred times their weight in water and store nutrients, reducing how often you need to water your houseplants.

- *USA Today.* To avoid getting water on furniture or walls, hold a section of *USA Today* behind the plant when watering houseplants with a mister.

- **Windex.** To use a clean, empty Windex bottle as a mister for plants, clean the bottle with a few drops of dishwashing liquid and water to remove any traces of harsh chemicals.

Wintering

- **Glad Trash Bags** and **Bubble Wrap.** To help an outdoor potted plant survive the winter, place the pot inside a Glad Trash Bag, fill the bag with Bubble Wrap to insulate the roots, seal the bag securely around the trunk of the plant, and set the pot on top of a wooden block to raise it off of the cold ground.

Strange Facts

- The number one cause of houseplant deaths is overwatering, which causes root rot.

- Underwatering a houseplant causes far less damage than overwatering. To revive a plant wilted from dryness, mist the leaves lightly, water the soil, and place the plant in direct sunlight.

- Plants are phototrophic, meaning they grow toward a light source. To help a houseplant grow evenly, turn the planter regularly so all sides of the plant get sufficient light.

- Plants with leaves of several colors require more sunlight than those with only green leaves.

- Plants typically do most of their growing at night, so houseplants need a daily period of darkness to develop.

- The 1988 children's book *The Plant That Ate Dirty Socks* by Nancy McArthur has inspired several sequels, including *The Escape of the Plant That Ate Dirty Socks* and *The Plant That Ate Dirty Socks Goes Hollywood*.

Insects

Ants

- **Arm & Hammer Baking Soda.** To kill ants in your home without using insecticide, sprinkle Arm & Hammer Baking Soda in cracks, corners, and crevices. Baking soda is poison to ants.

- **Crayola Chalk.** Draw a thick line of Crayola Chalk around windows and doors outside your home, and around water pipes inside your home. Ants will not cross chalk lines. You can also draw mazes on the patio floor to keep those ants entertained for hours.

- **Cream of Wheat.** Sprinkle uncooked Cream of Wheat wherever ants are giving you a problem. The ants take the farina back to their nest, and when they eat it, the farina swells in their stomachs, killing them without insecticide.

- **Dawn Dishwashing Liquid.** For a nontoxic way to kill ants, pour one teaspoon Dawn Dishwashing Liquid into a sixteen-ounce trigger-spray bottle, fill the rest of the bottle with water, shake well, and spray the ants with the soapy solution. They die instantly. The soap penetrates their exoskeletons, and you just wipe them up with a sponge. So you're cleaning the countertop while you're getting rid of ants.

- **Formula 409.** Spray ants with Formula 409 instead of Dawn Dishwashing Liquid (see above) and wipe clean, giving you clean walls and countertops at the same time.
- **Gillette Foamy.** In a pinch, you can kill ants by spraying them with Gillette Foamy shaving cream. The condensed soap in the shaving cream penetrates the ants' exoskeletons and kills them.
- **Gold Medal Flour.** Fill cracks and make a line with Gold Medal Flour wherever ants enter your home. Ants will not walk through flour.
- **Heinz White Vinegar.** To repel ants, mix equal parts Heinz White Vinegar and water in a trigger-spray bottle and mist the solution around door jambs, window sills, water pipes, and foundation cracks. The acetic acid in vinegar kills ants.
- **Johnson's Baby Powder.** Sprinkle Johnson's Baby Powder in cracks, along windowsills, or under doors where ants enter. Ants will not walk through baby powder.
- **Lysol Disinfectant.** To exterminate ants, spray them with Lysol Disinfectant.
- **Maxwell House Coffee.** Sprinkle unused Maxwell House Coffee grounds outside doors and cracks or around the outside perimeter of your home along the foundation. Coffee fertilizes the soil and simultaneously deters ants.
- **McCormick Black Pepper.** Sprinkle McCormick Black Pepper in cracks and crevices. Pepper repels ants.
- **McCormick Chili Powder.** To repel ants, sprinkle McCormick Chili Powder around the outside perimeter of your home along the foundation. The fiery spice repulses ants.

- **McCormick Cream of Tartar.** Sprinkle McCormick Cream of Tartar into cracks and crevices. When ants ingest cream of tartar, they die, unable to digest it.
- **McCormick Ground Cinnamon.** Keep ants far away by sprinkling cracks and crevices with McCormick Ground Cinnamon, which gives your home a nice smell and simultaneously repels ants.
- **Morton Salt.** To repel ants, sprinkle the problem area with Morton Salt. Ants hate salt and will not walk across it.
- **Scotch Packaging Tape.** Wrap a strip of Scotch Packaging Tape adhesive side out around your hand and use it to pick up an advancing line of ants.
- **20 Mule Team Borax.** Sprinkle a thin trail of 20 Mule Team Borax around the outside perimeter of your house along the wall near the foundation. This also kills carpenter ants.
- **20 Mule Team Borax, C&H Sugar,** and **Johnson & Johnson Cotton Balls.** Mix one cup 20 Mule Team Borax, two-thirds cup C&H Sugar, and one cup water. Dip Johnson & Johnson Cotton Balls in the solution and place them around the house, wherever ants are giving you trouble. The ants eat the sugar-coated borax and quickly kick the bucket.
- **Windex.** To exterminate ants, spray the invading insects with Windex. The soapy window cleanser kills ants on contact.

Bees and Wasps

- **Alberto VO5 Hair Spray.** To kill bees or wasps, spray the creatures with Alberto VO5 Hair Spray. The fixatives in the hair spray immobilize the insects.
- **Con-Tact Paper** and **C&H Sugar.** Sprinkle a very light coat of C&H Sugar over the sticky side of a sheet of Con-Tact Paper and hang or place the sugary adhesive strip wherever you wish to capture bees or wasps.

- **Formula 409.** One quick squirt of Formula 409 kills wasps and bees almost instantly.
- **Parsons' Ammonia.** To get rid of a wasp nest, fill a trigger-spray bottle with equal parts Parsons' Ammonia and water and carefully saturate the nest with the solution. Wait twenty-four hours, check the nest to make sure all the wasps are dead, and knock down the nest and discard it.
- **WD-40.** To get rid of a wasp nest, carefully spray the nest with WD-40. Wait twenty-four hours, check the nest to make sure all the wasps are dead, and knock down the nest and discard it.
- **Windex.** To kill a bee or wasp in your home without using insecticide, spray the intruder with a quick blast of Windex. The soap in the window cleanser kills insects.

Cobwebs

- **Wilson Tennis Balls.** To remove cobwebs from unreachable places, wrap a Wilson Tennis Ball inside a dust cloth secured with a few rubber bands (or inside a sock), then toss it at the distant cobweb.

Cockroaches

- **Alberto VO5 Hair Spray.** To freeze cockroaches in their tracks, spray the insects with Alberto VO5 Hair Spray. The fixatives in the hair spray immobilize insects.
- **Arm & Hammer Baking Soda** and **C&H Sugar.** Mix one-half cup Arm & Hammer Baking Soda and one tablespoon C&H Sugar and sprinkle the mixture in tight corners, cracks, and crevices. Lured by the sugar, the cockroaches walk through the baking soda, lick it off their legs, and, unable to digest it, leave this world.

- **Dawn Dishwashing Liquid.** Mix one teaspoon Dawn Dishwashing Liquid in a trigger-spray bottle filled with water, shake well, and spray the sudsy solution to kill cockroaches. The soap penetrates the insects' exoskeletons almost instantly, killing the bugs.

- **Kingsford's Corn Starch.** To kill cockroaches, mix equal parts Kingsford's Corn Starch and plaster of Paris. Sprinkle the mixture in cracks and crevices. Lured by the cornstarch, the cockroaches ingest the powdered concoction and "petrify." You'll have plaster statues of cockroaches, which can be used to decorate your home.

- **Lysol Antibacterial Kitchen Cleaner.** Spraying a cockroach with Lysol Antibacterial Kitchen Cleaner kills the insect instantly. After discarding the roach, wipe the puddle of Lysol clean, which conveniently disinfects the area.

- **Scrubbing Bubbles.** A quick spritz of Scrubbing Bubbles kills roaches dead in their tracks immediately.

- **20 Mule Team Borax** and **C&H Sugar.** Mix equal parts 20 Mule Team Borax and C&H Sugar and sprinkle the mixture in cracks and crevices where cockroaches are invading your home. Attracted by the sugar, the roaches ingest the borax, which kills them.

- **WD-40.** Spraying a little WD-40 on a cockroach kills the insect.

Crickets

- **Scotch Packaging Tape.** To capture crickets in a basement or garage, take a long strip of Scotch Packaging Tape and place it across the floor with the sticky side up. Crickets will get stuck in the adhesive.

Drains

- **Wilson Tennis Balls.** To prevent insects from crawling up through drains in a basement or laundry room floor, unscrew the faceplate from the drain, place a clean, used Wilson Tennis Ball inside the drain to block the hole, and screw the faceplate back in place. When the drain fills with water, the tennis ball will float, allowing water to go down the pipe. Once the water is gone, the ball will automatically reseal the hole.

Earwigs

- **Wesson Corn Oil.** To get rid of earwigs, fill a saucer with Wesson Corn Oil and sit it out in your backyard. Earwigs love oil, so they crawl into the saucer and drown.

Fleas

- **Hartz 2-in-1 Flea and Tick Collar.** Place a Hartz 2-in-1 Flea and Tick Collar in the bag of your vacuum cleaner. The chemicals on the flea collar inside the bag will kill any fleas sucked up by the vacuum cleaner.

- **Morton Salt.** To kill fleas in your house, pour plain Morton Salt (not iodized) on the carpet and upholstered furniture, let sit for three hours or longer, vacuum, and dispose of the vacuum bag.

- **Pine-Sol.** To rid fleas from your home, fill a trigger-spray bottle with equal parts Pine-Sol and water and mist your furniture and carpets. Pine-Sol kills fleas and deodorizes pet odors from sofas and chairs. Repeat daily until the fleas are gone.

- **20 Mule Team Borax.** Sprinkle a light coat of 20 Mule Team Borax on the carpets, floors, and furniture, use a broom to sweep the dry borax powder into the carpeting, let sit for twenty-four hours, and then vacuum clean. The borax absorbs all the moisture from the fleas, dehydrating the pests.

Flies

- **Alberto VO5 Hair Spray.** If you're unable to hit flies with a flyswatter, spray the pesky insects with Alberto VO5 Hair Spray. The fixative in the hair spray freezes their wings, and the flies fall to the floor, immobilized.

Insect Repellent

- **Dawn Dishwashing Liquid.** To prevent insects from entering your home, squeeze out a line of Dawn Dishwashing Liquid around the jamb of an entry door or the frame of a window. Invading insects—such as beetles, ants, and silverfish—will crawl into and get stuck in the soap.
- **Formula 409.** To kill invading insects quickly and cleanly, give them a quick spritz of Formula 409 all-purpose cleaner.
- **Skin So Soft Body Lotion.** To prevent insects from entering your home, put a tablespoon of Skin So Soft Body Lotion in a sixteen-ounce trigger-spray bottle, fill the rest of the bottle with water, shake well, and spray window screens, screen doors, and around door jambs.
- **WD-40.** To prevent insects and spiders from entering your house through windows and door, spray your doorjambs, windowsills and frames, and screens with WD-40. (Do not spray doors and windows with WD-40 if you have small children who might wipe their hands on it.)

Moths

- **McCormick Black Peppercorns** and **L'eggs Sheer Energy Panty Hose.** Use McCormick Black Peppercorns as an alternative to smelly mothballs. Cut off the foot of a clean, used pair of L'eggs Sheer Energy Panty Hose, fill it with peppercorns, and use it as a sachet. Pepper repels moths.

Plants

- **Listerine** and **Dawn Dishwashing Liquid.** To repel insects from plants, mix one teaspoon Listerine (regular flavor) and one teaspoon Dawn Dishwashing Liquid in a sixteen-ounce trigger-spray bottle, fill the rest of the bottle with water, shake well, and mist your houseplants with the solution once a week. (For more ways to repel insects from houseplants, see page 162.)

Slugs

- **Budweiser.** To kill slugs, fill jar lids with Budweiser beer and place them in your garden or wherever slugs are invading. Slugs love beer. They climb into the lid, drink the beer, and drown in it—which, if you're a slug, probably isn't such a bad way to go.
- **Crayola Chalk.** Draw a thick line of Crayola Chalk around windows and doors outside your home, and around water pipes inside your home. Slugs will not cross chalk lines.
- **Morton Salt.** Sprinkle Morton Salt on the sidewalk close to the grass. When slugs try to approach your house, the salt will kill them by reverse osmosis.

Snails

- **Budweiser.** Fill a saucer with Budweiser beer and set it in the garden or wherever snails are giving you problems. Snails love the taste of beer. They crawl in, get drunk, and drown.
- **Morton Salt.** To repel snails without hurting the environment, sprinkle salt lightly around your garden or by making a line of salt on the sidewalk close to the grass. Salt kills snails by reverse osmosis.

Spiders

- **Alberto VO5 Hair Spray.** If spiders have invaded your home, spray the arachnids with a little Alberto VO5 Hair Spray. The fixative in the hair spray freezes them in their tracks (or webs—whatever the case may be).
- **Formula 409.** To kill a spider, spray the creepy-crawly with Formula 409, which kills it on the spot.

Weevils

- **Rubbermaid.** To prevent weevils from getting into open packages of flour, noodles, macaroni, or spaghetti, store the foodstuffs in airtight, resealable Rubbermaid containers.
- **Wrigley's Spearmint Gum.** Place a few sticks of wrapped Wrigley's Spearmint Gum on the shelves in your panty near open packages of flour, noodles, macaroni, or spaghetti. The smell of spearmint repels weevils.

Strange Facts

- Bees pollinate fruit trees, vegetable plants, and flowers. One simple way to get rid of an abundance of bees is to call a local beekeeper, who will capture the bees and take them away.
- In the 1950s, Brazilian geneticist Warwick Kerr imported twenty-six queen killer bees from Africa to São Paulo in the hopes of crossbreeding them with Brazilian bees to create more prolific honey producers. Bees escaped from Kerr's laboratory and reproduced in the wild, spreading across South America and into Mexico and the United States.
- John Lennon and Stuart Sutcliffe named their band "The Beatles," changing the second letter *e* to *a*, to give the word a

double meaning—inspired by the way the name of Buddy Holly's band, the Crickets, played off cricket the game and cricket the insect. After achieving worldwide fame, the Beatles met the Crickets who had no idea cricket was a game in England.

- The Jitterbug, a type of swing dance, is not named after an insect. The name is derived from a slang term describing an alcoholic suffering from the "jitters" or delirium tremens. Bandleader Cab Calloway coined the term when he observed that the quirky and bouncy movements of the swing dancers made them look like a bunch of jitterbugs on the dance floor.

- In Czechoslovakian writer Franz Kafka's classic novella "The Metamorphosis," insurance salesman Gregor Samsa awakes one morning to discover that he has turned into a giant insect.

- In an episode of the 1960s television sitcom *Gilligan's Island*, a four-man mop-topped rock 'n' roll band named the Mosquitoes visits the island.

- Utah is known as the beehive state, despite the fact that in 1994, North Dakota led the nation in honey production with more than thirty-two million pounds, followed by South Dakota, California, and Florida with more than nineteen million pounds each.

- The most dangerous insect on Earth is the disease-carrying mosquito—delivering encephalitis, the West Nile virus, malaria, and Dengue fever. According to the World Health Organization, mosquitoes cause more than two million deaths a year worldwide.

Jewelry

Earrings

- **Maybelline Express Finish Clear Nail Polish.** To prevent inexpensive earrings from irritating skin, paint a protective coating of Maybelline Express Finish Clear Nail Polish over the posts and let dry completely. (Every few weeks, clean off the nail polish with Cutex Nail Polish Remover and apply a new coat of clear nail polish to the posts.)

Gold, Platinum, and Gem Stones

- **Alka-Seltzer.** To clean jewelry, drop two Alka-Seltzer tablets into a glass of water and immerse the jewelry for two minutes. The effervescent action of the sodium bicarbonate does the trick.
- **Arm & Hammer Baking Soda.** Instead of buying jewelry cleaner, make a paste from Arm & Hammer Baking Soda and water and use it to clean your jewelry. Baking soda is a mild abrasive.

- **Canada Dry Club Soda.** To clean diamonds, rubies, sapphires, and emeralds, soak the gems in Canada Dry Club Soda.
- **Colgate Regular Flavor Toothpaste.** To clean jewelry, squeeze a dab of Colgate Regular Flavor Toothpaste on a clean, soft cloth as a nontoxic cleaning agent. Then rinse clean.
- **Efferdent.** Drop two Efferdent denture cleansing tablets in a glass of water, soak the diamond jewelry in the solution until the water turns clear, and rinse the diamonds thoroughly. Efferdent is strong enough to clean gunk from dentures, but gentle enough not to harm the dentures. A diamond is one of the strongest substances known to man, so the Efferdent won't harm the diamond. Also, you can kill two birds with one stone by cleaning your diamond ring together with your dentures. (Do not use Efferdent to clean silver jewelry, otherwise you risk darkening and pitting the silver.)
- **Parsons' Ammonia** and **Oral-B Toothbrush.** Mix one part Parsons' Ammonia and two parts warm water and soak diamond and gold jewelry in the solution for five minutes. Brush the jewelry with a clean, used soft Oral-B Toothbrush and rinse clean with water.
- **Pink Pearl Eraser.** Use a Pink Pearl Eraser to gently scour gold-plated items to remove grease and grime.
- **Purell Instant Hand Sanitizer.** To clean gemstones and gold jewelry, use a few drops of Purell Instant Hand Sanitizer—the soapless, antibacterial hand sanitizer—and wipe clean with a soft cloth.
- **Scrubbing Bubbles.** To clean a diamond engagement ring, spray Scrubbing Bubbles into a small cup, drop in the ring, let sit overnight, and rinse clean with hot water in the morning.
- **Simple Green.** Place gold jewelry in a drinking glass, fill with Simple Green all-purpose cleaner (from the trigger-spray bottle), swirl the jewelry a few times, and let stand for one hour. Rinse thoroughly with water and dry.

- **Smirnoff Vodka.** Soak gold and diamond jewelry in Smirnoff Vodka for five minutes, then rinse and dry.

Pearls

- **Star Olive Oil.** To clean pearls, rub a dab of Star Olive Oil over each pearl individually and buff dry with a chamois cloth.

Restringing

- **Scotch Transparent Tape.** To restring a necklace of beads of graduated sizes, tape a strip of Scotch Transparent Tape, sticky side up, on a desktop. Arrange the beads in order on the tape, then restring.

Silver

- **Alberto VO5 Conditioning Hairdressing.** After cleaning your silver jewelry, prevent it from tarnishing by applying a thin coat of Alberto VO5 Conditioning Hairdressing with a soft cloth. Wipe off any excess, leaving behind a very thin, virtually invisible protective coating.
- **Arm & Hammer Baking Soda.** To remove tarnish on silver jewelry, mix a thick paste of Arm & Hammer Baking Soda with water, apply to the silver with a damp sponge, rub, rinse, and buff dry.
- **Arm & Hammer Baking Soda** and **Reynolds Wrap.** To clean tarnish from silver jewelry effortlessly, line a metal cake pan with Reynolds Wrap and fill with enough water to cover the silverware. Add two tablespoons Arm & Hammer Baking Soda per quart of water. Heat the water above 150 degrees Fahrenheit. Place the tarnished silver in the pan so it touches the aluminum foil. Do not let the water boil. The hydrogen produced by heated baking soda combines with the sulfur in the

tarnish, removing the stains. (This technique also removes the patina from silver jewelry, so make certain you're willing to do that before embracing this cleaning method.)

- **Colgate Regular Flavor Toothpaste.** A mild abrasive, Colgate Regular Flavor Toothpaste does an excellent job cleaning silver jewelry. Squeeze a dab of toothpaste on a soft, clean cloth, rub the jewelry vigorously, and rinse thoroughly with water.

- **Heinz Ketchup.** To remove black gunk from silver jewelry, squirt some Heinz Ketchup on a paper towel and rub it gently into the tarnish. For stubborn tarnish, coat the item with ketchup, wait fifteen minutes, then rub the item with a soft cloth, and rinse clean. (Do not soak silver jewelry in ketchup too long; the acids can ruin the finish.)

- **McCormick Cream of Tartar.** Use a paste made from McCormick Cream of Tartar and water to clean silver jewelry.

- **Morton Salt** and **ReaLemon.** To clean tarnish from silver jewelry, mix two tablespoons Morton Salt to one tablespoon ReaLemon lemon juice. Gently rub the paste on the tarnished silver item and then wipe clean with a dry cloth.

- **Parsons' Ammonia** and **Oral-B Toothbrush.** Mix one part Parsons' Ammonia and two parts warm water and soak silver jewelry in the solution for five minutes. Brush the jewelry with a clean, used, soft Oral-B Toothbrush and rinse clean with water.

- **Purell Instant Hand Sanitizer.** To clean silver jewelry, use a few drops of Purell Instant Hand Sanitizer—the soapless, antibacterial hand sanitizer—and wipe clean with a soft cloth.
- **Simple Green.** Place silver jewelry in a drinking glass, fill with Simple Green all-purpose cleaner (from the trigger-spray bottle), swirl the jewelry a few times, and let stand for one hour. Rinse thoroughly with water and dry.
- **Windex.** Windex removes light tarnish from silver. Spray and buff clean with a soft cloth.

Storing

- **Crayola Chalk.** To absorb moisture from a jewelry box and prevent jewelry from tarnishing as quickly, place a stick or two of Crayola Chalk in the box.
- **Ziploc Storage Bags.** Organize rings, earrings, necklaces, and brooches in Ziploc Storage Bags.

Stuck Rings

- **Alberto VO5 Conditioning Hairdressing.** To remove a ring stuck on a finger, rub a little Alberto VO5 Conditioning Hairdressing around the ring and finger and slide off the ring.
- **ChapStick.** Coat the affected ring and finger with ChapStick and slide the ring off.
- **Crisco All-Vegetable Shortening.** Use a dab of Crisco All-Vegetable Shortening to grease the ring and finger so you can glide the ring off the finger.
- **Jif Peanut Butter.** The oils in Jif Peanut Butter can lubricate that stuck ring enough to slide it off a finger.

- **Johnson's Baby Oil.** To remove a ring struck on a finger, lubricate the ring and finger with a few drops of Johnson's Baby Oil.
- **Land O Lakes Butter.** To get a stubborn ring off a finger, coat the affected area with Land O Lakes Butter and slide the ring right off.
- **Lubriderm.** To slide a ring off a finger easily, rub Lubriderm moisturizing lotion around the ring band and finger.
- **Miracle Whip.** Smear some Miracle Whip on the affected ring finger and slide the ring off.
- **Oral-B Dental Floss.** To get a stuck ring off a finger, tuck one end of a piece of Oral-B Dental Floss through the ring, then wrap the floss around the ring finger, making a spiral from the ring to the fingertip. Unwrap the floss starting at the base, and the ring will slowly and gently work itself off the finger.
- **Pam Cooking Spray.** Got a ring stuck on your finger? Spray the finger with Pam Cooking Spray and slide the ring off.
- **Preparation H.** To remove a ring stuck on a swollen finger, coat the finger with Preparation H cream to reduce the swelling and lubricate the finger, allowing the ring to slide off.
- **Vaseline Petroleum Jelly.** Coat a ring stuck on a finger with Vaseline Petroleum Jelly and slide the ring off.
- **WD-40.** Several medical journals suggest using WD-40 to remove a ring stuck on a finger. Afterward just wash the WD-40 off.
- **Windex.** Spraying a ring stuck on a finger with Windex makes the finger slippery enough to remove the ring with ease.

Tangles

- **Glad Flexible Straws.** To prevent tangles in a fine chain necklace when storing, feed the end of the chain through a length of Glad Flexible Straw and fasten the catch around the outside of the straw.

- **Johnson's Baby Oil** and **Reynolds Cut-Rite Wax Paper.** To detangle a knot from a fine chain necklace, place the chain on a sheet of Reynolds Cut-Rite Wax Paper and put a drop of Johnson's Baby Oil on the knot. Using two sewing pins, slowly and carefully pick out the knot.

- **Johnson's Baby Powder.** To untangle a fine chain necklace, dust the chain with Johnson's Baby Powder and slowly undo the knots. The baby powder lubricates the metal, helping the knots slip apart.

Tarnish

- **Crayola Chalk.** To prevent costume jewelry from tarnishing, place a stick of Crayola Chalk in your jewelry box. Chalk absorbs the moisture that causes jewelry to tarnish.

- **Maybelline Express Finish Clear Nail Polish.** To prevent inexpensive jewelry from turning your skin green, paint the inside of the ring or the back of the bracelet with Maybelline Express Finish Clear Nail Polish to create a protective barrier.

Wristwatches

- **ChapStick.** To clean a scratch from the glass face of a wristwatch, rub a little ChapStick lip balm over the mark and buff clean.

- **Colgate Regular Flavor Toothpaste.** To clean a scratch from the glass face of a wristwatch, rub a dab of Colgate Regular Flavor Toothpaste over the mark and buff well.

- **Cutex Nail Polish Remover** and **Q-Tips Cotton Swabs.** To repair scratches on the plastic face of a wristwatch, dip a Q-Tips Cotton Swab in Cutex Nail Polish Remover and gently rub it over the face of the watch until the scratches vanish, then wipe clean.

- **Purell Instant Hand Sanitizer.** To clean a scratch from the glass face of a wristwatch, put a few drops of Purell Instant Hand Sanitizer—the soapless, antibacterial hand sanitizer—on the mark and buff clean.

Strange Facts

- In 1522, Spanish Conquistador Gil Gonzalez Davila named Costa Rica (meaning "rich coast") because he saw natives wearing gold necklaces and thought the land was rich with gold. In fact, Costa Rica has less gold than any other country in Latin America.

- In 1607, the settlers in Jamestown, Virginia, the first colony in the New World, mined gold and sent a shipload back to London, where assayers identified the glittering metal as iron pyrite, better known as "fool's gold."

- In 1667, the *Wapen Van Amsterdam*, a Dutch ship carrying forty crates of gold and four tons of uncut diamonds, sank. In 1983, the government of Iceland located a sunken wooden ship and spent millions of dollars to raise the *Wapen Van Amsterdam*—only to bring up a German trawler that had sunk in 1903 carrying a cargo of herring.

- On May 10, 1869, the Union Pacific and Central Pacific railways were linked together with two golden spikes during a well-publicized ceremony at Promontory, Utah. Although the builders immediately replaced the golden spikes with steel spikes to avoid theft, within a few days souvenir hunters disconnected the transcontinental railroad at the historic spot, stealing twelve spikes, six ties, and two pairs of rails.

- *The Lord of the Rings*, an epic novel written by British professor J. R. R. Tolkien and originally published in three volumes in 1954 and 1955, follows the whereabouts of a powerful magic ring controlled by an evil entity.

- John Lennon did not write the 1967 Beatles song "Lucy in the Sky with Diamonds" to form the initials LSD. Lennon consistently claimed throughout his life that the song title had been inspired by his four-year-old son Julian, who came home one day with a picture he had drawn at school of his classmate Lucy O'Donnell against a backdrop of exploding, multicolored stars, which he called "Lucy in the Sky with Diamonds." Lennon repeatedly insisted that he had no idea the title formed the abbreviation LSD until someone pointed it out after the song had been released.

- Actor Richard Burton gave his wife, actress Elizabeth Taylor, some of the world's most magnificent jewelry, including the Krupp Diamond and the LaPeregina Pearl.

- Paul Simon's 1987 album *Graceland* includes a song titled "Diamonds on the Soles of Her Shoes," about a rich girl dating a poor boy and how their widely divergent economic stations in life come to bear on their romantic relationship.

Bottles

- **Alberto VO5 Hair Spray.** To remove dried glue from the outside of a glass bottles, spray Alberto VO5 Hair Spray on the dried glue, wipe off, and wash the bottle in soapy water. The propanes, butanes, and acetones in Alberto VO5 Hair Spray dissolve glue.

- **French's Mustard.** To deodorize the inside of a smelly glass bottle, mix two teaspoons French's Mustard with one quart water in the bottle, shake vigorously, and rinse well.

- **L'eggs Sheer Energy Panty Hose.** To wash the inside of a glass bottle, wrap a section of a clean pair of L'eggs Sheer Energy Panty Hose around the bristles of a bottle washer brush, fasten with a rubber band, and scrub. The nylon is a mild abrasive.

- **Parsons' Ammonia** and **Uncle Ben's Converted Brand Rice.** To clean narrow-necked glass bottles, fill the bottle with equal parts Parsons' Ammonia and water, add a handful of uncooked Uncle Ben's Converted Brand Rice, and swirl. Rinse with soapy water. The rice helps scrub the gunk from the inside of the bottle.

Butcher Block

- **Clorox Bleach.** To clean butcher block and prevent bacteria from breeding, wash the cutting board with hot sudsy water and rinse clean. Then apply a solution of three tablespoons Clorox Bleach per gallon of water, wait two minutes, and then rinse clean again.
- **Crisco All-Vegetable Shortening.** To oil butcher block, put a dab of Crisco All-Vegetable Shortening on a sheet of paper towel, rub it into the wood, and then wipe clean.
- **Pam Cooking Spray.** To preserve butcher block, spray the cutting board with Pam Cooking Spray, use a paper towel to rub the oil into the wood, and then wipe clean.
- **Wesson Corn Oil.** To oil butcher block, put a few drops of Wesson Corn Oil on a paper towel, rub it into the wood, and then wipe clean.

Cast Iron

- **Bounty Paper Towels.** To prevent cast-iron skillets from rusting, place a sheet of Bounty Paper Towel between your cast iron pots and pans in the cupboard. The quicker picker-upper absorbs moisture that would otherwise rust the skillets.
- **Canada Dry Club Soda.** To clean a cast-iron skillet, pour Canada Dry Club Soda over the skillet while it is still hot. The sodium bicarbonate in the club soda helps clean off the baked-on food left over from cooking.
- **Crisco All-Vegetable Shortening.** To season new cast-iron cookware, rub Crisco All-Vegetable Shortening into the cookware to create a thin coating and bake the cookware in an

oven heated to 200 degrees Fahrenheit for two hours. After using the new cookware a few times, repeat this procedure.

- **Easy-Off Oven Cleaner.** To clean baked-on food or grease from an aged cast-iron skillet or pot, spray the item with Easy-Off Oven Cleaner in a well-ventilated area, let sit for ten minutes, then wash thoroughly.

- **Morton Salt.** To clean a cast-iron pan, heat the pan on a stove burner set on high until the pan starts smoking. Pour one cup Morton Salt into the pan and use a wooden spoon to move the salt around the pan, allowing the salt to absorb any grease and grime from the pan. When the salt starts turning grey, discard it. The surface of the pan should appear dull; otherwise scrub it with salt again. Wash the pan clean with hot water, dry it thoroughly with a towel, let it air dry for thirty minutes, and then re-season the pan. (See "Wesson Corn Oil and Bounty Paper Towels" below.)

- **Mr. Coffee Filters.** To prevent cast-iron skillets from rusting on the shelf, place a Mr. Coffee Filter in the skillet to absorb moisture and avert rust.

- **Pam Cooking Spray.** To season new cast-iron cookware, wash the pot or pan in warm, soapy water after each use, wipe thoroughly dry, coat the inside with Pam Cooking Spray, then wipe clean with a sheet of paper towel.

- **Wesson Corn Oil.** To remove rust spots from a cast-iron skillet, apply Wesson Corn Oil, let stand, then wipe thoroughly. Repeat if necessary.

- **Wesson Corn Oil** and **Bounty Paper Towels.** To season a new cast-iron skillet, rub a few drops of Wesson Corn Oil into the inside of the pan with a sheet of Bounty Paper Towel and warm the skillet in an oven heated to 200 degrees Fahrenheit for two hours. Repeat after washing the skillet for several weeks.

China

- **Arm & Hammer Baking Soda.** To clean coffee or tea stains from fine china, dip a damp cloth in Arm & Hammer Baking Soda, use it to gently rub the china, and rinse clean. Baking soda is a mild abrasive that will clean, but won't scratch, china.

- **Clorox Bleach.** To remove coffee or tea stains from china, soak the blemished china cups and saucers for ten minutes in a solution of one tablespoon Clorox Bleach per gallon of water. Rinse thoroughly.

- **Elmer's Glue-All.** To repair a broken piece of fine china, glue the pieces back together with Elmer's Glue-All.

- **Morton Salt** and **Heinz White Vinegar.** To remove coffee or tea stains from china, mix equal amounts of Morton Salt and Heinz White Vinegar, dampen a soft cloth in the mixture, and use it to gently rub the china. Rinse clean.

- **Mr. Coffee Filters.** To protect china dishes stacked in your cabinet, place a Mr. Coffee Filter between each dish.

- **Nestlé Carnation Condensed Milk.** To repair broken porcelain china, glue the pieces back together with Nestlé Carnation Condensed Milk. The condensed milk works like strong glue and conceals the fracture.

- **Nestlé Carnation Evaporated Milk.** To make a slight crack in a china dish vanish, place the dish in a pan, cover it with Nestlé Carnation Evaporated Milk, bring to a boil, and then simmer for twenty-five minutes at low heat. The crack should disappear.

- **20 Mule Team Borax.** To shine china, fill a sink with water, add one-half cup 20 Mule Team Borax, rinse your fine china in the solution, and then rinse again in clean water.

Coffee Cups

- **Cascade.** To clean coffee or tea stains from cups, fill the sink with hot water, add one tablespoon Cascade dishwasher detergent, mix well, set the cups in the water, and let soak for twenty minutes. Then rinse clean with water.
- **Efferdent.** To clean coffee or tea stains from a cup, fill the stained cup with water, drop in one Efferdent denture cleansing tablet, and let sit overnight. Then rinse clean.

Cookware

- **Alka-Seltzer.** To clean baked-on food from pots, pans, or casserole dishes, fill the cookware with water, drop in six Alka-Seltzer tablets, let soak for one hour, and then scrub as usual.
- **Arm & Hammer Baking Soda.** To clean baked-on food from pots and pans, fill the pot or pan with enough water to cover the food baked inside, add one tablespoon Arm & Hammer Baking Soda, place on the stove, and bring to a boil for five minutes. Let cool and then scrub with a sponge, rinse, and dry.
- **Bounce.** To remove baked-on food and grime from a pot, pan, or casserole dish, go to your laundry and grab that box of Bounce dryer sheets. You'll notice that Procter and Gamble has conveniently designed a sheet of Bounce to fit perfectly in a Corningware or Pyrex casserole dish. Fill the pot, pan, or casserole dish with water, float a sheet of Bounce in it overnight, and in the morning, use the wet sheet of Bounce to wipe out the cookware. The antistatic elements in Bounce loosen the baked-on food. And there will be no static cling either.
- **Cascade.** To clean baked-on food from a pot or pan, pour two tablespoons Cascade dishwasher detergent in the cookware, fill with hot water, wait thirty minutes, and rinse clean. The phosphates in Cascade loosen all the baked-on food.

- **Coca-Cola.** If you burn a pot or pan on the stove and want to clean out a brown burn stain, boil some Coca-Cola in the pot or pan. The burn stain will come off.

- **Downy Fabric Softener.** To clean baked-on food from pots, pans, or casserole dishes, fill the cookware with water, add a cupful of Downy Fabric Softener, mix well, and let sit overnight. In the morning, scrub with a sponge and rinse clean.

- **Efferdent.** If you boil all the water out of a pot and want to clean out the brown burn stain, fill the pot with water and drop in two or three Efferdent denture cleansing tablets. Let the pot sit overnight. In the morning, use a sponge to wipe away that otherwise difficult burn stain. (You can also toss your dentures in the pot at the same time and kill two birds with one stone.)

- **Heinz White Vinegar.** To clean baked-on food from pots, pans, or casserole dishes, fill the cookware with equal parts Heinz White Vinegar and water; let stand for thirty minutes; scrub with a sponge in hot, soapy water; and rinse clean.

- **Jet-Dry.** Fill baking dishes, pots, or pans encrusted with baked-on food with water, add one tablespoon Jet-Dry, and let sit overnight. In the morning rinse clean. The surfactants in Jet-Dry loosen the baked-on food.

- **L'eggs Sheer Energy Panty Hose.** To make an excellent pot scrubber, ball up a clean, used pair of L'eggs Sheer Energy Panty Hose and insert it into a webbed onion bag.

- **Maxwell House Coffee.** Scrub baked-on food from pots and pans with used Maxwell House Coffee grounds, which are a nontoxic, readily available, mild abrasive.

- **McCormick Cream of Tartar.** Sprinkle McCormick Cream of Tartar on stubborn baked-on food in pots and pans and scrub with a sponge. The potassium bitartrate loosens the food particles.

- **Morton Salt.** To successfully scrub calcium deposits from glassware or baked-on food from pots and pans, use Morton Salt as if it was Comet cleanser. Salt is a highly effective abrasive.
- **Parsons' Ammonia** and **Glad Trash Bags.** To remove black burn marks from pots, pans, and casserole dishes, place the cookware in a Glad Trash Bag, pour in two cups Parsons' Ammonia, tie the bag securely shut, and let stand outside overnight. Open the bag outdoors, keeping your face away from the fumes. Rinse the ammonia off the dishes with a garden hose and then bring them back inside to wash thoroughly.
- **Reynolds Wrap.** Crumple a sheet Reynolds Wrap aluminum foil into a ball and use it as a pot scrubber to clean baked-on food from a pot or pan. The foil is soft and works like a steel wool pad, without scratching the cookware.
- **20 Mule Team Borax.** To clean baked-on food from pots, pans, or casserole dishes, sprinkle 20 Mule Team Borax on the cookware, rub with a damp sponge, and rinse thoroughly.

Copper Pots

- **A1 Steak Sauce.** To remove tarnish from copper pots, rub A1 Steak Sauce on the tarnish with a soft cloth. The acid from the tomato puree combined with the vinegar removes tarnish.

- **Heinz Ketchup.** Remove tarnish from the bottom of a copper pot or pan by covering the copper with Heinz Ketchup. Let sit for ten minutes. Then rinse off the pot or pan under running water. The acids from the tomatoes and the vinegar in the ketchup gently devour the tarnish.
- **Hunt's Tomato Paste.** Coat the copper pot with Hunt's Tomato Paste, let sit for ten minutes, and rinse off the tomato paste under running water. The acids from the tomatoes gently eliminate the tarnish.

- **Gold Medal Flour, Morton Salt,** and **Heinz White Vinegar.** In a bowl, mix one tablespoon Gold Medal Flour, one tablespoon Morton Salt, and one tablespoon Heinz White Vinegar to make a paste. Spread a thick coat of this paste on the copper and let dry, then rinse and wipe clean.
- **Lea & Perrins Worcestershire Sauce.** With a soft cloth, rub Lea & Perrins Worcestershire Sauce on the tarnish to remove it.
- **Morton Salt** and **ReaLemon.** Mix one tablespoon Morton Salt and two tablespoons ReaLemon lemon juice and rub the mixture into the copper until it sparkles shiny clean. The chemical reaction cleans the cooper instantly.
- **Tabasco Pepper Sauce.** To remove tarnish from copper pots, rub Tabasco Pepper Sauce on the tarnish with a soft cloth. The various acids in the sauce clean tarnish.

Crystal

- **Parsons' Ammonia.** To wash crystal sparkling clean, fill a sink full of warm water and add one-quarter cup Parsons' Ammonia. Soak the crystal in the sink for thirty minutes, then rinse clean with water.
- **Smirnoff Vodka.** Dampen a cloth with Smirnoff Vodka and gently wipe down crystal.

Cutting Boards

- **Arm & Hammer Baking Soda.** To clean and deodorize a cutting board, sprinkle Arm & Hammer Baking Soda on a damp sponge, rub the cutting board, and rinse clean.
- **Clorox Bleach.** To disinfect a cutting board, wash the cutting board with hot sudsy water and rinse clean. Then apply a solution of three tablespoons Clorox Bleach per gallon of water, wait two minutes, and then rinse clean again.

- **Crisco All-Vegetable Shortening.** To preserve a wooden cutting board, rub a few dabs of Crisco All-Vegetable Shortening into the cutting board, let sit overnight, then wipe off the excess shortening with a paper towel.
- **Pam Cooking Spray** and **Bounty Paper Towels.** To preserve a wooden cutting board, spray the cutting board with Pam Cooking Spray, use a sheet of Bounty Paper Towel to rub the oil into the wood, then wipe clean.
- **ReaLemon.** To deodorize a cutting board, wash the cutting board with ReaLemon lemon juice to eliminate the smell of garlic, onions, or fish.
- **Wesson Corn Oil** and **Bounty Paper Towels.** To preserve a wooden cutting board, put a few drops of Wesson Corn Oil on a sheet of Bounty Paper Towel, rub it into the wood, and then wipe clean.

Dishes

- **Clairol Herbal Essences Shampoo.** If you run out of dishwashing soap, wash your dishes in the kitchen sink with Clairol Herbal Essences Shampoo.
- **MasterCard.** To scrape food from dishes, use a clean, old MasterCard credit card.
- **Tide.** If you're having trouble scrubbing baked-on food from dishes, fill your sink with warm water, add one tablespoon liquid Tide, soak your dishes in the soapy solution, then scrub with a sponge and rinse well.

Dishwashing Liquid

- **Arm & Hammer Baking Soda.** To boost the strength of your regular dishwashing liquid, add two tablespoons Arm & Hammer Baking Soda to your dishpan along with the usual amount of detergent you use.

Drain Boards

- **Heinz White Vinegar.** To clean hard water stains from a drain board, soak the drain board in a sink filled with equal parts Heinz White Vinegar and water. Then rinse clean with water.

Food Graters

- **Oral-B Toothbrush.** To clean food particles from a grater, scrub the holes in the grater with a clean, used Oral-B Toothbrush dipped in your regular dishwashing liquid.
- **Pam Cooking Spray.** Before using a food grater, spray it with a light coat of Pam Cooking Spray to make cleaning up afterward easier.

Funnels

- **Clorox Bleach.** To improvise a funnel, cut an empty, clean Clorox Bleach jug in half and remove the cap.
- **Dixie Cups.** Punch a hole in the bottom of a Dixie Cup near the edge to devise an impromptu funnel.
- **Reynolds Wrap.** If you need a funnel in a pinch, double over a piece of Reynolds Wrap aluminum foil and roll it into the shape of a cone.

Glassware

- **Colgate Regular Flavor Toothpaste.** To clean superficial scratches on glassware, polish the marks with a dab of Colgate Regular Flavor Toothpaste.
- **Coppertone.** To pry apart two bowls or glasses, dribble a few drops of Coppertone sunscreen down the sides, then slip the bowls or glasses apart.

- **Johnson's Baby Oil.** To pry apart two bowls or glasses, dribble Johnson's Baby Oil between the stuck glassware, let it seep in, and gently tug the glasses apart.
- **Pam Cooking Spray.** When one drinking glass gets stuck inside another, spray a little Pam Cooking Spray between the two glasses, wait a few seconds, and pry them apart slowly.
- **Skin So Soft Body Lotion.** To pry apart two bowls or glasses, dribble a few drops of Skin So Soft Body Lotion down the sides, then slip the bowls or glasses apart.
- **Wesson Corn Oil.** When one drinking glass gets stuck inside another, trickle a few drops of Wesson Corn Oil between the two glasses, wait a few seconds, and pull them apart with ease.

Plasticware

- **Clorox Bleach.** To clean tomato sauce stains from the insides of Tupperware and Rubbermaid containers, fill the containers with one part Clorox Bleach to two parts water, let soak for ten minutes, wash with soapy water, and rinse clean.
- **Efferdent.** To clean tomato sauce stains from the insides of Tupperware and Rubbermaid containers, fill the plastic containers with hot water, drop in two Efferdent tablets, and let sit overnight. Then wash with soapy water and rinse clean.
- **Pam Cooking Spray.** To prevent tomato sauce from staining the insides of Tupperware or Rubbermaid containers, spray the plastic containers with Pam Cooking Spray before pouring in any tomato sauce.
- **Purell Instant Hand Sanitizer.** To clean tomato sauce stains from the insides of Tupperware and Rubbermaid containers, squirt some Purell Instant Hand Sanitizer into the containers when washing.

- **ReaLemon.** To safely bleach tomato sauce stains from the insides of Tupperware and Rubbermaid containers, rub ReaLemon lemon juice over the discolored plastic and let the containers sit in the sun for a day. The lemon juice bleaches the plastic back to its original color.

Sports Bottles

- **Efferdent.** To clean the inside of a sports bottle, fill the bottle with warm water, add two Efferdent tablets, let sit for five minutes, and then rinse thoroughly.

Teapots

- **Arm & Hammer Baking Soda.** To clean a teapot, wash in a solution of one-quarter cup Arm & Hammer Baking Soda and one quart warm water and then rinse clean.
- **Efferdent.** To clean the inside of a stained teapot, fill the teapot with warm water, add two Efferdent tablets, let sit for five minutes, and then rinse thoroughly.

Thermos Bottles

- **Alka-Seltzer.** Fill the Thermos bottle with water, drop in four Alka-Seltzer tablets, and let soak for an hour or longer if necessary. Rinse clean.
- **Arm & Hammer Baking Soda.** To clean coffee stains from the inside of a Thermos bottle, fill the bottle with two cups hot water, add two tablespoons Arm & Hammer Baking Soda, seal the lid, and shake vigorously. Remove the lid and let the solution stand overnight to soak away the stains.
- **Cascade.** Fill the bottle with two tablespoons Cascade dishwasher detergent and hot water. Let sit for thirty minutes, swish clean with a bottlebrush, and rinse thoroughly.

- **Clorox Bleach.** To deodorize the inside of a smelly Thermos bottle, fill the bottle with water, add one teaspoon Clorox Bleach, let sit for one hour, rinse clean with water, and let air dry.
- **Efferdent.** To clean coffee stains from the inside of a Thermos bottle, fill the bottle with water, drop in two Efferdent tablets, and let sit overnight. In the morning, rinse clean.
- **Uncle Ben's Converted Brand Rice.** To scrub stubborn coffee stains from the inside of a Thermos bottle, pour one cup warm water into the bottle and add one tablespoon uncooked Uncle Ben's Converted Brand Rice. Shake vigorously and then rinse clean.

Wooden Salad Bowls

- **Crisco All-Vegetable Shortening.** To revitalize a wooden salad bowl, rub Crisco All-Vegetable Shortening all over the inside and outside of the bowl, let sit overnight, and then remove the excess shortening by buffing with a paper towel. The shortening seals the wood.
- **Pam Cooking Spray** and **Bounty Paper Towels.** To preserve a wooden salad bowl, spray the bowl with Pam Cooking Spray, use a sheet of Bounty Paper Towel to rub the oil into the wood, then wipe clean.
- **Reynolds Cut-Rite Wax Paper.** To restore the luster to a wooden salad bowl, wash and dry the bowl completely, then rub the entire bowl with a sheet of Reynolds Cut-Rite Wax Paper.
- **Wesson Corn Oil** and **Bounty Paper Towels.** To preserve a wooden salad bowl, put a few drops of Wesson Corn Oil on a sheet of Bounty Paper Towel, rub it into the wood, and then wipe clean.

Wooden Spoons

- **Crisco All-Vegetable Shortening.** To treat new wooden spoons to prevent staining from tomato sauce, rub a dollop of Crisco All-Vegetable Shortening into the wood and buff well with a clean cloth or paper towel. The shortening seals the wood.

- **Pam Cooking Spray** and **Bounty Paper Towels.** To prevent tomato sauce from staining new wooden spoons, spray the spoons with Pam Cooking Spray, use a sheet of Bounty Paper Towel to rub the oil into the wood, then wipe clean.

- **Wesson Corn Oil** and **Bounty Paper Towels.** To preserve a wooden spoon, put a few drops of Wesson Corn Oil on a sheet of Bounty Paper Towel, rub it into the wood, and then wipe clean.

Strange Facts

- As early as the eighth century CE, Chinese and Japanese cultures began producing fine quality porcelain china.

- Only the Chinese and Japanese knew the well-guarded secret of how to make porcelain china—until 1708, when two German scientists by the names of J. F. Bottger and E. W. Von Tschirnhaus, commissioned by Augustus the Strong in the city of Dresden, mixed a white clay with alabaster powder to produce hard white porcelain.

- Dresden china is not made in Dresden, Germany, but rather in the nearby town of Meissen. In 1710, Augustus the Strong, Elector of Saxony and King of Poland, established the Meissen Royal Manufactory, today the oldest porcelain factory in Europe. Because most Meissen China was sold in Dresden, it was incorrectly referred to as Dresden china. The Meissen factory produces porcelain china and figurines to this very day.

- In 1913, Dr. Jesse Littleton, a scientist at the Corning Glass Works in Corning, New York, had his wife bake a chocolate cake in the sawed-off bottom of a battery jar made from heat-tempered glass, proving that food could be cooked in glass. Three years later, Corning introduced Pyrex ovenware.

- After World War II, plastics industrialist Earl Silas Tupper invented a method to transform polyethylene slag (a black, smelly byproduct of the crude oil refinement process) into a clean, clear plastic that was pliant, solid, and grease-free—a vast improvement over the brittle, slimy, and putrid plastics of the day. Tupper also developed an airtight and watertight seal for containers made of his improved plastic, creating Tupperware—the plastic storage container that still bears his name.

- A common method of protest throughout the world is for people to gather together on the streets of a city and bang pots and pans together. In 2001, hundreds of thousands of people filled the streets of Argentina banging pots and pans in loud protest against the bankrupt economy. In 2006, three thousand women banged pots and pans in the streets of Oaxaca, Mexico, to protest against the state governor.

- In a 2007 speech at a memorial service in Indianapolis for novelist Kurt Vonnegut, Mark Vonnegut said that his father used to recite Chaucer while his children were banging on pots and pans for background music.

Lawns

Bare Patches

- **Lipton Tea Bags.** To repair a bare patch on the lawn, place moist Lipton Tea Bags (new or used) on the spot and sprinkle with grass seed. The wet tea provides moisture and nutrients, and the tea bag itself eventually decomposes.
- **Nestea.** Repair a bare patch on the lawn by covering the bare spot with one-inch of unsweetened Nestea powdered mix, moisten with water, and sprinkle with grass seed. The wet tea provides moisture and nutrients for the seeds.

Crevices

- **Heinz White Vinegar.** To prevent grass from growing in crevices, pour Heinz White Vinegar in sidewalk cracks and between bricks.
- **Morton Salt.** To kill grass in cracks and crevices, sprinkle Morton Salt on the unwanted grass. Salt is a corrosive that kills plants.

Fences

- **Clorox Bleach.** To restore weathered wooden fences, put on rubber gloves, protective eyewear, boots, and rain gear and spray undiluted Clorox bleach directly on the wooden surfaces using a garden pressure sprayer. The bleach whitens the wood. Avoid getting the solution on the grass.

Fertilizing

- **Listerine, Epson Salt, Ivory Dishwashing Liquid, Parsons' Ammonia,** and **Budweiser.** Mix one cup Listerine, one cup Epsom Salt, one cup Ivory Dishwashing Liquid, and one cup Parsons' Ammonia in a one-quart jar, topping off the rest of the jar with Budweiser beer. Spray this on up to 2,500 square feet of lawn with a hose-attached sprayer in May and again in late June.

- **Maxwell House Coffee.** To fertilize your lawn with Maxwell House Coffee, sprinkle used coffee grounds over your yard. Filled with nutrients, coffee grounds stimulate grass.

- **Maxwell House Coffee.** To spread grass seed or fertilizer, punch several holes in the bottom of an empty Maxwell House Coffee can with a hammer and a punch, fill the can with grass seed or fertilizer, cover with the plastic lid, and shake the can like a big salt shaker as you walk across the lawn.

Garden Hoses

- **Con-Tact Paper.** To make finding the end of a hose easier, wrap the last six inches of your garden hose with Con-Tact Paper in a contrasting color.

- **Forster Toothpicks** and **Scotch Packaging Tape.** To repair a punctured garden hose, insert a Forster Toothpick into the hole, snap it off flush with the hose's outer skin, and then wrap a strip of Scotch Packaging Tape securely around the spot. The wooden toothpick will absorb water, swelling to seal the hole.

- **Wrigley's Spearmint Gum.** Patch a hole in a garden hose with a wad of Wrigley's Spearmint Gum (well chewed to remove all the sugar) and let it dry.

Raking

- **Forster Clothespins.** To hold a leaf bag open when raking leaves, use two or three Forster Clothespins to clip one side of the plastic trash bag to a chain-link fence. This way, you can easily hold the other side of the bag open to fill the bag with leaves.

Urine Spots

- **Arm & Hammer Baking Soda.** To repair yellow burn spots on a lawn caused by dog urine, dissolve one cup Arm & Hammer Baking Soda in one gallon water in a watering can and saturate the urine spots every three days. The baking soda neutralizes the acidity of the urine and simultaneously deodorizes the area, preventing the offending dog from recognizing the spot. (For more tips on repelling cats and dogs from your lawn, see page 61.)

Weeds

- **Clorox Bleach.** To kill weeds and grass growing between cracks in walkways, pour undiluted Clorox Bleach over the invading plants.
- **Heinz White Vinegar.** To kill weeds, pour Heinz White Vinegar directly on the intruding growth on your lawn or between the cracks in the sidewalk and driveway.

- **Morton Salt.** Pouring Morton Salt directly on weeds on a dry sunny day kills them. (Be sure to avoid getting salt on your healthy plants.)
- **Smirnoff Vodka.** To kill weeds, mix three tablespoons Smirnoff Vodka and two cups water in a sixteen-ounce trigger-spray bottle. Saturate the weeds with the solution, but do not get the alcohol solution on other plants. The vodka dehydrates the weeds.
- **Spray 'n Wash.** A quick spritz of Spray 'n Wash kills weeds without hurting the soil and leaves the weeds stain-free. Do not get the Spray 'n Wash on other plants.
- **20 Mule Team Borax.** To kill creeping Charlie on your lawn, dissolve exactly five teaspoons 20 Mule Team Borax in one quart of water. Fill a trigger-spray bottle with the solution and spray problem spots evenly. (The borax may cause the grass to yellow temporarily.)

Strange Facts

- No one knows who originated the proverb "The grass is always greener on the other side of the fence." As early as 25 BCE, the ancient Roman poet Ovid wrote in *The Art of Love*: "The crop seems always more productive in our neighbor's field."

- In his 1915 poem "Mending Wall," American poet Robert Frost noted that good fences make good neighbors.

- In the 1989 Disney movie *Honey, I Shrunk the Kids*, a nutty scientist (played by Rick Moranis) unwittingly miniaturizes his two kids and the two kids living next door and tosses them into the trash. The kids have to brave through the towering blades of grass—confronting gigantic bugs, sprinklers, and a lawn mower—to get back to the house. Along the way, two of the kids slide down an enormous blade of grass as if it were a sliding board.

- According to *The Guinness Book of World Records*, the world's largest hedge maze is the Pineapple Garden Maze located on the Dole Plantation in Wahiawa, Hawaii.

- In the United States alone, lawns cover an estimated thirty-two million acres of land. More than half of the water consumed by the average homeowner is used to water the lawn.

- In the United States, the word *sod* means a chunk of ground with grass growing in it. In England, the word *sod* means an oaf, and the phrase "sod off" is a profane way of saying "scram."

- The simplest way to prevent an abundance of weeds is to pull weeds before they seed.

Chandeliers

- **Smirnoff Vodka** and **Glad Trash Bags.** To clean a crystal chandelier, cut open a Glad Trash Bag and place the plastic sheet on the floor directly under the chandelier. Mix four teaspoons Smirnoff Vodka and two cups water in a sixteen-ounce trigger-spray bottle and mist the crystals with the solution. Let the crystals drip dry onto the plastic sheet.

Lightbulbs

- **Vaseline Petroleum Jelly.** Lubricate the threads of lightbulbs with a dab of Vaseline Petroleum Jelly to keep the threads free from corrosion, help the threads conduct electricity, and make the bulbs much easier to remove when they eventually burn out. This tip is particularly helpful for outdoor floodlights, whose threads are more apt to corrode and get stuck in the sockets.

Wiring

- **Dawn Dishwashing Liquid.** To fish electrical cable through conduits, mix one teaspoon Dawn Dishwashing Liquid and two cups water in a sixteen-ounce trigger-spray bottle, shake well, and spray the cable with the soapy solution. The soap will help the cable glide easily and effortlessly through winding conduits.

- **Glad Flexible Straws.** Before running thin low-voltage wires through drilled holes in studs or a wall, insert a Glad Flexible Straw (cut to whatever size you need) through the hole as a protective guide.

- **Pam Cooking Spray.** To thread electrical cable through conduits, spray the cable with Pam Cooking Spray. The oil will help the cable glide through winding conduits.

- **WD-40.** To thread electrical wire through conduits, spray WD-40 on the electrical wire to help it glide through winding conduits.

Strange Facts

- If a lightbulb breaks off in the socket, unplug the lamp or turn off the electrical power. Cut a raw potato in half, press the open face of one half potato into the broken glass, and unscrew the remaining bulb slowly and carefully.

- In the Bible, God's first words are "Let there be light."

- In the early seventeenth century, Italian scientist Galileo Galilei attempted an experiment to measure the speed the light by using two lanterns on two distant hilltops. The experiment failed because the speed of light was too fast to be measured from such a short distance.

- In 1801, English physicist Thomas Young proved that, under certain conditions, two light beams cancel each other out.

- In 1802, English chemist Sir Humphry Davy invented the first electric light by making a platinum wire glow by passing an electric current through it. Thomas Edison did not invent the first practical incandescent lamp until 1879.

- In 1923, President Calvin Coolidge ceremoniously flipped the switch to illuminate the first electric lights on an outdoor Christmas tree at the White House, launching that annual tradition.

- Light is produced when atoms are excited in one of several ways to emit photons. Light behaves like both waves and particles.

- The speed of light is 186,282 miles per second.

- The light emitted by the sun takes approximately eight minutes and twenty seconds to reach the Earth.

Mirrors

Cleaning

- **Arm & Hammer Clean Shower.** To clean a mirror, spray Arm & Hammer Clean Shower directly on the mirror, wipe it off with a sponge, spray the surface with water, and wipe dry.

- **Bounce.** Wipe down mirrors with a clean, used sheet of Bounce. The antistatic elements in Bounce prevent dust and lint from resetting on the mirrored glass.

- **Colgate Regular Flavor Toothpaste.** To clean tarnish from a mirror, squeeze a dollop of Colgate Regular Flavor Toothpaste on a soft, clean cloth and wipe clean.

- **Glade Air Freshener.** Spray Glade Air Freshener on a soft, clean cloth and wipe down the mirror, leaving the glass clean and smelling fresh.

- **Mott's Applesauce.** To clean mirrors, smear Mott's Applesauce on the glass, then wipe clean.

- **Mr. Coffee Filters.** Made from 100 percent virgin paper, Mr. Coffee Filters clean mirrors without leaving behind any lint.

- **Mrs. Stewart's Liquid Bluing.** Add a few drops of Mrs. Stewart's Liquid Bluing in a bucket of water and use the solution to clean a mirror.
- **Parsons' Ammonia.** Add six tablespoons Parsons' Ammonia to one quart warm water. Apply the solution to mirrors with a sponge, clean cloth, or trigger-spray bottle and wipe dry.

Defogging

- **Conair Pro Styler 1600.** To dry steam off a fogged-up bathroom mirror, use a Conair Pro Styler 1600 hair dryer to blow hot air at the mirror.
- **Gillette Foamy.** To keep your bathroom mirror from fogging up, spread Gillette Foamy shaving cream on the glass and wipe clean with a soft cloth. The thin coat of soap film left behind can prevent the mirror from steaming up for up to three weeks.
- **SPAM.** To keep the condensation off the bathroom mirror, rub SPAM luncheon meat on the glass and wipe clean with a soft cloth. The oils in SPAM prevent the mirror from fogging up.

Hair Spray

- **Smirnoff Vodka.** To clean hair spray from mirrors, saturate a soft, clean cloth with Smirnoff Vodka and wipe the glass spick-and-span.

Repairing

- **Reynolds Wrap.** To disguise the peeling silver on an old mirror, scrape off the flaked area on the back of the mirror, cut a piece of Reynolds Wrap to fit the spot, and tape into place with the shiny side facing the glass.

Strange Facts

- In Greek mythology, anyone who looked at the Gorgon Medusa (a monstrous female with living snakes as hair) was turned to stone. The hero Perseus killed Medusa by looking only at her reflection in a mirrored shield.

- In the Palace of Versailles, the Hall of Mirrors is a long corridor with large mirrors facing the seventeen arcaded windows that look out onto the extensive gardens outside. King Louis XIV had the Hall of Mirrors constructed in the seventeenth century. The Treaty of Versailles, which ended World War II, was signed in the Hall of Mirrors.

- In the story "Snow White," as told by the Brothers Grimm in their 1812 edition of *Grimm's Fairy Tales*, a wicked queen asks her talking mirror, "Mirror, mirror, on the wall, who's the fairest one of all?"

- In Lewis Carroll's 1871 children's book *Through the Looking-Glass*, the sequel to *Alice's Adventures in Wonderland*, Alice pretends the mirror on the wall is soft like gauze, climbs up on the mantelpiece, and when the glass turns into a silvery mist, she jumps through the mirror on the wall into the reflected room.

- In the 1897 novel *Dracula* by Irish author Bram Stoker, the vampire Dracula does not have a reflection in any mirror.

- A house of mirrors—a common carnival attraction—is a labyrinth with mirrored walls.

- The Harry Potter series of novels, by J. K. Rowling, feature the Mirror of Erised (*desire* spelled backward), a mirror that reflects how the viewer desires to be.

Odors

Air Fresheners

- **Arm & Hammer Baking Soda.** To deodorize a smelly room, place an open box of Arm & Hammer Baking Soda on a shelf in the room. Or dissolve two teaspoons Arm & Hammer Baking Soda in two cups of water in a sixteen-ounce trigger-spray bottle and spray the air.
- **Bounce.** To freshen the air in a dresser drawer, closet, or room, place an individual sheet of Bounce in a drawer, hang one from a hanger in the closet, or tape one to the front of a fan (or air-conditioning vent) and turn it on.
- **Car-Freshner Pine Trees.** To freshen the air in your home, hang a Car-Freshner Pine Tree in the house from the blinds.
- **Downy Fabric Softener.** Mix one tablespoon Downy Fabric Softener with two cups water in a sixteen-ounce trigger-spray bottle and spray the solution as an air freshener to make your home smell April fresh.
- **Heinz White Vinegar.** Fill a spray bottle with undiluted Heinz White Vinegar and spray it around your home as a natural air

freshener. The pungent smell of vinegar quickly dissipates, leaving your home smelling clean and fresh.

- **Ivory Soap.** To freshen the air in closed spaces, place unwrapped bars of Ivory Soap in drawers, linen closets, and storage trunks. Replace the bars of soap every few months.

- **Johnson & Johnson Cotton Balls.** To scent the air in your home, saturate a Johnson & Johnson Cotton Ball with perfume or cologne and place it in the bag of your vacuum cleaner before vacuuming the carpets.

- **Kingsford Charcoal Briquets.** A clean, used coffee can filled with untreated Kingsford Charcoal Briquets placed in a closet or chest absorbs odors.

- **Lipton Tea Bags, ReaLemon,** and **Mr. Coffee Filters.** Steep two Lipton Tea Bags in two cups of boiling water, let cool, add two tablespoons ReaLemon lemon juice, strain through a Mr. Coffee Filter, and pour the solution into a sixteen-ounce trigger-spray bottle. Spray it around your home. Tea is an all-natural air freshener, and the lemon juice adds a lemon scent.

- **Maxwell House Coffee.** A freshly opened can of Maxwell House Coffee deodorizes and freshens the air in a room. Or fill a small bowl with fresh coffee grounds and set it in a corner of the room.

- **McCormick Pure Vanilla Extract.** To scent the air in your home, saturate a cotton ball with McCormick Pure Vanilla Extract and place it in your vacuum cleaner bag before vacuuming the house. Or place a cotton ball saturated with vanilla extract on a saucer and set it in a corner of the room.

- **Mennen Speed Stick.** Apply Mennen Speed Stick to an incandescent lightbulb and then turn on the lamp. The heat from the lightbulb will slowly melt the deodorant, freshening the air in the room. You can also cut up chunks from the bar of deodorant and place them around the house. Or remove the lid from a Mennen Speed Stick and place it in a drawer or linen closet.

- **Nestea, ReaLemon,** and **Mr. Coffee Filter.** Mix up two cups Nestea, add two tablespoons ReaLemon lemon juice, and strain through a Mr. Coffee Filter. Pour the solution into a sixteen-ounce trigger-spray bottle and spray around your home to freshen the air.

- **Tidy Cats.** To prevent musty, damp odors in a closed summerhouse, fill shallow boxes with unused Tidy Cats. Place one box in each room before closing up the house. The cat box filler absorbs moisture and musty, lingering odors.

Diaper Pails

- **Bounce.** To help deodorize a diaper pail, place a sheet of Bounce in the lid of the diaper pail.

- **L'eggs Sheer Energy Panty Hose** and **Tidy Cats.** Cut off one leg from a clean, used pair of L'eggs Sheer Energy Panty Hose, fill it with unused Tidy Cats, and tie a knot at the top of the leg to seal it closed. Place the litter-filled panty hose leg in the bottom of a diaper pail to absorb odors and keep the pail smelling fresh. Replace the cat box filler when necessary.

Food

- **Heinz White Vinegar.** After cooking fish or broccoli, fill a drinking glass halfway with Heinz White Vinegar and set the glass on the kitchen counter. The vinegar neutralizes the smell of the fish or broccoli. You won't believe how amazingly strong vinegar is as a deodorizer until you give this simple trick a try.

Food Containers

- **Arm & Hammer Baking Soda.** To deodorize food containers, mix one-quarter cup Arm & Hammer Baking Soda with one quart water, swish the solution around in the food container, let soak overnight, and then rinse clean.

- **Heinz White Vinegar.** To eliminate odors from used jars, rinse the jars with Heinz White Vinegar, then rinse clean with water.

Humidifiers

- **ReaLemon.** To eliminate odors in a humidifier, pour three or four teaspoons of ReaLemon lemon juice into the water and run the machine.
- **20 Mule Team Borax.** To eradicate odors in a humidifier, dissolve one tablespoon 20 Mule Team Borax per gallon of water, add the solution to the unit, and run the machine. Use this treatment once or twice a year.

Mildew

- **Listerine.** To eliminate mildew odors, wipe the walls, tiles, or countertops with full-strength Listerine. The antiseptic kills mildew.

Shoes and Sneakers

- **Arm & Hammer Baking Soda.** In the evening, sprinkle Arm & Hammer Baking Soda inside shoes to absorb moisture and neutralize offending odors. In the morning, shake out the baking soda. (For more ways to deodorize shoes and sneakers, see page 260.)

Smoke

- **Heinz White Vinegar.** To eliminate the smell of cigarette or cigar smoke from a room in your home, fill a drinking glass halfway with Heinz White Vinegar and leave it in the room undisturbed. The vinegar absorbs the odors.

- **Smirnoff Vodka.** To deodorize cigarette smoke from clothing, mix one-half cup Smirnoff Vodka and one and one-half cups water in a sixteen-ounce trigger-spray bottle, spray the clothing with the solution, and let dry. Spraying smoky clothes with vodka neutralizes the reeking odor.

Spilled Milk

- **20 Mule Team Borax.** To neutralize the sour smell of spilled milk, dampen the spot, rub in 20 Mule Team Borax, let dry, then vacuum or brush clean.

Steamer Trunk

- **Tidy Cats** and **Maxwell House Coffee.** To deodorize a musty trunk, fill a clean, empty Maxwell House Coffee can with unused Tidy Cats, place the uncovered can inside the trunk, close the lid of the trunk, and let sit overnight. The next day, remove the can of cat box filler.

Suitcases

- **Bounce.** To prevent musty suitcases, place an individual sheet of Bounce inside the empty luggage before storing.

Urine

- **20 Mule Team Borax.** To neutralize urine odors from mattresses and mattress covers, dampen the spot, rub in 20 Mule Team Borax, let dry, then vacuum or brush clean.

Vomit

- **Arm & Hammer Baking Soda.** To neutralize vomit odor, sprinkle Arm & Hammer Baking Soda generously on the stained area, let sit for an hour, and then vacuum up.

Wastebaskets

- **Bounce.** To eliminate odors in wastebaskets, place a sheet of Bounce at the bottom of the wastebaskets.

Strange Facts

- Before buying an air freshener in a grocery store, most shoppers pick a can off the shelf, remove the cap, spray the air or their fingers, and breath deeply to test whether they like the fragrance. Most commercial air fresheners contain chemicals that mask odors and should not be inhaled.

- A person locked in a completely sealed room will die of carbon dioxide poisoning, not oxygen deprivation.

- In the 1890s, Joseph Pujol, a French music-hall entertainer who went by the stage name Le Petomane, was billed as "The Man with the Musical Derriere." Pujol used his uncanny ability to suck air into his rectum and expel it at will to imitate bird chirps and human voices, smoke cigarettes, and blow out candles—accompanied by an orchestra.

- In 1956, S.C. Johnson created Glade Air Freshener to eliminate hospital odors. An advertising campaign introduced Glade Air Freshener to consumers and boasted that the new product "makes indoor air fresh as all outdoors!"

- Body odor is merely the smell of bacteria growing on the human body. Washing with soap and water kills the bacteria, thus eliminating the odor.

- Human perspiration is virtually odorless, but bacteria multiply more prodigiously in sweat.

- Scientists believe that the average human being can recognize up to 10,000 different odors.

Painting

Buckets

- **Clorox Bleach.** To make a paint bucket, cut a hole in the side of an empty, clean Clorox Bleach jug opposite the handle.
- **Cool Whip.** Use clean, empty Cool Whip tubs to mix and store paints.

Cleaning

- **Coppertone.** To clean oil-based paint from your hands, rub a dollop of Coppertone sunscreen on your skin. Coppertone removes paint and stain from hands more gently than turpentine.
- **Cutex Nail Polish Remover.** To clean oil-based paint from your hands, dampen a cloth with Cutex Nail Polish Remover, wipe the skin, and then wash thoroughly with soap and water.
- **Gillette Foamy.** To wash latex paint from your skin, use a squirt of Gillette Foamy shaving cream. The emollients and moisturizers in shaving cream clean latex paint from skin.

- **Johnson's Baby Oil.** To clean oil-based paint from your hands, rub a few drops of Johnson's Baby Oil on your skin and then wash thoroughly with soap and water. Baby oil is gentler than turpentine.
- **Noxzema Deep Cleansing Cream.** Noxzema Deep Cleansing Cream cleans oil-based paint from hands with more mildness than turpentine or mineral spirits.
- **Pam Cooking Spray.** To clean oil-based paint from hands, spray Pam Cooking Spray on the skin and then wash thoroughly with soap and water.
- **Skin So Soft Body Lotion.** To clean paint and stain from hands, rub Skin So Soft Body Lotion on the painted or stained skin.
- **Spray 'n Wash.** To remove varnish from hands, spray Spray 'n Wash on the affected area, rub, then wash with soap and water. Spray 'n Wash typically works more effectively than turpentine, without burning the skin.
- **Wesson Corn Oil.** To clean oil-based paint from hands, use a few drops of Wesson Corn Oil rather than turpentine.

Doors

- *USA Today.* To avoid painting doors shut, fold a page of *USA Today* over the top of the door, close it so the jamb holds the newspaper in place, and then paint.

Drying

- **Conair Pro Styler 1600.** To dry small paint touch-ups quickly, use a Conair Pro Styler 1600 hair dryer to blow warm air back and forth over the new coat of paint.

Galvanized Metal

- **Heinz White Vinegar.** To prepare galvanized metal for a new coat of paint, damped a sponge with Heinz White Vinegar, use it to wipe down the galvanized metal, and let dry before painting. The acetic acid in the vinegar degreases and slightly etches the surface, which helps the paint adhere.

Gloves

- **Ziploc Storage Bags.** To improvise gloves, insert your hands into two Ziploc Storage Bags.

Latex Paints

- **Kool-Aid.** To color latex paint for home decorating projects, mix unsweetened Kool-Aid powdered drink mix with a couple of teaspoons of water, add the colored liquid to the paint, and stir well.

Mineral Spirits

- **Maxwell House Coffee.** To filter used mineral spirits for future use, pour the dirty mineral spirits into a clean Maxwell House Coffee can and seal the lid in place. Let sit undisturbed in a cool place for a few days to let the paint settle to the bottom of the can. Pour the top layer of clean mineral spirits into another can, leaving the paint residue in the coffee can. Discard the can of paint residue at a hazardous waste collection site.

Odors

- **McCormick Pure Vanilla Extract.** Mix two teaspoons McCormick Pure Vanilla Extract per gallon of paint, stir well, and paint as usual. The vanilla extract masks the smell of the paint, giving your newly painted home the pleasant aroma of freshly baked cookies.
- **Parsons' Ammonia.** To eliminate paint odor, fill a large pan with water, add one tablespoon Parsons' Ammonia, and place the pan in the freshly painted room overnight.

Outlets

- **Ziploc Storage Bags.** When you remove all the electrical outlet covers, place the plates and screws in a Ziploc Storage Bag and seal it shut so you'll know exactly where to find the plates and screws when you're finished painting the room.

Paint

- **Clairol Nice 'n Easy.** Mix up Clairol Nice 'n Easy hair coloring according to the directions, and use the hair coloring to paint on cardboard, poster board, or wooden furniture.

- **Kiwi Shoe Polish.** To stain wood or touch up scratches, scuff marks, and holes from picture hooks, use a dab of the appropriate color Kiwi Shoe Polish.

- **Nestlé Carnation NonFat Dry Milk** and **McCormick Food Coloring.** American colonists used to paint their homes with milk. They would boil berries in milk, which would thicken and color the milk. That's why so many houses in New England have that whitewashed look. Today, thanks to modern technology, we have the miracle of Nestlé Carnation Nonfat Dry Milk. Just mix one and one-half cups Nestlé Carnation Nonfat Dry Milk and one-half cup water until it is the consistency of paint, then add food coloring or pigment (available at art supply stores) to make whatever hue you desire. Once milk paint dries, it is incredibly durable. It won't wash off. Plus, you can have milk and cookies while you paint. Just try doing that with regular latex.

Paintbrushes

- **Downy Fabric Softener.** To keep paintbrushes soft, add a drop of Downy Fabric Softener to the final rinse.

- **Heinz White Vinegar** and **Ziploc Storage Bags.** To store clean paintbrushes used for latex paint and keep the bristles supple, place each brush in its own Ziploc Storage Bag, add one teaspoon Heinz White Vinegar, and seal the bag shut.
- **Jet-Dry.** To soften paintbrushes, add a few drops of Jet-Dry to the final rinse water. The surfactants help the water clean the soap film and paint residue from the brush.
- **L'eggs Sheer Energy Panty Hose.** A clean, used pair of L'eggs Sheer Energy Panty Hose makes a great substitute for a paintbrush. Ball up the panty hose and use it like a sponge or secure it to a stick with several rubber bands to apply wood stain, varnish, or polyurethane.
- **Maxwell House Coffee.** To prevent paintbrush bristles from bending while soaking in a solvent, pour the solvent into an empty Maxwell House Coffee can, cut an X in the plastic lid, and push the brush handle up through the slit so the brush hangs in the can about one-half inch from the bottom rather than resting on its bristles.
- **Oral-B Toothbrush.** To apply paint in a tight corner or crevice, use a clean, used Oral-B Toothbrush as a miniature paintbrush.
- **Q-Tips Cotton Swabs.** To paint crevices or tight corners, dip one end of a Q-Tips Cotton Swab into the paint and use it like a paintbrush.
- **Reynolds Wrap.** To store wet paintbrushes, wrap the wet brushes in Reynolds Wrap and store them in your freezer. The cold temperature in the freezer prevents the paint from drying. When you're ready to paint again, defrost the brushes for an hour or more.
- **Skin So Soft Body Lotion.** To keep paintbrushes feeling soft as new, add a drop of Skin So Soft Body Lotion to the final rinse.

- *USA Today.* To wipe paintbrushes clean after rinsing, place the bristles between the pages of a thick section of *USA Today*, squeeze the paper around the bristles, and remove the brush.

- **Ziploc Storage Bags.** To save a wet paintbrush saturated with oil-based paint overnight, place the entire paintbrush inside a Ziploc Storage Bag and store it in the freezer. The cold temperature in the freezer prevents the paint from drying. When you're ready to paint again, defrost the paintbrush for an hour or more.

Preparing

- **Alberto VO5 Conditioning Hairdressing.** To prevent spray paint from sticking in your hair, before your start the job, squeeze a dab of Alberto VO5 Conditioning Hairdressing about the size of a quarter into your palm, rub your palms together, and run your palms over your hair. The hairdressing will allow you to wash away the paint more easily.

- **Alberto VO5 Conditioning Hairdressing.** To make cleaning up after painting easy, lightly coat your hands with Alberto VO5 Conditioning Hairdressing before painting so you can clean them off afterward without harsh solvents.

- **Dawn Dishwashing Liquid.** Before starting a paint job, rub a dollop of Dawn Dishwashing Liquid straight from the bottle over your hands and arms and let dry. When you're finished painting, any paint will wash right off your skin.

- **Ivory Soap.** To prevent paint from getting under your fingernails, before starting the job, scrape your fingernails over a bar of Ivory Soap, filling the spaces with the soap.

- **Pam Cooking Spray.** Before painting a room, spray your hands and arms with a thin coat of Pam Cooking Spray, rubbing the oil into your pores. When you finish the job, wash clean with soap and water.

- **Vaseline Petroleum Jelly.** To make cleaning up after painting easy, coat your hands and arms with Vaseline Petroleum Jelly. When the job is done, wipe the splattered paint from your hands and arms and then wash clean with soap and water.

Rollers

- **Glad Trash Bags.** To avoid having to clean paint out of a roller tray, before filling with paint, place the roller tray inside a kitchen-size Glad Trash Bag and fold the excess bag under the tray. After painting, pour any excess paint back into the can, carefully remove the trash bag by turning it inside out, and discard.

- **Pringles.** To clean a paint roller, fill an empty Pringles can with solvent, put the roller inside, and seal the can with the plastic lid. Shake the can, let sit for two hours, then remove the roller and wash with soapy water.

- **Reynolds Wrap.** To avoid having to clean paint out of a roller tray, before filling it with paint, line the roller tray with Reynolds Wrap, overlapping all four sides. After painting, pour any excess paint back into the can, carefully roll up the aluminum foil, and throw it away.

- **Ziploc Storage Bags.** To remove a roller cover filled with paint from the roller handle without getting paint all over yourself, place a large Ziploc Storage Bag over the roller cover and pull the roller cover off the handle. If you don't wish to clean the roller cover for next time, seal the bag shut and discard.

- **Ziploc Storage Bags.** To save a wet roller saturated with oil-based paint overnight, place the entire roller inside a Ziploc Storage Bag and store it in the freezer. The cold temperature in the freezer prevents the paint from drying. When you're ready to paint again, defrost the roller for an hour or more.

Rust

- **Coca-Cola** and **Scotch-Brite Heavy Duty Scrub Sponge.** To remove rust from wrought iron to prepare for painting, saturate a Scotch-Brite Heavy Duty Scrub Sponge with Coca-Cola and scrub the rusty spots on the wrought iron. The phosphoric acid in Coke removes the rust.

Scraper

- **MasterCard.** To scrape off peeling paint, use an old Master-Card to master the possibilities.

Spills

- **Gold Medal Flour.** If you spill paint on carpeting, blot up as much of the paint as possible and then pour a mountain of Gold Medal Flour over the spill and let sit overnight. In the morning, sweep up the flour. Repeat several times if necessary. The flour absorbs most of the paint.

Splatters and Smears

- **Alberto VO5 Conditioning Hairdressing.** Coat windows, hinges, doorknobs, and lock latches with Alberto VO5 Conditioning Hairdressing to prevent paint from adhering to the surfaces. When the paint dries, wipe off the hairdressing with a cloth.
- **ChapStick.** Before painting a room, rub ChapStick on hinges, doorknobs, and around the edges of the glass next to the trim. Paint smears will wipe off easily with a cloth.
- **Dixie Paper Plates.** Use a Dixie Paper Plate as a drip pan for a can of paint. Attach the plate to the bottom of the paint can with a little putty or some adhesive tape.

- **Dixie Paper Plates.** To prevent paint from dripping when painting the ceiling, carefully cut an X through the center of a Dixie Paper Plate. Insert the handle of the paintbrush through the X, allowing the paper plate to catch any paint drips.
- **Glad Trash Bags.** To protect chandeliers and hanging lamps when painting a ceiling, pull a Glad Trash Bag up over the lighting fixture and tie it up as high on the chain as possible.
- **Huggies Baby Wipes.** To clean up paint splatters, wipe the spots with a Huggies Baby Wipe.
- **Ivory Soap.** Before painting a room, run a bar of Ivory Soap on hinges, on doorknobs, and along the edges of the glass next to the trim. Paint smears will wipe off with a cloth.
- **Maxwell House Coffee.** To prevent paint from dripping when painting the ceiling, carefully cut an X through the center of the plastic lid from a can of Maxwell House Coffee. Insert the handle of the paintbrush through the X in the lid, allowing the coffee lid to catch any paint drips.
- **Post-it Notes.** To avoid splattered paint on windows, metalwork, and floors, before painting a room, place Post-it Notes along the edge of the glass, over door hinges, and along a vinyl or tile floor where it meets the wall.
- **Reynolds Wrap.** To prevent paint splatters on hardware, mold a sheet of Reynolds Wrap around doorknobs, electrical switches, faucets, and handles before painting.
- **Scotch-Brite Heavy Duty Scrub Sponge.** To remove latex paint from electrical outlet covers, remove the outlet covers from the wall, soak in a sink filled with water for one hour, and then scrub lightly with a Scotch-Brite Heavy Duty Scrub Sponge.
- **Stayfree Maxi Pads.** When painting, use Stayfree Maxi Pads to help absorb any drips on the walls. When painting in a tight corner, peel off the adhesive strip and stick the maxipad to the

floor so it catches all the paint. You can use a pair of scissors to cut the maxipad to any shape you need.

- **Vaseline Petroleum Jelly** and **Q-Tips Cotton Swabs.** Before painting a room, dip a Q-Tips Cotton Swab in Vaseline Petroleum Jelly and run it around the edges of the glass; coat door hinges, doorknobs, lock latches; and spread a thin coat of Vaseline Petroleum Jelly along a vinyl or tile floor where it meets the wall. Paint smears will wipe off easily with a cloth.
- **Ziploc Storage Bags.** To avoid paint splatters on a doorknob, cover the doorknob with a Ziploc Storage Bag.

Spray Paint Cans

- **WD-40.** To clean a clogged spray paint can nozzle, remove the nozzles from the spray paint can and a WD-40 can, place the nozzle from the spray paint can on the WD-40 can, give it a couple of quick squirts, and replace both nozzles.

Stain

- **Kiwi Shoe Polish.** To stain wood to a high polish, apply Kiwi Shoe Polish to the wood, repeating to attain a deeper color, if desired. Buff with a soft cloth to achieve a glossy finish.
- **L'eggs Sheer Energy Panty Hose.** To apply stain without getting lint all over the wood, ball up a pair of clean, used L'eggs Sheer Energy Panty Hose. The nylon makes an excellent applicator that doesn't leave any lint behind.
- **Nestea.** To stain wood, mix a couple of teaspoons of Nestea Iced Tea Mix with enough water to make a thick paste and apply with a paintbrush. Let dry, buff with a soft cloth, and seal with lacquer.
- **Red Devil Lye.** To stain unfinished cherry wood, mix three tablespoons Red Devil Lye in one gallon of warm water and, wearing rubber gloves and protective eyewear, sponge this

solution on the wood in a well-ventilated area. Wait one minute, rinse clean, and dry. The more lye you use, the redder the cherry wood will become. Repeat to attain a deeper color, if desired.

- **Rit Dye.** Mix up Rit Dye according to the directions on the box and use a sponge brush to give wood one coat of the dye. Let dry.

Storing

- **Reynolds Cut-Rite Wax Paper.** Place the paint can lid on a sheet of Reynolds Cut-Rite Wax Paper, trace around the lid, and cut a pattern from the wax paper. Lay the wax paper directly on the surface of the paint in the can (letting the wax paper float on top of the paint) and replace the lid. The wax paper creates a barrier, preventing the oxygen in the can from drying up the paint, and helps keep the oil- or water-based paints fresh for months.

- **Reynolds Wrap.** To prevent a layer of skin from forming over the paint surface, set the paint can on top of a sheet of Reynolds Wrap, trace around it, cut out a disc of foil, and place it on the paint surface before sealing the can closed.

- **Saran Wrap.** Place a sheet of Saran Wrap over the open paint can before tapping the lid closed with a hammer. The Saran Wrap improves the airtight seal.

- **Ziploc Storage Bag.** To keep leftover paint fresh, pour the remaining paint into a Ziploc Storage Bag, carefully squeeze out the air, and seal the bag shut. Store the bag in the paint can and tap the lid closed with a hammer.

Straining

- **L'eggs Sheer Energy Panty Hose.** To strain lumps from a can of paint, cut off one of the legs from a clean, used pair of

L'eggs Sheer Energy Panty Hose, stretch it across the mouth of the paint can, and pour. To paint directly from the can, stretch the panty hose leg across the mouth of the paint can, secure in place with a large rubber band, and using a paintbrush, push the stocking toe into the paint, and use the freshly strained paint rising up through the mesh.

Stripping

- **Clorox Bleach.** After stripping wood, lighten stain that has permeated deeply into the wood by applying a liberal coat of Clorox Bleach to the wood. Let dry for several days and then neutralize the bleach with vinegar (see below).

- **Easy-Off Oven Cleaner.** To strip paint from metal lawn furniture or wooden picture frames, put on rubber gloves and protective eyewear and, working outdoors or with ample ventilation, spray Easy-Off Oven Cleaner on the item, let sit for fifteen minutes, and then wash clean with the highest pressure from the nozzle of a garden hose.

- **Heinz White Vinegar.** Neutralize any residual paint stripper chemical (or bathroom cleaner, oven cleaner, or ammonia) by washing the stripped surface with Heinz White Vinegar. Then rinse clean with water.

- **Parsons' Ammonia.** To strip milk paint from furniture or walls, wearing rubber gloves and protective eyewear, and working outdoors or with ample ventilation, rub full-strength Parsons' Ammonia on the area and then rub off with medium-grade steel wool.

- **Scrubbing Bubbles.** To strip the paint off wooden furniture, put on rubber gloves and protective eyewear and spray Scrubbing Bubbles on the furniture. Let sit until the paint or varnish bubbles up. Then use a putty knife to scrape off the paint or use an old rag to wipe it off.

Windows

- **Alberto VO5 Conditioning Hairdressing.** To prevent paint from adhering to windows, coat the glass with Alberto VO5 Conditioning Hairdressing. After painting, wipe the glass clean with a cloth.

- **ChapStick.** Before painting a room, rub ChapStick around the edges of the glass next to the trim. Paint smears will wipe off with a cloth.

- **Ivory Soap.** Before painting a room, run a bar of Ivory Soap around the edges of the glass next to the trim. Paint smears will wipe off with a cloth.

- **Post-it Notes.** To avoid splattered paint on windows, before painting a room, place Post-it Notes along the edge of the glass where it meets the wall.

- **Vaseline Petroleum Jelly** and **Q-Tips Cotton Swabs.** Before painting a room, dip a Q-Tips Cotton Swab in Vaseline Petroleum Jelly and run it around the edges of the glass. Paint smears will wipe off with a cloth.

Strange Facts

- To avoid having to deal with a skin of dried paint on the surface of a used can of paint, store used cans of paint upside down. This way, the inevitable paint skin will form on the bottom of the can, leaving fresh paint on top.

- To keep an accurate record of what color you painted each room in your home, remove the plastic switch plate from the light switch in the room, attach a piece of masking tape to the back of the switch plate, write the color of the paint on the tape, and screw it back into place. Next time you want to paint the room or make touch-ups, simply remove the switch plate to confirm the color of the paint.

- To prevent used paint from hardening inside a resealed can, before resealing the can, exhale into it several times. Air is the natural enemy of paint. Exhaling carbon dioxide into the can removes the air from the can because carbon dioxide is heavier than air.

- As early as 2000 BCE, Egyptians painted tombs with paints made from refined pigments, natural resins, and drying oils—much like paints today.

- American colonists made paints from eggs, coffee grounds, and milk.

- President Gerald R. Ford Jr., born Leslie Lynch King Jr., was raised by his mother and his adopted father, Gerald R. Ford, the owner of the Ford Paint and Varnish Company.

- In September 1978, a worker dropped a fifty-cent paint scraper into a torpedo launcher of the U.S. nuclear submarine *Swordfish*—costing the U.S. government $171,000 in repairs.

Patios, Decks, and Outdoor Furniture

Birds

- **Johnson's Baby Powder.** To prevent bird droppings on patio furniture or fence posts, sprinkle Johnson's Baby Powder wherever the birds perch. Birds dislike the way baby powder feels on their feet and will find other places to roost.

Chair Legs

- **Wilson Tennis Balls.** To prevent metal patio chairs from noisily scraping along the concrete patio floor, carefully cut a two-inch slit in four Wilson Tennis Balls and put one ball on the bottom of each leg of the chair. The tennis balls eliminate the noise problem.

- **Wilson Tennis Balls.** To prevent the legs of a wooden deck chair from slipping through the slats of wood on a deck, cut an

X in the side of four Wilson Tennis Balls and fit them on the feet of the deck chair.

Cleaning

- **Arm & Hammer Baking Soda.** To clean plastic or metal patio furniture, sprinkle Arm & Hammer Baking Soda on a damp sponge, wipe clean, and dry.

- **Arm & Hammer Clean Shower.** To clean mold and mildew from plastic patio furniture, spray the furniture and the pads with Arm & Hammer Clean Shower and wipe clean with a sponge.

- **Armor All.** Spray Armor All on plastic patio furniture and wipe clean with a dry cloth. Armor All gives plastic furniture a shine and prevents dirt from adhering to it.

- **Cascade.** To clean patio furniture, dissolve one-quarter cup Cascade dishwasher detergent in one gallon of hot water. Scrub the patio furniture with the solution and then wipe clean with a dry cloth.

- **Clorox Bleach.** To clean mold and mildew from outdoor siding, tile, brick, stucco, and patios, mix three-quarters cup Clorox Bleach per gallon of water. Wearing rubber gloves, scrub the affected area with the solution to kill and remove the mold and mildew.

- **Clorox Bleach.** Mix three-quarters cup Clorox Bleach and one gallon of water, fill a trigger-spray bottle with the solution, spray it on plastic patio furniture, and dry with a cloth.

- **Crisco All-Vegetable Shortening.** To preserve a wooden bench or any other wooden patio furniture, apply Crisco All-Vegetable Shortening to the wood and buff with a clean, soft cloth. The oils in the shortening give wood a healthy, protective shine.

- **Gillette Foamy.** To clean mold from patio furniture, spray Gillette Foamy shaving cream on the patio furniture cushions and scrub with a sponge. Kids love to lather up patio tables with shaving cream. Then hose down the cushions, table, and the children. Presto! You've got clean patio furniture and clean kids for the price of one.

- **Heinz White Vinegar.** To clean mildew stains from patio furniture or a wooden deck, spray the furniture and deck with undiluted Heinz White Vinegar and then wipe clean.

- **Pam Cooking Spray.** To clean and revitalize wooden patio furniture with a natural finish, spray the items with Pam Cooking Spray and buff with a clean, soft cloth. The oils rejuvenate the wood.

- **Pledge.** To clean plastic lawn chairs and tables, spray the furniture with a light coat of Pledge and buff with a clean cloth. The Pledge shines the plastic and prevents dirt from adhering to it.

- **Tide.** To clean mildew from vinyl-covered cushions for outdoor furniture, mix one cup liquid Tide in three gallons of water. Dunk the cushions in the soapy solution, scrub with an abrasive sponge, rinse well, and let dry in the sun.

- **Turtle Wax.** To restore the sheen to aluminum garden furniture, give the metal a light coat of liquid Turtle Wax.

- **20 Mule Team Borax, Parsons' Ammonia,** and **Ivory Dishwashing Liquid.** To clean patio furniture, use a cleaning solution made from one-half cup 20 Mule Team Borax, one teaspoon Parsons' Ammonia, one-half teaspoon Ivory Dishwashing Liquid, and two gallons warm water.

- **WD-40.** To rejuvenate the color of faded plastic patio furniture, spray WD-40 on the discolored plastic and then wipe with a clean cloth.

Decks

- **Arm & Hammer Baking Soda.** To weather replaced portions of a deck, mix one cup Arm & Hammer Baking Soda and one gallon water, apply to the wood, let dry, and rinse clean. Then apply a water sealant to the wood.

- **Clorox Bleach.** To restore a weathered wooden deck to its original condition (without having to paint it), put on protective eyewear, rubber gloves, boots, and rain gear, and spray full-strength Clorox Bleach directly on the wood surfaces using a garden pressure sprayer. The bleach makes the wood look brand new again.

- **Heinz White Vinegar.** To clean mildew stains from a wooden deck, spray the deck with undiluted Heinz White Vinegar, let sit for one hour, and then rinse clean.

Painting

- **Coca-Cola.** To strip paint off metal patio furniture, cover the painted surface for one week with a bath towel saturated with Coca-Cola. Add more Coke daily to keep the towel drenched. The paint strips off effortlessly.

- **Easy-Off Oven Cleaner.** To strip paint from metal lawn furniture, put on rubber gloves and protective eyewear and, working outdoors, spray Easy-Off Oven Cleaner on the item, let sit for fifteen minutes, and then wash clean with the highest pressure from the nozzle of a garden hose.

- **Kiwi Shoe Polish.** To stain wooden patio furniture to a high polish, apply Kiwi Shoe Polish to the wood, repeating to attain a deeper color, if desired. Buff with a soft cloth to achieve a glossy finish.

- **Nestlé Carnation NonFat Dry Milk** and **McCormick Food Coloring.** Paint wooden patio furniture with milk paint. Mix three cups Carnation Nonfat Dry Milk and one cup water until it is the consistency of paint. Then add food coloring or pigment (available at art supply stores) to make whatever hue you desire. Thin the paint by adding more water; thicken the paint by adding more powdered milk. Brush on as you would any other paint. Apply the paint with a brush or roller. Let the first coat dry for at least twenty-four hours before adding a second coat. Let the second dry for three days. American colonists painted their homes with milk. They boiled berries in milk to thicken and color the milk. Once milk paint dries, it is incredibly durable. It won't wash off. Plus, you can have milk and cookies while you paint. Just try doing that with regular latex.

- **Rit Dye.** Stain wooden patio furniture by mixing up Rit Dye according to the directions on the box and using a sponge brush to give wood one coat of the mixture. Let dry thoroughly.

Picnic Tables

- **Forster Clothespins.** To prevent the wind from blowing a tablecloth off an outdoor picnic table in your backyard, glue Forster Clothespins to the underside of the table with a strong all-purpose glue. Then you can clip the tablecloth directly to the table with ease.
- **Scotch Packaging Tape.** Tape the corners of a tablecloth to the picnic table with Scotch Packaging Tape to prevent the wind from blowing the tablecloth away.
- **Velcro.** Adhere strips of Velcro on the four corners of the tablecloth and the four corners of the picnic table to keep the tablecloth from blowing off the table.

Strange Facts

- The word *patio* is Spanish for "backyard" or "back garden."
- In the 1950s, the United States Office of Civil Defense informed Americans that they could survive an atomic bomb

blast in fallout shelters, buried under three feet of earth in the backyard, built with concrete walls at least twelve inches thick.

- In Alfred Hitchcock's 1954 movie *Rear Window*, Jimmy Stewart stars as a photojournalist homebound by a broken leg. With nothing to do but observe the goings on outside his back window, he comes to suspect a dubious neighbor of murder.

- The 1955 movie *Picnic* stars William Holden as a drifter who shows up in a small town in Kansas on Labor Day and falls in love with his friend's fiancée, played by Kim Novak.

- In 1990, after several homeowner associations in Palm Springs, California, banned satellite dishes to prevent the eyesores from becoming common adornments, a company called Under Cover Satellite Systems created satellite antennas disguised as patio umbrellas, sold with a table and four matching chairs.

- In 2005, former Beatle Paul McCartney released his solo album *Chaos and Creation in the Backyard*, which was nominated for three Grammy Awards. The photograph on the cover of the album shows a young McCartney strumming a guitar in his family's backyard in Liverpool, England.

- In the United States alone, hundreds of independent restaurants share the name "The Patio."

Pests

Gophers and Moles

- **Bounce.** To repel gophers and moles, shove a few sheets of Bounce into the tunnel openings and then fill the tunnels with dirt. Oleander, the fragrance in Bounce, is a natural repellent that repulses gophers and moles.

- **Castor Oil** and **Ivory Dishwashing Liquid.** To repel moles, mix one-half cup castor oil, four tablespoons Ivory Dishwashing Liquid, and two gallons water and drench the molehills with the solution. Castor oil naturally fends off moles.

- **Maxwell House Coffee.** Spreading Maxwell House Coffee grounds around your yard repels moles—and simultaneously fertilizes your lawn and garden.

- **Parsons' Ammonia** and **Tampax Tampons.** To repel moles or gophers, saturate a Tampax Tampon with Parsons' Ammonia, insert the engorged cotton deeply into the tunnel opening, and fill the tunnel with dirt. The pungent fumes will prompt the animals to tunnel elsewhere.

- **Tidy Cats.** Pour used Tidy Cats cat box filler into the mole, gopher, or groundhog tunnels. The animals take one whiff of the scent of their natural enemy and quickly tunnel elsewhere.

- **Ziploc Freezer Bags.** Place a portable radio inside a gallon-size Ziploc Freezer Bag, turn the radio on, seal the bag shut, and place it near mole and gopher tunnels. The sounds of Black Sabbath, Snoop Dogg, or Rush Limbaugh will repel moles and gophers.

Mice and Rats

- **Bounce.** To stop mice and rats from entering your home, place sheets of Bounce wherever you wish to repel them. The fragrance of oleander naturally repels rodents.

- **Hershey's Chocolate Syrup.** Bait a mouse or rat trap with Hershey's Chocolate Syrup to create a sweet temptation the rodents find irresistible.

- **Jif Peanut Butter.** Mice and rats can easily get cheese out of a trap without springing it, but they're even more attracted to Jif Peanut Butter, which is almost impossible to remove from a trap without setting it off.

- **S.O.S Steel Wool Soap Pads.** To prevent mice and rats from squeezing through small cracks and holes in wallboards, plug the openings with S.O.S Steel Wool Soap Pads.

- **Tabasco Pepper Sauce, McCormick Garlic Powder,** and **Wesson Corn Oil.** Mix four tablespoons Tabasco Pepper Sauce, four tablespoons McCormick Garlic Powder, and one-half teaspoon Wesson Corn Oil in one quart of water. Fill a trigger-spray bottle with the spicy solution and apply it wherever mice and rats are giving you trouble. The spicy solution keeps them away.

Raccoons and Squirrels

- **Castor Oil.** To keep squirrels out of your attic, mix one-half cup castor oil and two gallons water, fill a trigger-spray bottle with the solution, and spray it around your attic. Castor oil repels rodents. You can also keep squirrels out of your garden by watering the plants with this castor oil solution, which also enriches the soil.

- **Crisco All-Vegetable Shortening.** To prevent squirrels from climbing into a bird feeder, grease the pole to the birdhouse with Crisco All-Vegetable Shortening.

- **Epsom Salt.** To repel raccoons, sprinkle a few tablespoons of Epsom Salt around your garden and garbage cans. Raccoons dislike the taste of salt.

- **Jif Peanut Butter.** Bait a humane box trap, available from your local animal control center, with Jif Peanut Butter to attract squirrels or raccoons. The animal control center will tell you where to release the animals.

- **McCormick Black Pepper.** McCormick Black Pepper does an excellent job of getting rid of unwanted raccoons, squirrels, dogs, or cats—without harming the animals. Simply sprinkle the area around your garbage cans (and around flower beds or vegetable gardens as well) with black pepper. These creatures all share a highly sensitive sense of smell, and the pepper will keep them far away. The neighbors may think you're crazy when they see you sprinkling pepper on your lawn, but at least you'll be rid of those pests. Want proof this trick works? Whenever you go to a fancy restaurant and the waiter comes over to put pepper on your salad, you'll notice there are no raccoons around.

- **McCormick Ground (Cayenne) Red Pepper.** To keep squirrels out of a bird feeder, sprinkle McCormick Ground (Cayenne) Red Pepper over the birdseed. Birds cannot taste red pepper, but squirrels can and stay far away from it.

- **McCormick Pure Peppermint Extract, Johnson & Johnson Cotton Balls,** and **L'eggs Sheer Energy Panty Hose.** To keep squirrels and raccoons at bay, cut the foot off a pair of clean, used L'eggs Sheer Energy Panty Hose, saturate a few Johnson & Johnson Cotton Balls with McCormick Pure Peppermint Extract, and place the cotton balls inside the panty hose foot. Hang the sachet from a fence post, tree branch, or rafter in the attic. The smell of mint repels squirrels and raccoons.

- **Old Spice Aftershave Lotion.** To repel squirrels from your chimney or attic, spray the area with Old Spice Aftershave Lotion. The brisk fragrance repels squirrels.

- **Pam Cooking Spray.** To keep squirrels out of a bird feeder, coat the pole with Pam Cooking Spray so squirrels attempting to climb up slide right back down.

- **Quaker Oats.** Bait a humane box trap, available from your local animal control center, with uncooked Quaker Oats to attract squirrels or raccoons. The animal control center will tell you where to release the animals.

- **Slinky.** To prevent squirrels from climbing up the pole to a bird feeder, secure a Slinky to the bottom of the bird feeder and let it hang down the pole. Any squirrel that tries to climb up the pole will be frightened away by the recoiling springs.

- **Tabasco Pepper Sauce, McCormick Chili Powder,** and **Ivory Dishwashing Liquid.** To repel squirrels, mix three teaspoons Tabasco Pepper Sauce, one teaspoon McCormick Chili Powder, one-half teaspoon Ivory Dishwashing Liquid, and two cups water in a sixteen-ounce trigger-spray bottle. Spray the solution around your yard or attic.

- **Tidy Cats.** Repel squirrels from flower beds by sprinkling a tablespoon of used Tidy Cats cat box filler on the ground.

(Do not use the cat box filler in vegetable or herb gardens.) Squirrels catch one whiff of the scent of their natural enemy and flee.

- **Vaseline Petroleum Jelly.** To prevent squirrels from being able to climb up the pole to a bird feeder, coat the pole with Vaseline Petroleum Jelly. Even the most ambitious squirrels slip right back down.

- **Ziploc Freezer Bags.** To keep raccoons away from your garbage cans or garden, place a portable radio inside a gallon-size Ziploc Freezer Bag, turn the radio on, and seal the bag shut. The noise from a radio, particularly one tuned to a heavy metal station or all-night talk show, repels raccoons.

Strange Facts

- Gophers push out dirt from their holes, creating a fan-shaped mound. Moles create a circular mound of dirt.

- The Gopher Gang was a notorious street gang in Hell's Kitchen in New York City in the early part of the twentieth century.

- Actor Fred Grandy starred as Gopher, the purser on the television series *The Love Boat*. Grandy was elected to Congress for four terms to represent his home state of Iowa.

- The state of Minnesota is nicknamed the Gopher State, and the University of Minnesota is home to the Golden Gophers sports teams, which compete in the Big Ten Conference.

- English chemist Joseph Priestley (1733–1804) discovered oxygen by accident. Priestly believed that anything that could burn contained a special substance called phlogiston. When the object was burned, phlogiston escaped into the atmosphere. In 1774, Priestly heated red oxide of mercury and red oxide of lead, captured the resulting gas, and found that a mouse would stay conscious twice as long in a sealed container of the gas as it would in a sealed container of air. Priestly called his new gas "dephlogisticated air." In reality, it was simply oxygen.

- In his 1815 book, *Histoire Naturelle Des Animaux Sans Vertèbre*, botanist Chevalier de Lamarck (1744–1829), attempting to explain why many animals possess vestiges of organs or bodily appendages, incorrectly insisted that chopping off the tails of mice and letting them breed would produce tail-less mice.

- Walt Disney provided the original voice of Mickey Mouse in animated cartoons.

- Scientists at the Stanford Research Institute named the computer mouse after the rodent, because the device, with its attached cord, vaguely resembled a mouse with a tail.

- Raccoon coats became popular in the 1920s, and Walt Disney's three-part television series *Davy Crockett* and the accompanying theme song "The Ballad of Davy Crockett" popularized raccoon caps among boys in the 1950s.

Picture Frames and Photo Albums

Cleaning

- **Wonder Bread.** To clean dust and grime from an oil painting, rub a slice of crustless Wonder Bread over the painting and then wipe off the crumbs. The bread works like a mild abrasive to clean the dirt and film from the oil painting.

Frames

- **Alberto VO5 Conditioning Hairdressing.** To prevent silver frames from tarnishing, apply a thin coat of Alberto VO5 Conditioning Hairdressing with a soft cloth to clean, polished, silver picture frames. Wipe off the excess hairdressing, leaving behind a very thin, virtually invisible, protective coating. VO5's organic protectants actually prevent tarnishing.

- **Kiwi Shoe Polish.** To stain a wooden frame, wipe on your favorite color Kiwi Shoe Polish, wait a few minutes to allow the polish to soak into the wood, then buff with a soft, lint-free cloth to achieve a glossy finish. Repeat to achieve a deeper color, if desired.

Hanging

- **Glad Flexible Straws.** Having difficulty getting the wire behind a picture frame to slip over the hook in the wall? Cut a section from a Glad Flexible Straw and place it over the end of the hook to lengthen it. Hang the wire over the straw, let it slide down to the hook, and remove the straw. Presto! You've hung up a picture without mussing up the wall.
- **Mr. Coffee Filters.** To avoid damaging the wall surface and creating a pile of dust on the floor, tape an open Mr. Coffee Filter under the spot you plan to drill. The tape prevents the plaster from crumbling, and the coffee filter catches the ensuing mess.
- **Oral-B Dental Floss.** When it comes to hanging framed pictures on a wall, Oral-B Dental Floss is stronger and more durable than ordinary string.
- **Pink Pearl Eraser.** To prevent framed pictures from tilting or scratching the wall, glue at least two Pink Pearl Erasers to the bottom edge of the back of the frame. The rubber erasers give the picture frame sufficient traction to stay in place against the wall.
- **Scotch Transparent Tape.** To prevent a plaster wall from crumbling when driving a nail into it, make a small X over the spot with two strips of Scotch Transparent Tape and then drive the nail into the center of the X.

Photo Albums

- **Conair Pro Styler 1600.** To free a snapshot stuck in a magnetic photo album, blow warm air from a Conair Pro Styler 1600 hair dryer underneath the plastic page.

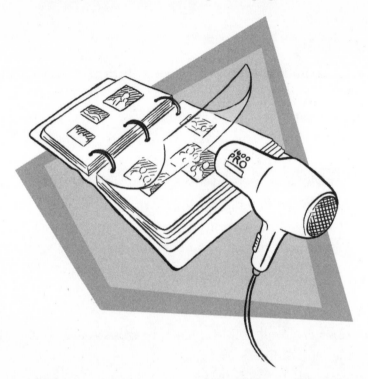

- **Oral-B Dental Floss.** Remove photographs stuck to pages of a self-adhesive photo album by gently gliding a piece of Oral-B Dental Floss behind the photos.

Plexiglas

- **Colgate Regular Flavor Toothpaste.** To hide scuff marks on clear Plexiglas acrylic glass, use a dab of Colgate Regular Flavor Toothpaste to polish the sheet of glass.

Strange Facts

- On October 18, 1961, the New York Museum of Modern Art opened an exhibit of the works of French impressionist Henri Matisse, accidentally displaying one of the artist's paintings titled *Le Batuea* (The Boat) upside down for a total of forty-seven days. An estimated 116,000 museum visitors viewed the upside-down painting, including Matisse's son, Pierre. Wall Street stockbroker Genevieve Habert brought the mistake to the museum's attention—after visiting the exhibit for the third time.

- When natural catastrophes strike, the first possessions people take with them are photo albums and pets.

- In 1971, British rock band Emerson, Lake, & Palmer released a live album called *Pictures at an Exhibition*, which included a rock version of Russian composer Modest Mussorgsky's 1874 classical piece "Pictures at an Exhibition."

- To play the Parker Brothers game Masterpiece, players bid in auctions for twenty-four famous paintings from the Art Institute of Chicago.

- People have been putting together scrapbooks ever since printed material became available to the average person. In 1981, Marielen Christensen opened the worlds' first scrapbooking store in Spanish Fork, Utah, and the rapid growth of the company—today called Keeping Memories Alive—fueled a scrapbooking craze.

- In the hit television sitcom *Friends*, a decorative picture frame hangs over the peep hole on Monica and Chandler's apartment door.

- At wedding celebrations in Germany, guests are handed large decorative picture frames to hold in front of themselves to pose for photographs.

Plumbing

Disconnecting

- **Coca-Cola.** To loosen two pipes rusted together, pour Coca-Cola over the threaded joint, wait ten minutes, and then unscrew the pipes. The phosphoric acid in Coke dissolves rust.

- **Kool-Aid.** Mix the contents of one packet of any flavor Kool-Aid with two quarts water and soak the rusted pipe joint in the drink. The citric acid in Kool-Aid dissolves rust.

- **Morton Salt** and **ReaLemon.** To free two pipes rusted together, make a paste using two tablespoons Morton Salt and one tablespoon ReaLemon lemon juice. Apply the paste around the threaded joint, wait ten minutes, and then pry the pipes apart.

- **Pam Cooking Spray.** To disconnect two pipes rusted together, spray the juncture with Pam Cooking Spray to loosen the stubborn bond.

Frozen

- **Conair Pro Styler 1600.** To defrost frozen pipes, set a Conair Pro Styler 1600 hair dryer on hot, aim the nozzle at the pipes, and move back and forth, leaving the pipes cool enough to touch.
- **Morton Salt.** To thaw frozen pipes (or prevent them from freezing in the first place), sprinkle Morton Salt down waste pipes in cold weather.

Hot Water Heaters

- **Wrigley's Spearmint Gum.** To temporarily repair a small leak in a hot water tank, chew a stick of Wrigley's Spearmint Gum well (until all the sugar is gone) and seal it over the hole.

Leaks

- **Forster Toothpick.** To temporarily fix a small leak in a waste pipe, insert a Forster Toothpick into the hole, break off the end, and wrap duct tape at least three times around the pipe over the toothpick.

Pipe Joints

- **Alberto VO5 Conditioning Hairdressing.** A thin layer of Alberto VO5 Conditioning Hairdressing on pipe connections will make them fit together more easily.
- **Coppertone.** Coppertone sunscreen works as an oil lubricant for fitting pipe joints together.
- **Noxzema Deep Cleansing Cream.** Noxzema Deep Cleansing Cream doubles as a lubricant for fitting pipe joints together.
- **Skin So Soft Body Lotion.** Coat the threads of pipes with Skin So Soft Body Lotion so you can fit them together without difficulty.

- **Vaseline Petroleum Jelly.** Dab a little Vaseline Petroleum Jelly on the ends of pipes so they fit together smoothly.
- **WD-40.** WD-40 works as an effective lubricant for fitting pipe joints together.

Soldering

- **Wonder Bread.** When soldering a joint in a copper pipe, the heat from a blowtorch turns excess water in the pipe to steam, which pushes the solder out of the joint. To prevent this, tear off a piece of bread from the center of a slice of Wonder Bread, ball it up, and push it approximately ten inches into the open pipe. The bread will absorb the steam or excess water, and when you eventually turn the water back on, the water will quickly dissolve the bread.

Sweating

- **Bounce.** To prevent puddles on your basement floor from sweating pipes, tie used Bounce sheets around exposed water pipes. The fabric softener sheets will absorb the condensation from the pipes.

Strange Facts

- Victor Hugo's 1862 novel *Les Misérables* features a history of the Paris sewers, and the hero, Jean Valjean, journeys through the sewers of Paris.

- On February 10, 1935, the *New York Times* reported that boys found a six-foot alligator in an East Harlem manhole and killed the reptile with a shovel. The urban legend that swarms of alligators live in the sewers beneath New York City most likely originated with the 1959 publication of the book *World Beneath the City*, in which author Robert Daley reported that New York's superintendent of sewers, Teddy May, known for spinning fanciful yarns, claimed that he had personally seen a colony of alligators in the sewers in 1935.

- In 1972, a group of seven members of President Richard M. Nixon's reelection committee broke into the Democratic National Committee Headquarters in the Watergate Building and bugged the offices. When the group, nicknamed the "plumbers" (in the hopes they would stop leaks), returned to the scene to fix a broken listening device, the police arrested them, eventually leading to Nixon's resignation.

- The Alaska Pipeline, with a diameter of forty-eight inches, stretches some eight hundred miles, from Prudhoe Bay to Valdez.

- The longest oil pipeline in the world is the Baku-Tbilisi-Ceyhan pipeline, which stretches one thousand miles from the Azeri-Chirag-Guneshli oil field in the Caspian Sea to Ceyhan, a port on the Mediterranean Sea.

- The *Musée des Egouts de Paris*, or Paris Sewers Museum, is located in the sewers beneath the Quai d'Orsay on the Left

Bank. It features a peek at some of the more than 1,312 miles of sewer tunnels built under Paris since 1850. In the late nineteenth century, tourists traveled through the sewer tunnels in mechanized carts.

- In October 1978, a pressure relief valve in the cooling system around the core of one of three nuclear reactors at Three Mile Island near Harrisburg, Pennsylvania, began leaking, but the management of the General Public Utilities Corporation that ran the facility did nothing to fix it. Around the same time, the Nuclear Regulatory Commission, having discovered that nine out of 150 pressure relief valves in U.S. nuclear power plants were faulty, failed to notify any nuclear power plant to check its pressure relief valves. On March 28, 1979, the malfunctioning pressure relief valve at Three Mile Island got stuck open for more than two hours. This mishap allowed thousands of gallons of cooling water to escape and caused the core of the nuclear reactor to overheat to within less than an hour of a meltdown.

- In 1999, when sanitation engineers at a sanitation plant in Los Angeles cycled the power off and on to conduct a Y2K readiness test, a valve defaulted to its open position, causing millions of gallons of raw sewage to spill into Balboa Park in Encino.

- In 2005, sewer workers in Jerusalem, Israel, discovered the biblical Pool of Siloam, where the New Testament reports that Jesus cured a man who had been blind since birth.

Refrigerators and Freezers

Cleaning

- **Arm & Hammer Baking Soda.** To clean and deodorize a refrigerator or freezer, sprinkle Arm & Hammer Baking Soda on a damp sponge, scrub, and rinse clean.

- **L'eggs Sheer Energy Panty Hose.** To clean the dust from under a refrigerator, cut off one leg from a clean, used pair of L'eggs Sheer Energy Panty Hose, place it over the end of a broomstick, and secure it in place with a rubber band. Slide the nylon-covered broomstick under the refrigerator and move it back and forth. The dust bunnies will cling to the nylon.

- **Pam Cooking Spray.** If the colored print from the packages of frozen food has made a mess on the inside walls of your freezer, spray the walls with Pam Cooking Spray and wipe clean.

- **20 Mule Team Borax.** To clean and deodorize a refrigerator or freezer, mix one tablespoon 20 Mule Team Borax in one quart of warm water. Wash spilled food with a sponge dipped in the solution. Rinse with cold water and dry with a soft cloth. Borax is a natural deodorizer.

Defrosting

- **Pam Cooking Spray.** To make defrosting a freezer a breeze, after defrosting and cleaning the freezer, spray a thin coat of Pam Cooking Spray on the inside walls. The next time you defrost the freezer, the ice will fall off the walls within minutes of unplugging the freezer.

Deodorizing

- **Kingsford Charcoal Briquets.** A cup of untreated Kingsford Charcoal Briquets set in the back of the refrigerator absorbs odors. For really bad odors, place cups of charcoal briquets on different shelves.

- **Maxwell House Coffee.** To cover up unpleasant odors inside a refrigerator, place a bowl filled with Maxwell House Coffee grounds on the back shelf. The coffee grounds simultaneously absorb foul odors and mask them.

- **McCormick Pure Vanilla Extract** and **Johnson & Johnson Cotton Balls.** To mask the odors inside a refrigerator, dampen a Johnson & Johnson Cotton Ball with McCormick Pure Vanilla Extract (or lemon or peppermint extract) and place it on a saucer inside the refrigerator. Or wipe down the inside walls of the refrigerator with a sponge saturated with vanilla extract.

- **Tidy Cats.** To deodorize a clean, empty, unplugged refrigerator, pour unused Tidy Cats in a flat box, place it on the middle shelf, and shut the door for five days. The cat box filler absorbs moisture and musty, lingering odors.

- *USA Today.* To deodorize a clean, empty, unplugged refrigerator, crumple pages of *USA Today* into balls and fill the appliance with them. The newsprint absorbs nasty odors.

Drawers

- **Alberto VO5 Conditioning Hairdressing.** To prevent refrigerator drawers from getting stuck, coat the edges of the drawers with a thin layer of Alberto VO5 Conditioning Hairdressing so the drawers glide easily.

- **Vaseline Petroleum Jelly.** Coat the edges of the drawers in the refrigerator with Vaseline Petroleum Jelly to keep them gliding open and shut smoothly.

Gaskets

- **DAP Caulk.** To repair a torn refrigerator gasket, fill the tear with DAP Caulk and let dry.

- **Vaseline Petroleum Jelly.** To prolong the life of refrigerator gaskets, put a thin coat of Vaseline Petroleum Jelly on the seals of refrigerator doors to prevent the rubber gaskets from drying out and cracking.

Ice Cube Tray

- **Pam Cooking Spray.** To prevent ice cubes from sticking to the inside of the tray of an automatic icemaker, wash and dry the tray, spray the inside of the tray with a light coat of Pam Cooking Spray, and wipe off the excess.

Icemaker

- **Conair Pro Styler 1600.** To defrost a jammed automatic icemaker, hold a Conair Pro Styler 1600 hair dryer eight inches from the frozen mass of ice cubes until they melt apart.

Mold

- **Arm & Hammer Clean Shower.** To prevent mold in a refrigerator, spray the inside walls with Arm & Hammer Clean Shower and let dry.
- **Clorox Bleach.** To clean mold from refrigerator drains, mix three-quarters cup Clorox Bleach and one gallon water and use a turkey baster to inject the sanitizing solution into refrigerator drains.

Strange Facts

- Professional football player William Perry, best known for his years as a defensive lineman for the Chicago Bears, was nicknamed "the Refrigerator" for his large rectangular frame.
- In 1989, during the U.S. invasion in Panama, Pentagon spokesmen announced finding fifty kilograms of cocaine in General Manuel Antonio Noriega's refrigerator. The Pentagon later admitted that the white powder was actually fifty kilograms of cornmeal intended for making tamales.

- In the United States and many other industrialized nations, people hang children's artwork and family photos on their refrigerator doors with magnets.

- Crime prevention experts suggest storing valuables or money in the freezer, a place where burglars are less likely to ransack. The tip gives new meaning to the phrase "cold cash."

- Placing a can of Coca-Cola in a freezer causes the liquid in the can to expand, and the can, pressurized from the carbonation, may explode, spraying the inside walls of the freezer with slushy Coca-Cola.

- Putting a jar of mayonnaise in a freezer causes the mayonnaise to turn to large chunks of white curds floating in yellow oil. As mayonnaise freezes, the oil globules expand and break away from the film that surrounds them. The oil congeals and rises to the surface, and no amount of mixing can make the mayonnaise look appetizing again.

- California governor and action movie hero Arnold Schwarzenegger, born in the Austrian village of Thal to a police officer and housekeeper, lived in a house without a refrigerator or indoor toilet until he was fourteen years old.

Shoes and Sneakers

Blisters

- **Vaseline Petroleum Jelly.** To avoid getting blisters from new shoes, rub a dab of Vaseline Petroleum Jelly into the leather of the new shoes wherever you feel friction against your feet. The lubricant allows your feet to glide against the leather.

Deodorizing

- **Arm & Hammer Baking Soda.** In the evening, sprinkle Arm & Hammer Baking Soda inside shoes to absorb moisture and neutralize offending odors. In the morning, shake out the baking soda.

- **Bounce.** To eliminate odors from sneaker or shoes, place a sheet of Bounce in the footwear overnight so it will smell great in the morning.

- **Dial.** To deodorize shoes or sneakers, place a wrapped bar of Dial soap in the footwear overnight.
- **Febreze.** Spray Febreze inside stinky shoes and sneakers to eradicate offending odors.
- **L'eggs Sheer Energy Panty Hose** and **Tidy Cats.** Take a clean, used pair of L'eggs Sheer Energy Panty Hose, cut off the legs at the knee, fill the feet with unused Tidy Cats, tie the ends with a knot, and place inside shoes or sneakers overnight. The cat box filler absorbs moisture and musty, lingering odors.
- **20 Mule Team Borax.** To deodorize shoes or sneakers, in the evening sprinkle 20 Mule Team Borax into the footwear to absorb moisture and neutralize offending odors. In the morning, shake out the borax.
- *USA Today.* To deodorize shoes or boots, crumple up a few pages of *USA Today*, shove them inside the footwear, and let sit overnight. By morning the newsprint will absorb the odors.

Drying

- **Conair Pro Styler 1600.** To dry wet boots or sneakers, insert the nozzle of a Conair Pro Styler 1600 hair dryer into the boots or sneakers and blow warm air into the footwear for five minutes.
- *USA Today.* To dry wet shoes or boots, stuff the footwear with crumpled pages from *USA Today* and let sit overnight (away from a heat source). The newsprint will absorb moisture from the shoes or boots. In the morning, remove the crumpled-up newspaper.

Galoshes

- **Crisco All-Vegetable Shortening.** To polish rubber galoshes, rub a few dabs of Crisco All-Vegetable Shortening into the rubber and buff with a soft, clean cloth.

Gum

- **Cutex Nail Polish Remover.** To clean chewing gum from the bottom of a shoe or sneaker, saturate a cotton ball with Cutex Nail Polish Remover and use it to rub off the wad of gum.
- **Jif Peanut Butter.** Step in gum? A dab of Jif Peanut Butter (creamy, not chunky) removes gum from the bottom of a shoe, boot, or sneaker.

- **WD-40.** To remove chewing gum from the bottom of a shoe or sneaker, spray on WD-40, wait, and pull the gum free.

Heels

- **Krazy Glue.** To reattach a broken heel, use a few drops of Krazy Glue and hold the heel in place until the glue dries.

Patent Leather

- **Vaseline Petroleum Jelly.** To shine patent leather shoes, coat the shoes with Vaseline Petroleum Jelly and buff with a soft cloth.
- **Wonder Bread.** To clean and shine patent leather shoes, take a slice of Wonder Bread and rub it over the shoes. The dough

works like an kneaded eraser, simultaneously cleaning scuff marks and giving the patent leather an exquisite shine.

Polish

- **A1 Steak Sauce.** If you run out of shoe polish, use A1 Steak Sauce on a soft cloth.
- **Geritol.** In a pinch, you can polish brown leather shoes with a few drops of Geritol on a soft cloth.
- **Maxwell House Coffee.** To polish suede shoes, make a cup of Maxwell House Coffee and brush the black coffee onto black suede shoes to revive them.
- **Reynolds Cut-Rite Wax Paper.** To prevent shoe polish from smearing on your shoes, let the shoe polish dry, then rub the shoes with a sheet of Reynolds Cut-Rite Wax Paper to remove the excess polish. The wax paper also helps buff the shoes. Use a second sheet of wax paper as a work surface to prevent shoe polish from spattering the floor.

Scuff Marks

- **Alberto VO5 Hair Spray.** To clean scuff marks from shoes, spray a little Alberto VO5 Hair Spray on the mark and rub forcefully with a towel or washcloth.
- **Colgate Regular Flavor Toothpaste.** Squeeze a dab of Colgate Regular Flavor Toothpaste on a soft cloth, rub it over the scuff marks, and—presto!—the marks vanish like magic.
- **Cutex Nail Polish Remover.** A cotton ball dampened with Cutex Nail Polish Remover cleans scuff marks off white shoes.
- **Fantastik.** Spray scuff marks on shoes with Fantastik and wipe clean with a soft cloth.
- **Liquid Paper.** To cover up scuff marks on white shoes in a pinch, touch up the spots with Liquid Paper.

- **Mr. Clean Magic Eraser.** To clean dirt, grime, and scuff marks from sneakers, wipe footwear clean with a Mr. Clean Magic Eraser.

- **Noxzema Deep Cleansing Cream.** To clean scuff marks from patent leather shoes, apply Noxzema Deep Cleansing Cream to a soft cloth and rub it into the patent leather.

- **Skin So Soft Body Lotion.** To clean scuff marks from patent leather shoes, apply Skin So Soft Body Lotion to a soft cloth and rub it into the patent leather.

- **Smirnoff Vodka.** Rub scuff marks off shoes with a cotton ball saturated with Smirnoff Vodka.

Shining

- **Alberto VO5 Conditioning Hairdressing.** Rub in a little Alberto VO5 Conditioning Hairdressing, then buff. Aside from shining shoes, the hairdressing protects leather shoes and boots from winter salt and ice.

- **ChapStick.** To shine shoes in a pinch, rub ChapStick over the leather and buff with a dry, clean cloth.

- **Heinz White Vinegar.** To clean white stains left by rock salt (used for melting ice on roads in winter) from leather shoes, rub Heinz White Vinegar on the stain and wipe with a with clean, wet cloth.

- **Huggies Baby Wipes.** To shine shoes in a pinch, wipe the shoes with a Huggies Baby Wipe.

- **Johnson's Baby Oil.** To shine shoes, put a few drops of Johnson's Baby Oil on a paper towel, rub it into the shoes, and buff with a clean cloth.

- **L'eggs Sheer Energy Panty Hose.** Ball up a clean, used pair of L'eggs Sheer Energy Panty Hose and use it to shine shoes. The nylon is a mild abrasive.

- **Lubriderm.** To shine shoes, rub a dab of Lubriderm on each shoe and buff with a soft cloth.
- **Mr. Coffee Filter.** If you don't have a soft cloth to buff shoes, use a balled-up, lint-free Mr. Coffee Filter.
- **Pledge.** For a long-lasting and beautiful shine, spray your shoes with Pledge furniture polish and buff dry with a soft cloth. The waxes in Pledge also help the shoes repel water.
- **Star Olive Oil.** Polishing shoes with a few drops of Star Olive Oil revitalizes the leather.
- **Stayfree Maxi Pads.** After applying polish to shoes, buff the leather with Stayfree Maxi Pads.
- **Tampax Tampons.** To shine shoes, use the cotton tip of a Tampax Tampon to buff.
- **Turtle Wax.** In a pinch, dab Turtle Wax on leather shoes and buff with a clean, soft cloth to achieve a glimmering shine.
- **Vaseline Petroleum Jelly.** Apply a few dabs of Vaseline Petroleum Jelly on your shoes or boots and buff with a cloth.
- **Windex.** To shine shoes in a pinch, spray Windex on the leather and buff with a soft, clean cloth.

Shoelaces

- **Elmer's Glue-All.** To prevent broken shoelaces from fraying, dip the ends into Elmer's Glue-All and let dry.
- **Maybelline Express Finish Clear Nail Polish.** To repair frayed shoelaces, dip the tattered ends of the shoelaces in Maybelline Express Finish Clear Nail Polish and let dry so the unraveled threads hold together and fit through the holes.
- **Scotch Packaging Tape.** To mend frayed shoelaces, wrap the frayed ends with a small strip of Scotch Packaging Tape.
- **Scotch Transparent Tape.** To fix frayed shoelaces in a pinch, wrap the frayed ends with a small strip of Scotch Transparent Tape.

Sneakers

- **Colgate Regular Flavor Toothpaste** and **Oral-B Toothbrush.** To clean the white rubber part of sneakers, squeeze some Colgate Regular Flavor Toothpaste on a clean, used Oral-B Toothbrush, dampen with water, and scrub the rubber until it comes clean.
- **S.O.S Steel Wool Soap Pads.** Use an S.O.S Steel Wool Soap Pad dampened with water to gently clean dirty sneakers.
- **Scrubbing Bubbles.** To clean sneakers, spray Scrubbing Bubbles on the footwear, let sit for two minutes, and then rinse clean.

Squeaks

- **Alberto VO5 Conditioning Hairdressing.** To remove the squeak from a new pair of shoes, coat the shoes with a thin layer of Alberto VO5 Conditioning Hairdressing.
- **WD-40.** To stop shoes from squeaking, spray WD-40 on the spot where the sole joins the heel and wipe off the excess. (Be careful to avoid lubricating the shoe too much and slipping when you walk.)

Strange Facts

- Nearly 80 percent of all corporate executives believe that well-cared for shoes are very important to a person's success.

- A version of the Bible translated into an Eskimo dialect included one misplaced letter so the verse "nation shall rise up against nation" (Mark 13:8) became "a pair of snowshoes shall rise up against a pair of snowshoes."

- In the 1997 movie *Wag the Dog*, Americans tie pairs of shoes together by the shoelaces and hurl them over telephone pole wires to show support for American Sgt. William Schumann (nicknamed "Shoe"), who is held hostage in Albania.

- The plot of Louis Sachar's 1998 novel *Holes* and the 2003 movie version of the book revolves around a pair of stolen sneakers.

- The standard clown shoe is fifteen inches long, two-colors, and comically enlarged at the toes.

- To make a pair of sandals from a used automobile tire, use a utility knife or table saw to cut two flat sections from the tire, each approximately 6 x 12 inches. Using a piece of chalk, trace around the outside of each foot, leaving one inch extra around and adding wings at the toe and heel. Cut out the pattern, cut slits in the wings, thread leather straps through the slits, and hold the straps together with rivets.

- American parents traditionally bronze their children's first pairs of baby shoes as cherished keepsakes.

Showers

Doors

- **Hydrogen Peroxide.** To clean shower door tracks, pour hydrogen peroxide into the tracks, wait a few minutes, then rinse and wipe.
- **Pledge.** To make sliding shower doors glide more easily, spray Pledge furniture polish into the tracks and wipe clean. The waxes in Pledge help keep dirt out and lubricate the wheels.
- **WD-40.** To clean sliding shower door tracks, spray WD-40 into the grooves and wipe off the excess. This petroleum distillates clean the tracks, and the water displacement liquid lubricates them.

Faucets

- **Cover Girl Continuous Color Classic Red.** To adjust the water in the shower effortlessly, turn on the shower faucet(s) to the temperature you prefer, then mark the faucet(s) and the wall with dots of Cover Girl Continuous Color Classic Red

Nail Polish so they can be aligned immediately every time you shower.

Grout

- **Coca-Cola.** To clean stained grout, pour Coca-Cola over the affected area, let sit for five minutes, and wipe clean. The phosphoric acid in Coke cleans the grout.
- **Heinz White Vinegar** and **Oral-B Toothbrush.** To clean grout, fill a sixteen-ounce trigger-spray bottle with Heinz White Vinegar, spray the grout with the vinegar, wait five minutes, then scrub with a clean, used Oral-B Toothbrush.
- **Listerine.** To clean mold and mildew in grout, fill a sixteen-ounce trigger-spray bottle with Listerine antiseptic mouthwash, wait two minutes, and wipe clean. The antiseptic kills mold and mildew.

Leaks

- **DAP Caulk.** If the shower seems to be leaking, water may be leaking into walls through the seams from around a soap dish, faucet, or drain. Caulk around these areas.

Mildew

- **Clorox Bleach.** To kill mildew, combine three-quarters cup Clorox Bleach and one gallon water and fill a trigger-spray bottle with the solution. Spray the bleach mixture on the pink stains on the shower walls, wait five minutes, and rinse clean.
- **Listerine.** If you don't like using bleach to kill mildew, dampen a sponge with Listerine antiseptic mouthwash and wipe the pink stains with it. Listerine kills mildew, and it leaves your shower smelling all nice and medicine-y.

- **Parsons' Ammonia.** To remove mildew from shower walls, scrub it with a mixture made from equal parts Parsons' Ammonia and water.
- **Tidy Cats.** To prevent mildew in a shower when you leave your home for a long time, pour unused Tidy Cats in a flat box and place it in your shower. (If you have cats, be sure to keep the bathroom door closed so they don't use the cat box filler in the shower.)

Shower Curtains

- **Alberto VO5 Conditioning Hairdressing.** To keep shower curtains gliding easily, apply a thin coat of Alberto VO5 Conditioning Hairdressing to the curtain rod.
- **Clorox Bleach.** To clean mildew from shower curtains, shower caddies, bath mats, and plastic soap dishes, place all the bathroom accessories into a bathtub, fill with two gallons water, and add one and one-half cups Clorox Bleach. Let sit for ten minutes, rinse, and drain. (The Clorox Bleach also will have cleaned the bathtub, so rinse it well too.)
- **Conair Pro Styler 1600.** To remove wrinkles from a shower curtain, blow the curtain with a Conair Pro Styler 1600 hair dryer set on hot until the plastic softens.
- **Heinz White Vinegar.** To clean soap scum from a vinyl shower curtain, place the curtain in the washing machine, set for warm rinse with your regular laundry detergent, and add one cup Heinz White Vinegar. The moment the rinse cycle ends, remove the shower curtain and rehang it immediately so it doesn't get wrinkled.
- **Jet-Dry.** To clean a vinyl shower curtain, place the curtain in the washing machine, set for warm rinse with your regular laundry detergent, and add four ounces Jet-Dry. When the rinse cycle finishes, immediately remove and rehang the

shower curtain. The Jet-Dry does double duty in the washing machine, simultaneously cleaning soap scum from the tubes and pipes in the washing machine.

- **Pledge.** To make your shower curtain glide over the rod, wipe Pledge furniture polish on your shower curtain rod to give it a slick, waxy coating.
- **Vaseline Petroleum Jelly.** To keep a shower curtain gliding easily, apply a thin coat of Vaseline Petroleum Jelly to the curtain rod.
- **Velcro.** To keep a shower curtain in place while taking a shower, attach a piece of self-adhesive-backed Velcro to the side of the bathtub and the bottom of the shower curtain so you can adhere the curtain in place.

Showerheads

- **ChapStick.** If the showerhead is leaking from the connection to the shower arm, unscrew the showerhead, apply ChapStick to the threads, and screw the showerhead back in place. The ChapStick seals any small gaps in the threads.
- **Forster Toothpicks.** To unclog a showerhead filled with mineral deposits, unblock the clogged holes with a Forster Toothpick.
- **Heinz White Vinegar.** To unclog a showerhead filled with mineral deposits, unscrew the showerhead, remove the rubber washer, place the head in a pot filled with equal parts Heinz White Vinegar and water, bring to a boil, then simmer for five minutes—and you've got showerhead soup. Or soak the showerhead in Heinz White Vinegar overnight, if necessary. (Do not use vinegar on a brass showerhead.)
- **Jet-Dry.** To clean mineral deposits from a showerhead, unscrew the showerhead and soak it in a mixture of four ounces Jet-Dry and four ounces water. The Jet-Dry removes the mineral deposits, enabling your showerhead to run clean.

- **Ziploc Storage Bags** and **Heinz White Vinegar.** If a shower-head cannot be removed for cleaning, fill a Ziploc Storage Bag with Heinz White Vinegar, wrap it around the showerhead (with the showerhead inside the bag so it can soak in the vinegar), and secure in place overnight with a rubber band.

Soap Scum and Mineral Deposits

- **Armor All.** To prevent soap scum from sticking to shower doors and walls, polish the doors and walls with Armor All. (Do not use Armor All on the shower floor; otherwise you risk slipping on the floor.)
- **Bon Ami.** To clean mineral deposits from glass shower doors, sprinkle Bon Ami on a damp sponge and scrub the doors clean.
- **Bounce.** To clean soap scum from shower doors, wipe the glass doors with a used sheet of Bounce dampened with water. The antistatic elements in Bounce and the abrasiveness of the sheet help remove the soap scum.
- **Cascade.** To clean soap scum from shower doors and walls, dissolve one-quarter cup Cascade dishwasher detergent in one gallon hot water. Wearing rubber gloves, scrub the walls and doors with the solution and then rinse clean.
- **Downy Fabric Softener.** To clean soap scum and mineral deposits from a shower door, mix one capful Downy Fabric

Softener and one quart warm water in a plastic bucket, dampen an abrasive sponge in the solution, and scrub the shower doors and walls clean.

- **Easy-Off Oven Cleaner.** To clean soap scum and mineral deposits from shower doors and walls, open the doors and windows and put on protective eyewear and rubber gloves and spray Easy-Off Oven Cleaner on the walls and glass shower doors and let sit for ten minutes, making sure the room is well ventilated. Wash away any residual oven cleaner with regular cleanser and rinse well with very hot water. (Do not get oven cleaner on any metal surfaces; it eats away chrome.)

- **Heinz White Vinegar.** Fill a trigger-spray bottle with Heinz White Vinegar, spray it on glass shower doors, and wait a few minutes. Wipe clean with a sponge. Rinse.

- **Jet-Dry.** To clean soap scum and hard water mineral deposits from shower doors, fill a clean, empty sixteen-ounce trigger-spray bottle with four ounces Jet-Dry, fill the rest of the bottle with water, and shake well. Spray the glass shower doors with this solution, wipe with a mildly abrasive scrub pad, and rinse clean.

- **Johnson's Baby Oil.** Put a few drops of Johnson's Baby Oil on a clean cloth and use it to wipe soap scum from shower doors. To prevent water spots and soap scum on shower walls and doors, wipe the walls and doors with a few drops of Johnson's Baby Oil on a damp cloth once a week. (Do not use Johnson's Baby Oil on the shower floor; otherwise you risk slipping on the floor.)

- **Morton Salt** and **Heinz White Vinegar.** To scrub hard water stains and soap scum from shower walls and doors, fill a measuring cup with three-quarters cup Morton Salt and add enough Heinz White Vinegar to make one cup of solution. Using a sponge, spread the abrasive mixture on tile walls and shower doors. Scrub well and rinse clean.

- **Pam Cooking Spray** and **Dawn Dishwashing Liquid.** To clean soap scum and mineral deposits from shower doors, spray the glass with Pam Cooking Spray. Wait five minutes and then wash clean with a few drops of Dawn Dishwashing Liquid in a bucket of water.
- **Pledge.** To prevent water spots and soap scum on shower walls and doors, coat the walls and doors with Pledge furniture polish and wipe clean. This also removes the existing soap scum buildup from the walls and doors. (Do not use Pledge on the shower floor; otherwise you risk slipping on the floor.)
- **Rain-X.** To prevent mineral deposits from adhering to glass shower doors, treat the shower doors with Rain-X.
- **Turtle Wax.** Give your glass shower doors a coat of Turtle Wax to prevent water spots from forming on the glass.

Tile

- **Arm & Hammer Baking Soda.** To clean tile, sprinkle Arm & Hammer Baking Soda on a damp sponge, scrub, and rinse clean. (For more ways to clean tile, see page 299.)

Strange Facts

- As a law student at Duke University, Richard Nixon lived in a primitive cabin, ate a Milky Way candy bar each morning for breakfast, shaved each morning in the men's room at the law library, and took a shower every afternoon in the gym after playing handball.
- Jane Fonda made her screen debut in the 1960 movie *Tall Story*, in which she makes out with actor Anthony Perkins while standing in a shower stall. Later that year Perkins, star-

ring as Norman Bates in the Alfred Hitchcock movie *Psycho*, would become renowned for a more macabre shower scene.

- In Alfred Hitchcock's 1960 horror film *Psycho*, the famous shower scene ends with an extreme close-up of Janet Leigh's eye, with her pupil tightly contracted. When people die, their pupils dilate.

- Russian cosmonaut Valery Polyakov, who lived aboard the Mir Space Station for 437 days (from January 8, 1994 to March 22, 1995), used wet towels to wash his skin and hair.

- Pop star Madonna claimed that to achieve success, every time she took a shower, she visualized being showered with money.

- Amtrak trains with bedroom sleeping cars now have showers either in the cabins or down the hall.

Silverware

Silverware

- **Alberto VO5 Conditioning Hairdressing.** Once you've cleaned those silver candlesticks, picture frames, and silverware sets, you can prevent them from tarnishing by applying a thin coat of Alberto VO5 Conditioning Hairdressing with a soft cloth. Wipe off the excess, leaving behind a very thin, virtually invisible protective coating. VO5's organic protectants actually prevent tarnishing. Just be sure to wash the silverware thoroughly before using.

- **Arm & Hammer Baking Soda.** To remove tarnish from silver, mix a thick paste of Arm & Hammer Baking Soda with water, apply to the silver with a damp sponge, rub, rinse, and buff dry.

- **Arm & Hammer Baking Soda** and **Reynolds Wrap.** For the best and easiest way to polish silver, line a metal cake pan with Reynolds Wrap and fill with enough water to cover the silverware. Add two tablespoons baking soda per quart of water.

Heat the water above 150 degrees Fahrenheit. Place the tarnished silverware in the pan so it touches the aluminum foil. Do not let the water boil. The hydrogen produced by heated baking soda combines with the sulfur in the tarnish, removing the stains. (This technique also removes the patina from silverware, so make certain you're willing to do that before embracing this cleaning method.)

- **Colgate Regular Flavor Toothpaste.** To clean silverware, squeeze a dollop of Colgate Regular Flavor Toothpaste on a soft, clean cloth and rub the silverware. The toothpaste is a mild abrasive, so it does a great job cleaning the silverware. Rinse thoroughly. And now you won't have to brush after meals (just kidding).

- **Crayola Chalk.** Place a piece of Crayola Chalk in your silverware chest to absorb moisture and prevent tarnish from forming on silverware.

- **Heinz Ketchup.** To remove tarnish from silverware, squirt some Heinz Ketchup on a paper towel and rub it gently into the tarnish. For stubborn tarnish, coat the silver item with ketchup, wait fifteen minutes, rub the item with a soft cloth, and rinse clean. (Do not soak silver in ketchup too long; the acids can ruin the finish.)

- **Kingsford's Corn Starch.** To polish silverware, make a paste with Kingsford's Corn Starch and water. Apply with a damp cloth, let dry, and then rub off with cheesecloth, which is a mild abrasive.

- **McCormick Cream of Tartar.** To clean silver, make a paste with McCormick Cream of Tartar and water. Apply with a damp cloth, let dry, rub off, and rinse clean.

- **Morton Salt** and **ReaLemon.** Mix two tablespoons Morton Salt and one tablespoon ReaLemon lemon juice. Gently rub the paste on the tarnished silver, wipe clean with a dry cloth, and rinse. Repeat if necessary.

- **Nestlé Carnation Nonfat Dry Milk** and **Heinz White Vinegar.** To polish silverware, mix five ounces Nestlé Carnation Nonfat Dry Milk powder, twelve ounces water, and one table-spoon Heinz White Vinegar (or ReaLemon lemon juice) in a pan. Let the silver stand overnight in the mixture, rinse clean, and dry thoroughly.

- **Parsons' Ammonia.** To polish silverware, mix equal parts Parsons' Ammonia with silver paste polish, apply with a soft cloth, and rinse clean.

- **Purell Instant Hand Sanitizer.** Squirt a few drops of Purell Instant Hand Sanitizer on a clean cloth and rub it on the silver to remove the tarnish.

- **Windex.** Spray some Windex on the silver and wipe clean with a soft clean. Windex removes minor tarnish from silver. Rinse the silverware thoroughly.

Strange Facts

- Tarnish results on the surface of silver objects. The silver combines with sulfur in the air to form silver sulfide, which is black.

- Polishing silverware with an abrasive cleanser removes the silver sulfide and some of the silver from the surface. Other chemical tarnish removers dissolve the silver sulfide, but they also remove some of the silver. The technique on page 276 using baking soda and aluminum foil coverts the silver sulfide into silver and transfers the sulfur to the aluminum foil.

- Silver conducts heat and electricity better than any other metal.

- Silver was mined in Asia Minor as early as 2500 BCE.

- According to the New Testament, the high priests of Jerusalem paid thirty silver coins to Judas Iscariot to turn Jesus over to the Romans.

- Eggs tarnish silverware rapidly because they contain a substantial amount of sulfur.

- The Lone Ranger, best known from radio and television programs, has a horse named Silver and leaves behind a silver bullet as his calling card.

- The five leading silver-mining countries are Mexico, Peru, Russia, the United States, and Canada.

Sinks

Chrome Faucets and Handles

- **Alberto VO5 Conditioning Hairdressing.** To shine chrome faucet and handles, squeeze some Alberto VO5 Conditioning Hairdressing on a soft, dry cloth and buff lightly.

- **Alberto VO5 Conditioning Hairdressing.** To stop a faucet from screeching, remove the handle and stem, coat both sets of metal threads with Alberto VO5 Conditioning Hairdressing, and replace.

- **Arm & Hammer Clean Shower.** To clean chrome fixtures, simply spray on Arm & Hammer Clean Shower, wait twenty minutes, and wipe clean.

- **Canada Dry Club Soda.** To polish chrome, fill a trigger-spray bottle with Canada Dry Club Soda, spray the fixtures, and wipe clean.

- **Colgate Regular Flavor Toothpaste.** To clean chrome faucets and handles, squeeze a dollop of Colgate Regular Flavor

Toothpaste on a soft, clean cloth and rub the fixture. The toothpaste is a mild abrasive that cleans chrome beautifully. Rinse thoroughly.

- **Huggies Baby Wipes.** Use a Huggies Baby Wipe to clean chrome faucets.
- **Johnson's Baby Oil.** Apply a few drops of Johnson's Baby Oil with a damp cloth to faucets and handles and polish with a clean, soft cloth.
- **Parsons' Ammonia.** To clean chrome faucets and handles, mix one-quarter cup Parsons' Ammonia and one quart hot water. Apply with a soft cloth and rinse clean.
- **Reynolds Wrap.** Crumple up a sheet of Reynolds Wrap and use the balled-up aluminum foil as a gentle scrubber to polish chrome fixtures.
- **Smirnoff Vodka.** Dampen a clean, soft cloth with Smirnoff Vodka and wipe chrome faucets and handles clean. The alcohol removes soap scum and calcium and lime deposits.
- **Turtle Wax.** To prevent water spots from forming on chrome faucets and handles, rub a little Turtle Wax into the fixtures and buff well with a clean cloth.
- **Vaseline Petroleum Jelly.** To stop a faucet from screeching, coat the threads on the handle and stem with Vaseline Petroleum Jelly.

Cleaning

- **Arm & Hammer Baking Soda.** To clean a sink, sprinkle Arm & Hammer Baking Soda on a damp sponge, scrub the sink, and rinse clean.
- **Arm & Hammer Clean Shower.** Spray the sink with Arm & Hammer Clean Shower, let sit twenty minutes, and wipe clean.

- **Cascade.** To clean a sink, sprinkle a little Cascade dishwasher detergent in the sink, add just enough water to make a paste, and gently rub the paste over the sink with a sponge. Let sit for fifteen minutes, then rinse clean.

- **Colgate Regular Flavor Toothpaste.** To clean a ceramic or stainless steel sink, apply Colgate Regular Flavor Toothpaste and scrub with a sponge. Toothpaste is a mild abrasive that safely cleans any finish.

- **Listerine.** To clean hard water stains from a sink, sponge down the sink with Listerine antiseptic mouthwash, which conveniently disinfects the sink at the same time.

- **ReaLemon** and **Morton Salt.** To clean a sink, make a paste from ReaLemon lemon juice and Morton Salt, scrub the sink with a sponge dipped in the paste, and then rinse with water.

Drains

- **Wilson Tennis Balls.** If you lose the drain plug for your sink, use a Wilson Tennis Ball to block the drain. The suction holds the rubber ball in place.

Garbage Disposers

- **Arm & Hammer Baking Soda.** To freshen the smell of a garbage disposer, instead of throwing out that old box of Arm & Hammer Baking Soda that's been sitting in the refrigerator or freezer, gradually pour it down the drain and flush with water. Or better yet, pour two tablespoons Arm & Hammer Baking Soda down the garbage disposer every week.

- **Clorox Bleach.** To clean a garbage disposer, pour Clorox Bleach down your sink, being careful to avoid splashing any bleach on your skin. (Do not pour bleach down your sink if you have a septic tank; otherwise the bleach will kill the beneficial bacteria.)

- **Heinz White Vinegar.** Fill an ice cube tray with Heinz White Vinegar, place in the freezer until frozen, grind the ice cubes through the disposer, and flush with cold water. Just be sure to leave a note on the ice cube tray in the freezer to prevent anyone from using the cubes of frozen vinegar in a tall glass of iced tea.

- **ReaLemon.** Pour one-quarter cup ReaLemon lemon juice down the drain into your garbage disposer, let sit for fifteen minutes, and flush with clean water.

- **20 Mule Team Borax.** To neutralize acidic odors, sprinkle two to three tablespoons 20 Mule Team Borax in the drain, let stand for fifteen minutes, then flush with water while running the disposer.

Porcelain

- **Canada Dry Club Soda.** To clean a porcelain sink, pour Canada Dry Club Soda over the bowl and wipe clean.

- **Clorox Bleach.** To whiten a porcelain sink, fill the sink with a solution of three-quarters cup Clorox Bleach per gallon of water. Let sit for five minutes, then rinse clean.

- **McCormick Cream of Tartar.** Sprinkle McCormick Cream of Tartar on a damp cloth and rub the porcelain sink to clean it thoroughly.

Rust Stains

- **Cascade.** To clean rust stains from a sink, fill the sink with hot water, add one tablespoon Cascade dishwasher detergent, and let stand for about ten minutes. Use an abrasive sponge to scrub the stains, then rinse clean with water. Repeat if necessary.

- **Coca-Cola.** To clean rust stains from a sink, cover the stains with Coca-Cola, let sit for one hour, and rinse clean. The phosphoric acid in Coke removes the rust.

- **20 Mule Team Borax** and **ReaLemon.** To clean rust stains from a sink, scrub with a paste made from 20 Mule Team Borax and ReaLemon lemon juice. Rinse with water.

Shutoff Valves

- **WD-40.** To avoid causing a leak when turning off a shutoff valve that hasn't been used for a long time, spray a little WD-40 on the spot where the stem meets the packing nut. Turn the handle one turn, return the handle to its original position, and wait a few minutes to allow the oil to seep inside before using.

Sink Mats

- **Clorox Bleach.** To clean a rubber sink mat, fill the sink with water, add one-quarter cup Clorox Bleach, and soak the mat for five to ten minutes. Rinse clean.

Stainless Steel

- **Alberto VO5 Conditioning Hairdressing.** Shine a stainless steel sink with a dab of Alberto VO5 Conditioning Hairdressing on a soft cloth.

- **Arm & Hammer Clean Shower.** To clean limestone deposits from a stainless steel sink, spray on Arm & Hammer Clean Shower, wait a minute, then wipe off with a soft towel.

- **Canada Dry Club Soda.** To clean a stainless steel sink, fill a trigger-spray bottle with Canada Dry Club Soda, spray the sink, and wipe clean.

- **Easy-Off Oven Cleaner.** To clean persistent stains from a stainless steel sink, put on protective eyewear and rubber gloves, apply Easy-Off Oven Cleaner to the sink (making sure the room is well ventilated), let sit for a few minutes, then rinse well with soap and water.

- **Efferdent.** Fill the sink with water, drop in two to four Efferdent denture cleansing tablets, let sit for one hour, and rinse clean for a shiny stainless steel sink.

- **Johnson's Baby Oil.** Clean a stainless steel sink with a drop of Johnson's Baby Oil, dry with a paper towel, and polish with a few more drops of oil.

- **Pam Cooking Spray.** To shine a stainless steel sink, give the sink a quick spritz of Pam Cooking Spray and buff with a soft cloth.

- **Star Olive Oil.** To polish a stainless steel sink, use a few drops of Star Olive Oil on a paper towel or soft cloth.

- **Wesson Corn Oil.** Shine a stainless steel sink with a few drops of Wesson Corn Oil on a soft cloth.

Strange Facts

- In 1912, British metallurgist Harry Brearley, seeking a steel with better resistance to erosion, began experimenting with steels containing chromium, creating the first true stainless steel on August 13, 1913 (containing 0.24 percent carbon and 12.8 percent chromium) in Sheffield, England. Discovering that this new steel strongly resisted chemical attack from vinegar and lemon juice, Brearley realized that his "rustless steel" could revolutionize the cutlery industry. He had knives made at a local cutler's, R. F. Mosley, where cutlery manager Ernest Stuart called the new metal "stainless steel."

- The phrase "Everything but the kitchen sink" originated during World War II as military slang for massive bombardment.

- On the animated television series *The Flintstones*, Fred and Wilma Flintstone own a buzzard that lives under their kitchen sink as a garbage disposer.

- In the 1970s, Jan's Ice Cream Parlor, with locations in Brooklyn, New York, and South Florida, offered a dish called "the Kitchen Sink," a massive bowl of scoops of various flavors of ice cream and covered with a wide array of toppings.

- Beaches and Cream Soda Shop at Walt Disney World near Orlando, Florida, sells a sundae called "the Kitchen Sink Sundae." It includes every flavor of ice cream in the place, tons of toppings, and an entire can of whipped cream, and it's served in a container that looks like a kitchen sink.

Small Appliances

Cleaning

- **Arm & Hammer Clean Shower.** Clean the exterior of a blender, coffeemaker, or food processor by spraying with Arm & Hammer Clean Shower and wiping off.

- **Cascade.** To clean dirt, grease, and grime from the outside of a blender, coffeemaker, or food processor, dissolve one-quarter cup Cascade dishwasher detergent in one gallon of hot water. Dampen a sponge in the solution and scrub the appliance, then wipe clean with a dry, soft cloth.

- **Clorox Bleach.** Clean the exterior of a white blender, coffeemaker, or food processor by mixing three-quarters cup Clorox Bleach and one gallon water. Apply with a sponge, let stand for ten minutes, then rinse and dry thoroughly.

- **Forster Toothpicks.** To clean tight crevices on the outside of a blender, coffeemaker, or food processor, dip a Forster Toothpick in water or rubbing alcohol and work along the tight spaces.

- **Huggies Baby Wipes.** To clean smudge marks, grease, or food stains from the outside of a blender, coffeemaker, or food processor, simply wipe clean with a Huggies Baby Wipe.
- **Liquid Paper.** Cover up dings or chips on a white blender, coffeemaker, or food processor by touching up the spot with a touch of Liquid Paper.
- **Oral-B Toothbrushes.** To clean tight crevices on the outside of a blender, coffeemaker, or food processor, scrub with a clean, used Oral-B Toothbrush.
- **Parsons' Ammonia.** Clean the outside of a blender, coffeemaker, or food processor with a sponge dampened with equal parts Parsons' Ammonia and water.
- **Q-Tips Cotton Swabs.** Dip a Q-Tips Cotton Swab in water or rubbing alcohol to clean the crevices between the push buttons on a blender, coffeemaker, or food processor.
- **Reynolds Cut-Rite Wax Paper.** To give your blender, coffeemaker, or food processor a shine, buff the exterior with a sheet of Reynolds Cut-Rite Wax Paper.

Coffeemakers

- **Alka-Seltzer.** To clean the pipes and tubes in a coffeemaker, fill the water chamber with water, drop in four Alka-Seltzer tablets, and run the coffeemaker through a regular cycle. The ascorbic acid in Alka-Seltzer cleans the system. Then run clean water through the cycle twice.
- **Coca-Cola.** To clean a stained glass coffeepot, fill the coffeepot with Coca-Cola, let stand overnight, and then rinse clean. The phosphoric acid and ascorbic acid in Coke clean the grime from the pot.
- **Efferdent.** Fill a stained glass coffeepot with water, drop in two Efferdent tablets, let sit for twenty minutes, then

rinse clean. The denture cleansing tablets clean the gunk from the glass.

- **Jet-Dry.** To clean stains and calcium buildup from a coffeemaker, pour four ounces Jet-Dry into your coffeemaker, fill the rest of the way with water, and let sit overnight.

- **Morton Salt.** To clean all the baked-on coffee from the bottom of a glass coffeepot, pour in enough Morton Salt to cover the bottom of the glass, fill the coffeepot with ice cubes, and then holding the pot handle, shake the pot back and forth for several minutes so the ice and salt swirl around the pot, scrubbing the inside of the glass. Rinse clean.

Curling Irons

- **S.O.S Steel Wool Soap Pads.** To clean hairspray baked onto a curling iron, unplug the cooled curling iron and use an S.O.S Steel Wool Soap Pad to gently scrub the curling iron clean.

Microwave Ovens

- **Arm & Hammer Baking Soda.** To clean and deodorize the inside of a microwave oven, sprinkle Arm & Hammer Baking Soda on a damp sponge, scrub, and rinse. Or mix two tablespoons Arm & Hammer Baking Soda in one cup of water. Boil in the microwave for five minutes, allowing the steam to condense on the inside walls of the oven, then wipe clean.

- **Bounce.** Dampen a clean, used sheet of Bounce with water and use it to wipe clean your microwave. A dryer sheet makes a mildly abrasive scrubber, and the fragrance helps cover up pungent odors.

- **Dixie Paper Plates.** Save your microwave from splatters and spills by placing a Dixie Paper Plate under cups or dishes and inverting a second paper plate over dishes as a splatter screen.

- **Heinz White Vinegar.** If there's a stench inside your microwave oven, unplug the microwave and place a drinking glass filled with Heinz White Vinegar inside the oven, with the door open. Let sit for 24 hours, or longer if necessary. Vinegar absorbs foul odors.

- **Mr. Coffee Filters.** Prevent spatters in the microwave in the first place by covering dishes or bowls of spaghetti and meatballs, chili, or other saucy foods with a Mr. Coffee Filter.

- **ReaLemon.** Add four tablespoons ReaLemon lemon juice to one cup water in a microwave-safe four-cup bowl. Boil for five minutes in the microwave, allowing the steam to condense on the inside walls of the oven. Then wipe clean.

- **Reynolds Cut-Rite Wax Paper.** Prevent spatters in the microwave in the first place by simply covering dishes or plates of spaghetti and meatballs, chili, or other saucy foods with a sheet of Reynolds Cut-Rite Wax Paper.

Teakettles

- **Coca-Cola.** To clean hard water stains, lime scale, or calcium buildup from a teakettle, fill the teakettle with Coca-Cola and let sit overnight. The phosphoric acid and ascorbic acid in Coke dissolve the buildup, and all you need to do is rinse the teakettle clean.

- **Efferdent.** Is the inside of your teapot or teakettle stained? Fill it with water, drop in two Efferdent tablets, let sit overnight, then scrub with a bottle brush and rinse clean with hot water.

- **Heinz White Vinegar.** To remove stains or calcium buildup from the inside of a teakettle, pour three cups Heinz White Vinegar into the teakettle, fill the rest of the way with water, stir well, and let sit overnight. In the morning, rinse clean. The acetic acid in vinegar dissolves calcium carbonate.

- **Jet-Dry.** To clean stains and calcium buildup from an electric teapot, pour four ounces Jet-Dry into your teakettle, fill the rest of the way with water, and let sit overnight. In the morning, rinse clean with water.

Toasters

- **Arm & Hammer Baking Soda.** To remove melted bread bags from the exterior of a toaster, sprinkle Arm & Hammer Baking Soda on a damp cloth or sponge, scrub gently, and wipe clean. Buff dry. The baking soda works like a polishing compound, increasing the shine.
- **Colgate Regular Flavor Toothpaste.** To shine up your toaster, use a dollop of Colgate Regular Flavor Toothpaste on a sponge or a soft, clean cloth. Then wipe clean.

Strange Facts

- In 1915, Stephen J. Poplawski, a Polish-American from Racine, Wisconsin, began designing a gadget to mix his favorite drink—malted milk shakes. Seven years later, Poplawski patented the "vibrator," the first mixer with a wheel of blades mounted inside the bottom of a pitcher and activated only when the pitcher is placed in a base containing the motor. Picturing every soda fountain in America using his mixer, Poplawski struck a deal with the Racine-based Horlick Corporation, the largest manufacturer of the powdered malt used in soda fountain shakes. Obsessed with malted milk shakes, Poplawski never thought of using his mixer to blend fruits and vegetables.
- During World War I, master mechanic Charles Strite, tired of the burnt toast served in the company cafeteria in Stillwater, Minnesota, used springs and a variable timer to create the world's first pop-up toaster. After Strite received a patent in

1919, the Childs restaurant chain placed an order for the first batch of one hundred pop-up toasters (assembled by hand), but it returned every toaster to be mechanically adjusted. In 1926, Strite introduced the Toastmaster, the first pop-up toaster for the home—complete with a dial to adjust to the desired degree of darkness. Unfortunately, the Toastmaster grew hotter after making each slice of toast. The first slice popped up underdone, and the sixth slice popped up burned.

- In 1936, Fred Waring, the famous bandleader of the Pennsylvanians, witnessed a demonstration of one of Poplawski's blenders and decided to finance the development and marketing of a food liquefier to be sold to bars to mix daiquiris as the Waring Blendor—spelled with the letter O to make his blender stand out.

- In 1945, shortly after World War II, self-taught electrical engineer Percy Spencer was touring a laboratory at the Raytheon Company where he worked in Waltham, Massachusetts, and stopped in front of a magnetron—a device invented in 1940 by Sir John Randall and Dr. H. A. Boot to create radar to help England fight the Nazis. Suddenly, Spencer noticed that the chocolate bar in his pocket had begun to melt. Intrigued, he held a bag of unpopped popcorn next to the magnetron, only to discover that the radio waves popped the kernels into popcorn. Spencer used the magnetron to develop the first microwave oven, weighing 750 pounds and standing five feet, six inches tall. Two years later, Raytheon marketed the Radarange microwave oven (named by an employee in a company contest) to restaurants, passenger railroad dining cars, and cruise ships. Unfortunately, the original microwave ovens could not brown meat and left French fries white and limp.

- The 1967 novel *Coffee, Tea or Me? The Uninhibited Memoirs of Two Airline Stewardesses*, spawned three sequels and was made into a television movie in 1973 staring Karen Valentine and John Davidson. The novels were attributed to Trudy Baker and Rachel Jones, but they were actually written by male author Donald Bain.

- In 1971, three coffee aficionados—Jerry Baldwin, Gordon Bowker, and Zev Siegl—founded Starbucks in Pike Place Market, Seattle's legendary open-air farmer's market. They named their company after the coffee-loving first mate in the 1851 novel *Moby-Dick* by Herman Melville.

- While attending a Paris housewares show in 1971, retired physicist Carl Sontheimer, a graduate of MIT and an accomplished cook, and his wife, Shirley, witnessed a demonstration of the Magimix, a compact food processor invented by French chef Pierre Verdun. Eager to distribute the food processor in the United States, Sontheimer founded the Cuisinart company and began importing the Magimix into the United States. The following year, Sontheimer began building a prototype of his own vastly improved version of the food processor, extending the feed tube, enhancing the cutting blade and discs, and adding safety features to meet American standards.

Stoves and Ovens

Broiler Pans

- **Pam Cooking Spray.** To make cleaning a broiler pan trouble-free, spray the pan with Pam Cooking Spray before cooking.

Drip Pans and Rings

- **Arm & Hammer Baking Soda.** To clean burner rings, fill a large pot with water, add two tablespoons Arm & Hammer Baking Soda, drop in the burner rings, place on the stove, and bring to a boil. Let cool and then rinse the burner rings clean.

- **Cascade.** To clean stove top burner drip pans, fill the kitchen sink with very hot water, add one-half cup Cascade dishwasher detergent, and let the pans soak for a few minutes in the solution.

- **Efferdent.** Are the drip pans under your stove top burners all gunked up? Fill the kitchen sink with water, drop in two to four Efferdent denture cleansing tablets, let the pans soak in the blue solution for one hour, and rinse clean.

- **Parsons' Ammonia** and **Glad Trash Bags.** To clean burner rings and drip pans, put the pieces in a Glad Trash Bag, pour in two cups Parsons' Ammonia, tie the bag securely shut, and leave it outside for several hours. The ammonia fumes loosen grease and grime from the rings and pans. Open the bag outdoors, keeping your face away from the fumes. Rinse the ammonia off the rings with a garden hose and then bring the items back inside to wash thoroughly.

Drips

- **Reynolds Wrap.** To catch messy oven drips, tear off a sheet of Reynolds Wrap a few inches larger than the baking pan you're using. Place the foil on the oven rack below the food being baked. (To prevent damage to the oven, do not use aluminum foil to line the bottom of the oven.)

Oven Racks

- **Easy-Off Oven Cleaner** and **Glad Trash Bags.** To clean oven racks, place the racks in a Glad Trash Bag and take it outside. Wearing rubber gloves and protective eyewear, spray the racks with Easy-Off Oven Cleaner, close the bag securely with a twist tie, and let stand overnight. Open the bag outdoors, keeping your face away from the fumes. Rinse the oven cleaner off the racks with a garden hose and then bring the racks back inside to wash thoroughly.

- **Parsons' Ammonia** and **Glad Trash Bags.** Put oven racks and broiler pans in a Glad Trash Bag, take the bag outside, add one cup Parsons' Ammonia, close the bag securely with a twist tie, and let stand overnight. The ammonia fumes loosen the baked-on food and grease from the racks and pans. Open the bag outdoors, keeping your face away from the fumes. Rinse the ammonia off the racks and pans with a garden hose and then bring them back inside to wash thoroughly.

- **Tide.** To clean oven racks, pour one cup liquid Tide into a clean, empty, plastic garbage can, fill the can halfway with water, and place the oven racks in the garbage can. Let sit for one hour, then rinse clean.

Ovens

- **Cascade** and **Bounty.** To clean an oven, sprinkle the bottom of the oven with Cascade dishwasher detergent and cover with wet sheets of Bounty Paper Towels. Let stand for a few hours. Then wipe clean.

- **Kool-Aid.** For a nontoxic oven cleanser, mix the contents of one packet of any flavor Kool-Aid with two quarts water and use it like cleanser. The citric acid in Kool-Aid cuts through the gunk in the oven.

- **Parsons' Ammonia.** Warm the oven slightly, turn it off, then set a small bowl of Parsons' Ammonia inside the oven, close the oven door securely, and let sit undisturbed overnight. In the morning, open all the kitchen windows (making sure the room is well ventilated), stand back, open the oven, and let the oven air out for one hour. Wash the oven walls and floor with soap and water and wipe clean. The ammonia fumes loosen grease and grime from the oven walls.

- **Tang.** To clean an oven, mix two tablespoons Tang and one cup water and use the orange drink mix like cleanser. The citric acid in Tang cuts through the grease and grime in the oven.

Stoves

- **Colgate Regular Flavor Toothpaste.** To scrub grease from the stove top after cooking, squeeze a dollop of Colgate Regular Flavor Toothpaste on a clean cloth and wipe the stove top. Then wipe off the toothpaste with a damp cloth.

- **Heinz White Vinegar.** To clean a stove top, fill a trigger-spray bottle with Heinz White Vinegar, spray the stove, and wipe clean with a sponge. Vinegar shines and deodorizes the stove top.

- **Jet-Dry.** To clean a stove, fill a clean, empty sixteen-ounce trigger-spray bottle with water, add one tablespoon Jet-Dry, and shake well. Spray the stove and use a sponge to clean off grease and food stains. Jet-Dry leaves the stove clean, shiny, and smelling fresh.

- **Lipton Tea Bags.** Use one Lipton Tea Bag to brew a strong cup of tea, let cool, and use the tea on a sponge to clean grease from a stove top.

- **Morton Salt.** To clean a grease spill from a stove top, sprinkle Morton Salt over the spill and wipe clean. The salt absorbs liquids and acts as a mild scouring agent.

- **Shout.** To clean baked-on grease from a stove top, spray the spot with Shout Stain Remover, wait five minutes, and wipe clean.

Strange Facts

- In the Grimm's fairytale "Hansel and Gretel," a wicked witch living in a gingerbread house captures two lost children and attempts to fatten them up, bake them in her oven, and eat them. Gretel pushes the witch into the oven, and the children escape.

- In the 1790s, British statesman and inventor Count von Rumford, born Benjamin Thompson, designed the first practical wood-burning cooking stove—a box built from bricks with holes in the top to hold pots.

- In 1802, British iron founder George Bodley invented and patented a compact cast-iron, closed-top, even-heating cooking range, fueled by coal, with a modern flue. That same year, German inventor Frederick Albert Winson produced a makeshift gas cooking range. Unfortunately, permanent gas range stoves tended to leak fumes and explode—until European manufacturers perfected the devices thirty years later.

- In 1855, German chemist Robert W. Bunsen invented the first practical gas burner (giving birth to the Bunsen burner), and the following decade, Americans who had gas piped into their homes to fuel gaslights began embracing the gas range.

- In 1890, manufacturers introduced the first electric stoves. Unfortunately, these contraptions, equipped with crude thermostats, tended to incinerate meals and send electric bills through the roof. Luckily for consumers, most homes in America were not yet wired for electricity.

- In 1963, the Kenner toy company introduced the Easy-Bake Oven, a toy oven that let children cook small cakes using an ordinary lightbulb as a heat source.

Tile

Cleaning

- **Arm & Hammer Baking Soda.** To clean tile, sprinkle Arm & Hammer Baking Soda on a damp sponge, scrub, and rinse clean.
- **Bounce.** Place a sheet of Bounce on the bottom of a dry sponge mop and dust the tile floor with it. The Bounce will cling to the dry sponge mop without having to be attached.
- **Cascade.** To clean tile, mix one-quarter cup Cascade dishwasher detergent in a bucket of hot water. Scrub the tiles with a scrub brush dipped in the solution and then rinse clean with a mop (or sponge) and water.
- **Downy Fabric Softener.** To eliminate the stickiness on tiles left by typical cleansers, add one-half capful Downy Fabric Softener to a bucket of sudsy water. The surfactants in Downy boost the cleaning power of the water, and the fragrance in the fabric softener leaves behind a fresh scent.

- **Epsom Salt** and **Dawn Dishwashing Liquid.** Mix equal parts of Epsom Salt and Dawn Dishwashing Liquid, apply the gritty paste to grimy tiles, and scrub with a brush. The Epsom Salt gives the dishwashing liquid abrasiveness.
- **Gillette Foamy.** To clean the tiles surrounding a bathtub and let your kids have a blast at the same time, give your kids a can of Gillette Foamy shaving cream to entertain themselves in the bathtub. They can use the shaving cream to draw on the tile walls, and when you wash the condensed soap off with water, the tiles will be sparkling clean.
- **L'eggs Sheer Energy Panty Hose.** To scrub tiles with a mildly abrasive scouring pad, use a balled-up pair of clean, used L'eggs Sheer Energy Panty Hose.
- **Listerine.** To clean tile floors and kill germs, mix one cup Listerine antiseptic mouthwash in one gallon water and mop the tile floor or sponge a tile wall with this antiseptic cleanser.
- **Maxwell House Coffee.** To clean tiles, pour hot, freshly brewed Maxwell House Coffee on the tile and wipe clean immediately with a damp sponge. The coffee helps dissolve grease and soap scum.
- **Spray 'n Wash.** To clean tiles, spray with Spray 'n Wash, wait three minutes, then wipe clean with a sponge.
- **Turtle Wax.** After cleaning tiles, apply Turtle Wax and buff with a soft cloth. The wax prevents future stains from sticking. (Don't do this on a tile floor, to keep from slipping.)

Grout

- **Coca-Cola.** To clean stained grout, pour Coca-Cola over the affected area, let sit for five minutes, and wipe clean. The phosphoric acid in Coke cleans the grout.
- **Heinz White Vinegar** and **Oral-B Toothbrush.** To clean grout, fill a sixteen-ounce trigger-spray bottle with Heinz

White Vinegar, spray the grout with the vinegar, wait five minutes, then scrub with a clean, used Oral-B Toothbrush.

- **Listerine.** To clean mold and mildew from grout, fill a sixteen-ounce trigger-spray bottle with Listerine antiseptic mouthwash, wait two minutes, and wipe clean. The antiseptic kills mold and mildew.

Grouting

- **Ziploc Storage Bags.** When grouting tiles, mix the grout in a Ziploc Storage Bag, seal the bag closed, cut off a bottom corner of the bag, and pipe the grout like frosting to fill the spaces between tiles.

Re-Adhering

- **Forster Toothpicks.** To make sure a new, replaced tile is squarely aligned, use four round Forster Toothpicks as spacers to hold the tile in place.

- **Reynolds Wrap.** To re-adhere a vinyl floor tile, put a piece of Reynolds Wrap on top of the tile and run a hot iron over it several times to melt the glue underneath. Place several books on top of the tile until the glue dries completely.

- **Wrigley's Spearmint Gum.** If a tile comes loose, put a little piece of Wrigley's Spearmint Gum (well-chewed so the sugar is gone) on each corner on the bottom of the tile and press the tile back in place.

Removing

- **Procter-Silex Iron.** To remove a vinyl floor tile, place a cloth over the tile and iron it with medium heat. The heat from the iron will soften the tile and the adhesive under it, making it easy to pry the tile from the floor with a putty knife.

Strange Facts

- As early as 8000 BCE, mankind developed ceramic tiles. Around 3000 BCE, people first manufactured glass as a glaze on ceramic vessels, but artisans did not develop glass tiles until the third century BCE.

- During the Byzantine Empire (from the sixth to fifteen centuries), artisans developed Byzantine tile—opaque glass tiles (sometimes topped with gold leaf) used to create stunning mosaics.

- Because Islamic law prohibits the depiction of living things, Muslims have adorned mosques with mosaics with intricate geometric designs that create complex spatial decorations.

- In Venice, Italy, the interior of St. Mark's Basilica is adorned with intricate and grandiose mosaics depicting biblical scenes.

- In 1931, unemployed New England architect Alfred Mosher Butts turned the crossword puzzle into a workable board game, by cutting one hundred wooden tiles from quarter-inch balsa wood and hand-lettering each one with a letter of the alphabet and a point value. For a playing board, he used his drafting tools to draw a grid of boxes. The game eventually became known as Scrabble. Today, Scrabble is the second best-selling American board game, behind Monopoly.

- In German, the word for floor tile is *fliese*, the word for wall tile is *kachel*, and the word for roof tile is *ziegel*.

Toilets

Cleaning

- **Alka-Seltzer.** To clean a toilet, drop in two Alka-Seltzer tablets, wait twenty minutes, then brush and flush. The sodium bicarbonate and the effervescent action of Alka-Seltzer clean the toilet.

- **Cascade.** Pour one teaspoon Cascade dishwasher detergent into the toilet, brush well, let sit for ten minutes, brush again, and flush. The phosphates in Cascade will make the toilet sparkling clean.

- **Clorox Bleach.** Pour one cup Clorox Bleach into the toilet bowl, let stand for ten minutes, brush, and flush.

- **Coca-Cola.** Pour a can of Coca-Cola into your toilet, let sit for one hour, brush, and flush. The citric acid, ascorbic acid, and phosphoric acid in Coke remove stains from vitreous china. Better yet, when a two-liter bottle of Coca-Cola goes flat in

your refrigerator, don't throw it out. Use it to clean your toilet. Is it a soft drink or is it a toilet bowl cleaner? Why, it's both!

- **Efferdent.** Drop two Efferdent tablets in the toilet bowl, wait five minutes, scrub, and flush. To avoid an unforeseen calamity, do not clean your dentures at the same time you're cleaning the toilet.

- **Heinz White Vinegar.** Pour one cup Heinz White Vinegar into the toilet bowl, let stand for five minutes, brush, and flush.

- **Kool-Aid.** Empty a packet of any flavor Kool-Aid into the toilet, scrub with a toilet brush, and flush clean. The citric acid in Kool-Aid cleans toilets.

- **Listerine.** Pour one-quarter cup Listerine into the toilet, let sit for thirty minutes, then brush and flush. The antiseptic mouthwash disinfects germs, and the alcohol cleans the toilet.

- **Tang.** Put two tablespoons Tang powdered drink mix in the toilet bowl, wait fifteen minutes, brush, and flush. The citric acid in Tang removes stains from vitreous china.

Flappers

- **Vaseline Petroleum Jelly.** To revive a leaking flapper in a toilet tank, give the flapper a thin coat of Vaseline Petroleum Jelly to rejuvenate the rubber, giving the flapper sufficient suppleness to seal the valve.

Flush Chains

- **Glad Flexible Straws.** To prevent the flush chain in the toilet tank from getting sucked under the flapper whenever someone flushes the toilet, thread the chain through a plastic Glad Flexible Straw cut to the desired length.

Hard Water Stains

- **Heinz White Vinegar.** To clean hard water stains from a toilet bowl, turn off the water to the toilet and flush a few times to empty all the water from the bowl. Place a small hand towel inside the bowl so that it covers the hard water stains. Saturate the towel with Heinz White Vinegar and let sit overnight. The acetic acid in the vinegar will dissolve the mineral deposits.

Leaks

- **McCormick Food Coloring.** To determine whether a toilet tank is leaking, put enough food coloring in the toilet tank to change the color of the water. Let the colored water sit overnight without flushing the toilet. If the water in the bowl has changed color in the morning, your tank is leaking into the bowl and wasting water. Stop the leak by adjusting the lift chain or replacing the flapper.

- **Mrs. Stewart's Liquid Bluing.** To detect a leak in a toilet tank, put a few drops of Mrs. Stewart's Liquid Bluing into the toilet's holding tank to determine whether the tank leaks into the bowl, wasting water. Stop the leak by adjusting the lift chain or replacing the flapper.

Rust

- **Maybelline Express Finish Clear Nail Polish.** To prevent rust on toilet seat screws, paint the heads of the screws with a protective coating of Maybelline Express Finish Clear Nail Polish.

Septic Tanks

- **Arm & Hammer Baking Soda.** To maintain your septic tank, flush one cup Arm & Hammer Baking Soda down the toilet once a week. Baking soda helps maintain proper pH and alkalinity, controlling sulfide odors.

Shutoff Valves

- **WD-40.** To avoid causing a leak when turning off a shutoff valve that hasn't been used for a long time, spray a little WD-40 on the spot where the stem meets the packing nut. Turn the handle one turn, return the handle to its original position, and wait a few minutes to allow the oil to seep inside before using.

Strange Facts

- The ruins of the Minoan Palace at Knossos, built in 2000 BCE on the island of Crete, contain a toilet that was used by the royal family.

- In 1596, Englishman John Harington, a writer and godson of Queen Elizabeth I, invented a valve that when pulled would release water from a reservoir tank, building the first flush toilet in his manor in Kelston, a village near Bath. Soon after, Harington installed a flush toilet at the Royal Palace, emptying directly into a cesspool.

- In 1775, British watchmaker Alexander Cummings improved upon Harington's design by adding an S-shaped "stink trap" in the pipe that connected to the cesspool, allowing water to block the route by which foul aromas would waft up through the sewer pipe.

- In 1819, Albert Giblin produced the "Silent Valveless Water Waste Preventer," a siphon discharge system.

- During the 1880s, British plumber Thomas Crapper began manufacturing toilets based on Giblin's design, popularizing the flush toilet, supplying toilets for residences of the royal family. Crapper did not devise any improvements to the flush toilet.

- While the Beatles performed at the Star Club in Hamburg, Germany, in 1961, John Lennon appeared on stage wearing only his briefs and a toilet seat around his neck.

- Toilet paper and facial tissues are made from wood pulp treated with plant resins to make them absorbent.

Tools and Workshops

Boots

- **Glad Trash Bags.** To make emergency snow boots or flood boots (when the toilet, washing machine, or bathtub flood the floor with water), insert each foot into a Glad Trash Bag and secure the bags in place with masking tape.
- **Ziploc Storage Bags.** In a pinch, make emergency flood or snow boots by putting each foot inside a one-gallon Ziploc Freezer Bag as if it were a sock. Then put your shoes on over the plastic bags to keep your feet dry and warm.

Brooms

- **Playtex Living Gloves.** To prevent broom handles from falling over when leaning them against a wall, cut the fingers off of a clean, used pair of Playtex Living Gloves and slip them onto broom handles.

Caulk Guns

- **Glad Flexible Straws.** To elongate the nozzle of a caulk gun for hard-to-reach spots, use a Glad Flexible Straw as an extension tube.

Chalk Tape Lines

- **Crayola Chalk** and **Ziploc Storage Bags.** To make a chalk tape line, place a stick of colored Crayola Chalk in a Ziploc Storage Bag, seal the bag shut, and use a hammer to crush the chalk into powder. Place a piece of string in the bag, reseal, and shake well to cover the string in colored chalk powder.

Circular-Saw Blades

- **Easy-Off Oven Cleaner** and **Oral-B Toothbrush.** To clean a circular saw blade gummed up with sap, remove the blade from the saw. Wearing rubber gloves and eye protection, spray it with Easy-Off Oven Cleaner in a well-ventilated area (or outdoors) and let soak for fifteen minutes. Use a clean, used Oral-B Toothbrush to scrub around the teeth. Wash the blade clean with soap and warm water, rinse clean, and dry.

Clamps

- **Wilson Tennis Balls.** To prevent injuries caused by accidentally walking into protruding metal guides on clamps, carefully cut an X into a Wilson Tennis Ball and fit it onto the end, creating a homemade protective cap.

Cleaning

- **Alberto VO5 Hair Spray.** Protect the wooden handles of tools by spraying the wood with a thin coat of Alberto VO5 Hair Spray. The hair spray acts like shellac, preserving the wood.

- **Arm & Hammer Clean Shower.** To prolong the life of sharp tools, such as pruning shears, hatchets, and saws, spray Arm & Hammer Clean Shower on a the blades after each use.
- **Colgate Regular Flavor Toothpaste.** Shine up your tools with a squirt of Colgate Regular Flavor Toothpaste. Rub with a soft cloth, then rinse thoroughly.
- **Crisco All-Vegetable Shortening.** Preserve the wooden handles of gardening tools by coating them with a dab of Crisco All-Vegetable Shortening. Rub the shortening into the wood, then buff with a soft, clean cloth.
- **Cutex Nail Polish Remover.** To clean scissors, soak a cotton ball in Cutex Nail Polish Remover and cautiously wipe the blades.
- **Easy-Off Oven Cleaner.** To clean gardening tools, saw blades, or drill bits gummed up with sap, put on rubber gloves and eye protection and spray the tools with Easy-Off Oven Cleaner in a well-ventilated area (or outdoors) and let sit for twenty minutes. Rinse well with water.
- **Oral-B Toothbrushes.** To clean caked-on dirt from crevices of your tools, scrub with a clean, used Oral-B toothbrush.
- **Reynolds Wrap.** Crumple up a sheet of Reynolds Wrap and use the balled-up aluminum foil as a scrubber to clean tools.
- **Scrubbing Bubbles.** Spray Scrubbing Bubbles on filthy tools, let sit for a few minutes to give the scrubbing bubbles a chance to work, rinse clean with a hose, and dry.

Con-Tact Paper

- **Conair Pro Styler 1600.** To remove Con-Tact Paper from any surface, set a Conair Pro Styler 1600 hair dryer on warm, wave the nozzle back and forth over one section at a time to melt the adhesive under the Con-Tact Paper, and gently pull up the edges.

Drill Bits

- **Cool Whip.** Use a clean, empty Cool Whip tub to hold loose drill bits.
- **Huggies Baby Wipes.** Use a clean, empty Huggies Baby Wipes container in the workshop to hold assorted drill bits.
- **Maxwell House Coffee.** A clean, empty Maxwell House Coffee can makes a perfect storage container for drill bits.
- **Pink Pearl Eraser.** To store small drill bits, twist the tips of the bits into a large Pink Pearl Eraser.

Drill Caddies

- **Coca Cola.** To hang a drill in your workshop, cut the bottom off of a clean, empty, uncapped, two-liter Coke bottle in a diagonal, attach it upside-down to the wall using a screw and a washer, and insert the drill.
- **Clorox Bleach.** To make a hip holster for carrying a drill, cut off the bottom of an empty, clean, uncapped Clorox Bleach bottle in a diagonal opposite the handle, then string your belt through the handle.

Drill Presses

- **Johnson's Baby Powder.** Sprinkle the metal base of a drill press with Johnson's Baby Powder to fill in the metals pores, keep the metal shiny, prevent rust, and help whatever item you're drilling to glide smoothly.

Drilling

- **Scotch Transparent Tape.** To drill a hole without penetrating through the other side of the wood, place a strip of Scotch Transparent Tape around the drill bit to create a flag at the height on the drill bit where you wish to stop drilling.

Face Shields

- **Saran Wrap.** To prevent a face shield from getting scratched up, cover the front of the plastic shield with a sheet of Saran Wrap. When you're done with the job, simply peel off the protective plastic wrap.

Files

- **Scotch Packaging Tape.** To clean metal shavings from a metal file, adhere a piece of Scotch Packaging Tape over the length of the file, press firmly, then peel off. The shavings will stick to the tape.

Funnels

- **Clorox Bleach.** To improvise a funnel, cut an empty, clean Clorox Bleach jug in half and remove the cap.
- **Coca-Cola.** To make a funnel, cut an empty, clean two-liter Coca-Cola bottle in half and use the capless top half.
- **Dixie Cups.** Punch a hole in the bottom of a Dixie Cup near the edge to improvise a funnel.
- **Dixie Paper Plates.** Curl a Dixie Paper Plate to make an instant, disposable funnel.
- **Reynolds Wrap.** Double over a piece of Reynolds Wrap and roll it into the shape of a cone to create an impromptu funnel.

Goggles

- **Bounce.** To prevent sawdust from sticking to safety goggles due to static electricity, wipe the goggles with a clean, used sheet of Bounce. The antistatic elements in Bounce eliminate the static electricity.
- **Windex.** To keep safety goggles clean, wipe the lenses with a spritz of Windex and a paper towel.

Hand Cleaners

- **Arm & Hammer Baking Soda.** To clean dirt, grime, and oil from hands, sprinkle Arm & Hammer Baking Soda onto your wet hands along with liquid soap, rub vigorously, rinse, and dry.
- **C&H Sugar.** Sprinkle a little C&H Sugar on your hands, then lather with soap and water. The sugar works as an abrasive to remove grease and grime from hands.
- **Clairol Herbal Essences.** Using a dab of Clairol Herbal Essences Shampoo as soap cuts through the grime on your hands.
- **Crisco All-Vegetable Shortening.** To clean oil-based paint or grease from hands, rub in Crisco All-Vegetable Shortening before using soap. (For more ways to clean paint from hands, see page 220.)
- **Gillette Foamy.** Rubbing a little Gillette Foamy shaving cream between your hands will dissolve grime without water. Keep a can of Gillette Foamy in the workshop.
- **Skin So Soft Body Lotion.** To clean grease and grime from hands, rub Skin So Soft Body Lotion into the skin and wash clean with water.

Lawn Mowers

- **Bounce.** For a disposable air filter for use with any gasoline-powered lawn mower, fit one or two sheets of Bounce in place to protect the air-intake opening.
- **Jif Peanut Butter.** To lubricate a lawn mower, put a dollop of Jif Peanut Butter (creamy, not chunky) on the blade shaft of the underside of the lawn mower.
- **L'eggs Sheer Energy Panty Hose.** To improvise a filter for a lawn mower in a pinch, use scissors to cut a large piece of

nylon from a clean, used pair of L'eggs Sheer Energy Panty Hose, fold the nylon into four layers, and attach it to the carburetor intake horn with electrical tape or duct tape.

- **Maybelline Express Finish Clear Nail Polish.** To prevent screws from vibrating loose on a lawn mower, coat the ends of the screws with Maybelline Express Finish Clear Nail Polish.

- **Mr. Coffee Filters.** To filter sediment from a gas can when filing a lawn mower, place a Mr. Coffee Filter over the mouth of the plastic portable gas canister and screw on the threaded cap. The coffee filter prevents the sediment from getting into the gas tank of the lawn mower, and the sediment eventually sinks to the bottom of the gas canister. Change the coffee filter when necessary.

- **Pam Cooking Spray.** To prevent cut grass from sticking to the blades of a lawn mower, spray the cutting blade on the underside of the lawn mower with Pam Cooking Spray before cutting the lawn.

- **WD-40.** To prevent cut grass from sticking to the blades of a lawn mower, spray WD-40 on the underside of the lawn mower housing and blade before cutting the grass.

- **WD-40.** To start a sluggish lawnmower, spray WD-40 in the carburetor/air cleaner and then pull the starter cord.

Lubricating

- **ChapStick.** Rubbing ChapStick lip balm over the pivot joint of pliers provides ample lubrication to keep them working smoothly.

- **Crisco All-Vegetable Shortening.** Use a dab of Crisco All-Vegetable Shortening to lubricate the pivot joint of pliers.

- **Pam Cooking Spray.** A quick spritz of Pam Cooking Spray lubricates pliers.

- **Star Olive Oil.** A drop of Star Olive Oil on moving parts of pliers keeps them well lubricated and working smoothly.
- **Vaseline Petroleum Jelly.** Lubricate the pivot area of your pliers with Vaseline Petroleum Jelly.
- **WD-40.** Oil the pivot joint of your hedge clippers, pruning shears, pliers, and scissors with a short blast of WD-40.
- **Wesson Corn Oil.** Lubricate pliers with a few drops of Wesson Corn Oil.

Mallets

- **Wilson Tennis Balls.** To improvise a mallet, carefully cut an X in the side of a Wilson Tennis Ball and place the fuzzy rubber ball over the head of a hammer. Use the tool to hammer items you don't wish to damage.

Nails

- **ChapStick.** Nails rubbed with ChapStick will go into hardwood more easily.
- **Clorox Bleach.** To store nails, cut a large notch in the top of a empty, clean Clorox Bleach jug, opposite the handle. The jug can be stored on its side, enabling you to see what type of nails it contains, and the handle allows you to carry the nails easily.
- **Cool Whip.** Use empty, clean Cool Whip canisters in the workshop to hold loose nails. (For more ways to store nails, see "Storage" on page 323.)
- **Ivory Soap.** Nails rubbed with Ivory Soap will go into wood more readily.
- **Scotch Transparent Tape.** To caddy nails, place the nails between layers of Scotch Transparent Tape so they're easily accessible.

- **Ziploc Storage Bags.** To pick up spilled nails, place a magnet inside a Ziploc Storage Bag, hold the bag over the nails, and then turn the bag inside-out to capture them.

Nuts and Bolts

- **Alberto VO5 Conditioning Hairdressing.** To prevent nuts and bolts from rusting together, lubricate the nuts and bolts with a dab of Alberto VO5 Conditioning Hairdressing before screwing them together.
- **Canada Dry Club Soda.** To loosen rusty nuts and bolts, pour Canada Dry Club Soda over them.
- **Coca-Cola.** To loosen rusty nuts and bolts, apply a cloth soaked in a Coca-Cola to the rusted nuts and bolts for several minutes.
- **Heinz White Vinegar.** Soak a rusted nut and bolt in full-strength Heinz White Vinegar overnight.
- **Pam Cooking Spray.** To separate rusty nuts and bolts, spray them with Pam Cooking Spray.
- **Parsons' Ammonia.** Soak a rusted nut and bolt with Parsons' Ammonia.
- **ReaLemon.** To loosen a rusty nut and bolt, soak them in ReaLemon lemon juice.
- **Vaseline Petroleum Jelly.** To prevent nuts and bolts from rusting together, lubricate the nuts and bolts with a dab of Vaseline Petroleum Jelly before screwing them together.
- **WD-40.** To loosen rusty nuts and bolts, spray the parts with WD-40.

Oil

- **Glad Flexible Straws.** To extend the spout of an oil can and reach tight spots, put a Glad Flexible Straw over the end of the spout.

- **Q-Tips Cotton Swabs.** Dip a Q-Tips Cotton Swab in machine oil to lubricate tools and precision machine parts.

Picnic Coolers

- **Clorox Bleach.** To deodorize a cooler, wash it with three-quarters cup Clorox Bleach diluted with one gallon water, then rinse.
- **McCormick Pure Vanilla Extract.** After washing out a cooler, saturate a cloth with McCormick Pure Vanilla Extract and wipe down the insides. The vanilla adds a nice scent.

Plastic Wood

- **Cutex Nail Polish Remover.** To revive Plastic Wood that has started to harden in the can, add a few drops of Cutex Nail Polish Remover and mix.
- **MasterCard.** A clean, old credit card makes a great impromptu putty knife for applying Plastic Wood to a small hole.

Pliers

- **Playtex Living Gloves.** To prevent pliers from leaving marks, cut off two fingers from a clean, used pair of Playtex Living Gloves and slip them over the jaws of pliers as protective padding.

Putty

- **Ziploc Storage Bag.** To prevent putty from drying out in the can, place all the putty inside a Ziploc Storage Bag, remove all the air from the bag, and seal well. Store the bag of putty inside the original can. You can also cut a small hole in one of the bottom corners of the plastic bag to pipe out the putty, but be sure to secure the hole closed with a twist tie before storing.

Rubber Bands

- **Playtex Living Gloves.** When your Playtex Living Gloves wear out, slice up the cuff to make giant rubber bands.

Rulers

- **Cover Girl Continuous Color Red Nail Polish.** To renew the worn-out numbers and gradation marks on a ruler, paint the indentations of the numbers and marks with Cover Girl Continuous Color Red Nail Polish and wipe off the excess nail polish.
- **Liquid Paper.** To renew the worn-out numbers and gradation marks on a ruler, paint the indentations of the numbers and marks with Liquid Paper and wipe off the excess white.

Rust

- **Alberto VO5 Conditioning Hairdressing.** To prevent tools from rusting, give them a thin coat of Alberto VO5 Conditioning Hairdressing. Use a soft cloth to wipe off the excess, leaving behind a very thin, virtually invisible protective coating. VO5's organic protectants prevent rust.
- **Arm & Hammer Baking Soda.** To clean rust from tools, mix a thick paste of Arm & Hammer Baking Soda and water, apply to the tool with a damp sponge, rub, rinse, and dry.
- **Arm & Hammer Clean Shower.** Remove rust from tools by spraying them with Arm & Hammer Clean Shower, let dry, then rinse clean and dry.
- **Canada Dry Club Soda.** Loosen rusty tools by soaking them in Canada Dry Club Soda.
- **ChapStick.** Prevent tools from rusting by giving them a light coat of any flavor ChapStick.

- **Coca-Cola.** Soak a rusted tool in Coca-Cola overnight, then rinse clean. The Real Thing dissolves the rust.

- **Crayola Chalk.** Prevent tools from rusting by placing a piece of Crayola Chalk in your toolbox to absorb the moisture that causes tools to rust in the first place.

- **Heinz White Vinegar.** To remove rust from tools, soak the rusted items in a pan of full-strength Heinz White Vinegar overnight.

- **Kingsford Charcoal Briquets.** To prevent tools from rusting in the first place, place an untreated Kingsford Charcoal Briquet in your toolbox to absorb moisture.

- **Kool-Aid.** Mix the contents of one packet of any flavor Kool-Aid with two quarts water, soak the rusted tool in the drink over night, and then scrub well. The citric acid in Kool-Aid dissolves rust.

- **Morton Salt** and **ReaLemon.** To clean rust from tools, make a paste using two tablespoons Morton Salt and one tablespoon ReaLemon lemon juice. Apply the paste to the rusted tools with a dry cloth and rub clean.

- **Pam Cooking Spray.** To prevent tools from rusting, spray clean tools with a light coat of Pam Cooking Spray.

- **Turtle Wax.** Prevent tools from rusting by giving them a light coat of Turtle Wax.

- **Vaseline Petroleum Jelly.** Applying a generous coat of Vaseline Petroleum Jelly over tools prevents them from rusting.

Sawdust

- **Bounce.** Wipe up sawdust from drilling or sandpapering with a used sheet of Bounce. The dryer sheet, infused with anti-static elements, attracts sawdust just like a tack cloth.

- **Conair Pro Styler 1600.** Use a Conair Pro Styler 1600 hair dryer set on cool to blow away sawdust in the workshop.

Saws

- **Ivory Soap.** To lubricate a handsaw, rub a bar of Ivory Soap across the sides and teeth of the saw. Coating the saw blade with soap helps the saw blade glide through wood and also prevents sap from adhering to the blade.
- **Turtle Wax.** To prevent sap from adhering to a saw blade, polish the saw blade with Turtle Wax.

Scissors

- **Cutex Nail Polish Remover.** To clean gunk from a pair of scissors, use a cotton ball saturated with Cutex Nail Polish Remover to carefully clean the scissor blades.

Scoopers

- **Clorox Bleach.** To make a scooper, cap an empty, clean Clorox Bleach jug, cut it diagonally across the bottom, and use it to scoop up flour, sugar, rice, dog food, sand, fertilizer, snow, nuts, bolts, screws, or sawdust.

Screwdrivers

- **Cover Girl Continuous Color Red Nail Polish.** To make screwdrivers easy to identify, use Cover Girl Continuous Color Red Nail Polish to paint an X on the tops of the handles of your Phillips head screwdrivers and a minus sign on your slot screwdrivers.
- **Crayola Chalk.** To prevent a screwdriver from slipping out of the screw slot, rub Crayola Chalk on the blade.

Screws

- **ChapStick.** Screws rubbed with ChapStick penetrate wood more easily.
- **Cool Whip.** Use empty, clean Cool Whip canisters in the workshop to hold loose screws. (For more ways to store screws, see "Storage" on page 323.)
- **Forster Toothpicks** and **Elmer's Glue-All.** To tighten a loose screw, fill the screw hole with Elmer's Glue-All, insert a Forster Toothpick into the screw hole (making the hole narrower), break it off at the surface (or cut flush with a single-edge razor blade), and screw in the screw.
- **Ivory Soap.** Screws rubbed with a bar of Ivory Soap will go into wood with greater ease.
- **Johnson & Johnson Cotton Balls** and **Elmer's Glue-All.** When a screw hole is too worn out to hold a screw, soak a Johnson & Johnson Cotton Ball in Elmer's Glue-All, stuff it into the hole, and let dry for twenty-four hours. Use a screwdriver to put a new screw into the spot.
- **Maybelline Express Finish Clear Nail Polish.** To tighten a loose screw, paint Maybelline Express Finish Clear Nail Polish on the threads and screw it into the hole.
- **Pam Cooking Spray.** Spraying the threads of a screw with Pam Cooking Spray makes the screw easier to thread.
- **S.O.S Steel Wool Soap Pads.** To tighten a loose screw, wrap a few steel strands from an S.O.S Steel Wool Soap Pad around the threads of a screw.
- **Saran Wrap.** To hold a screw in position while using a screwdriver, push the screw through a small piece of Saran Wrap, fit the screwdriver into the slot in the head, hold the Saran Wrap back over the blade of the screwdriver, and screw.

- **Scotch Transparent Tape.** To caddy screws, place the screws between layers of Scotch Transparent Tape so they're readily available.
- **Scotch Transparent Tape.** To hold a screw in position while using a screwdriver, push the screw through the adhesive side of a piece of Scotch Transparent Tape, fit the screwdriver into the slot in the screw, and wrap the adhesive tape back over the blade of the screwdriver.
- **Ziploc Storage Bags.** To pick up spilled screws, place a magnet inside a Ziploc Storage Bag, hold the bag over the screws, and then turn the bag inside-out to capture them.

Shop Aprons

- **Glad Trash Bags.** To make a shop apron, cut open the bottom of a Glad Trash Bag, put it over your head, and slip your arms through the handles.

Shop Vacuums

- **Glad Trash Bags.** To make cleaning out the inside of a shop vacuum easier, line the inside of the vacuum with a large Glad Trash Bag, folding the top edge of the bag over the rim to hold it in place. This way, when it comes time to empty the shop vacuum, all you have to do is remove the trash bag and replace it with a new one.
- **L'eggs Sheer Energy Panty Hose.** To prolong the life of the filter in a shop vacuum and avoid having to clean it as often, cut off the legs from a clean, used pair of L'eggs Sheer Energy Panty Hose, tie a knot in each of the cut ends, and pull the waist band over the pleated paper filter to secure the filter inside the panty hose, creating a protective sheath.

Small Parts

- **Scotch Transparent Tape.** To avoid losing small parts when fixing an appliance, before dismantling the item, tape a strip of Scotch Transparent Tape, adhesive side up, on your worktable. Place the parts on the tape in the order you remove them, so they are ready to be reassembled.

Snow Shovels

- **Crisco All-Vegetable Shortening.** To prevent snow from sticking to a snow shovel, lubricate the shovel with Crisco All-Vegetable Shortening before you start shoveling snow from the driveway.
- **Pam Cooking Spray.** Spray Pam Cooking Spray on the snow shovel before shoveling the driveway so snow slides right off.
- **Turtle Wax.** To prevent snow from sticking to a snow shovel, cover the shovel with two thick coats of Turtle Wax.
- **Wesson Corn Oil.** To make snow slide right off a snow shovel, coat the shovel with Wesson Corn Oil before starting the job.

Soldering

- **Forster Clothespins.** Use a couple of Forster Clothespins to hold wires in place while soldering.
- **Scotch Packaging Tape.** To hold wires in place while soldering, use a few pieces of Scotch Packaging Tape.

Storage

- **Bubble Wrap.** To prevent chisel blades from smacking into other tools and dulling, wrap each chisel in a small sheet of Bubble Wrap.

- **Cool Whip.** Use empty, clean Cool Whip tubs in the workshop to hold loose screws, bolts, and nuts.

- **Gerber Baby Food.** Fill empty, clean Gerber Baby Food jars with leftover nails, screws, nuts, and bolts.

- **Huggies Baby Wipes.** Use empty Huggies Baby Wipes containers in the workshop to hold loose screws, bolts, nuts, nails, drill bits, and spare parts.

- **Maxwell House Coffee.** Maxwell House Coffee cans make perfect storage containers for nails and screws.

- **Scotch Packaging Tape.** Fold a piece of Scotch Packaging Tape over the edge of any small tool, punch a hole in the tape, and hang it on a peg in your workshop.

- *USA Today*. After cleaning and lubricating your garden tools at the end of the season, wrap them in sheets of *USA Today* and store. The newsprint absorbs moisture and prevents the tools from rusting.

- **Wilson Tennis Balls.** To prevent chisel blades from bumping into other tools and getting dull, make a slit in a Wilson Tennis Ball and insert the chisel blade into the homemade rubber protector.

- **Ziploc Storage Bags.** Organize nuts, bolts, drill bits, nails, washers, and screws in Ziploc Storage Bags.

String Dispensers

- **Coca-Cola.** To make a string dispenser, cut off the bottom half of an empty, clean, uncapped, two-liter Coca-Cola bottle. Use a screw and washer to mount the top half of the bottle upside-down on a wall in your workshop. Place a ball of string in the bottle, with the end of the string coming through the hole in the neck.

Table Saws

- **Easy-Off Oven Cleaner** and **Oral-B Toothbrush.** To clean table-saw blades gummed up with sap, remove the blade. Wearing rubber gloves and eye protection, spray it outdoors with Easy-Off Oven Cleaner in a well-ventilated location and let soak for a few minutes. Use a clean, used Oral-B Toothbrush to scrub around the teeth. Rinse clean with water.
- **Forster Clothespins** and **Glad Trash Bags.** To collect sawdust generated by a table saw, use Forster Clothespins to attach a thirty-gallon Glad Trash Bag to the underside of the table saw. Be sure to unplug the table saw before emptying the bag.
- **Pam Cooking Spray.** To prevent rust on a metal table-saw top, unplug the saw, spray the top with a thin coat of Pam Cooking Spray, and wipe off the excess oil with a paper towel. The cooking spray doubles as lubricant so wood glides smoothly across the tabletop.
- **Turtle Wax.** To protect a metal table-saw top from rust, unplug the saw and wax the metal surface with Turtle Wax.
- **Vaseline Petroleum Jelly.** To clean rust from a metal table-saw top, rub Vaseline Petroleum Jelly on the rust, let sit overnight, and wipe clean.
- **Wilson Tennis Balls.** To prevent injuries caused by accidentally walking into protruding metal fence guides on a table saw, carefully cut an X into two Wilson Tennis Balls and fit them onto the ends, creating homemade protective end caps.

Tape

- **Forster Toothpicks.** To mark the starting point of a roll of masking tape or packaging tape, stick a Forster Toothpick under the loose end of the tape so you can find it easily the next time you use the tape.

Tape Measures

- **Avery Laser Labels.** Adhere a blank Avery Laser Label to the side of your tape measure so you always have a convenient place to write down measurements (on a piece of paper that won't get lost).

Toolboxes

- **Bubble Wrap.** To cushion your tools and prevent them from clanking together when you carry your toolbox, line the bottom of your toolbox with a sheet of Bubble Wrap.

Toting and Using

- **Bubble Wrap** and **Scotch Packaging Tape.** Avoid blisters and make rakes, shovels, and hoes easier to handle by wrapping the handles with Bubble Wrap secured in place with Scotch Packaging Tape.
- **Clorox Bleach.** Cut off the top of an empty, clean Clorox Bleach jug above the handle to make a handy tool carrier.
- **Tide.** Make a tool bucket to tote trowels and small spades by cutting off the top of an empty, clean liquid Tide bottle just above the handle.

Wiring

- **Dawn Dishwashing Liquid.** To fish electrical cable through conduits, mix one teaspoon Dawn Dishwashing Liquid in a sixteen-ounce trigger-spray bottle filled with water, shake well, and spray the cable with the soapy solution. The soap will help the cable glide through winding conduits.
- **Glad Flexible Straws.** Before running thin low-voltage wires through drilled holes in studs or a wall, insert a Glad Flexible

Straw (cut to whatever size you need) through the hole as a protective guide.

- **Pam Cooking Spray.** To thread electrical cable through conduits, spray the cable with Pam Cooking Spray. The oil will help the cable glide through winding conduits.

- **WD-40.** To thread electrical wire through conduits, spray WD-40 on the electrical wire to help it glide through winding conduits.

Woodwork

- **Forster Toothpicks** and **Elmer's Glue-All.** To plug small nail or thumbtack holes in wood, dip the end of a Forster Toothpick in Elmer's Glue-All, insert into the hole, slice flush with a single-edge razor blade, sand smooth, and refinish the wood.

- **Lea & Perrins Worcestershire Sauce.** To repair scratched woodwork, use a cotton ball to apply Lea & Perrins Worcestershire Sauce to the scratched surface.

- **Maxwell House Instant Coffee.** To patch woodwork, mix dry Maxwell House Instant coffee grounds with spackling paste until you achieve the desired brown tone, fill the crack or hole, and smooth with a damp cloth.

- **Maxwell House Instant Coffee.** To repair scratched woodwork, mix one teaspoon Maxwell House Instant Coffee with two teaspoons water and apply the thick coffee to the scratch with a cotton ball.

- **Nestea Iced Tea Mix.** To repair scratched woodwork, mix one level teaspoon Nestea with two teaspoons water. Use a cotton ball to apply the paste to the scratched surface.

Strange Facts

- Legend holds that Santa Claus and his elves build toys at his workshop at the North Pole. In the town of North Pole, Alaska, located thirteen miles east of Fairbanks, tourists can visit Santa's workshop.

- The word *gadget* purportedly originated in 1886 when a Misseur Gaget, a partner in Gaget, Ganhier & Cie., the French company that built the Statue of Liberty, came up with the idea of selling miniature replicas of the statue in Paris. Americans supposedly called the souvenirs "gadgets," mispronouncing Gaget's name.

- In "The Turn of the Screw," the 1898 novella by Henry James, a guest at a Christmas Eve party tells a ghost story by reading a letter from his sister's governess about two children, Flora and Miles, and their interactions with two ghosts.

- The word *gizmo* originated in 1942, not for anyone named Gizmo, but as United States Navy and Marine Corps slang for a gadget or machine part.

- The word for tool is *werkseug* in German, *outil* in French, and *utensile* in Italian.

- The lyrics to the 1958 folksong "If I Had a Hammer (The Hammer Song)" by Lee Hays and Pete Seeger speak of hammering out danger and love between human beings.

- Aside from being a tool, a screwdriver is an alcoholic beverage made with vodka and orange juice.

Barbie Dolls

- **Johnson's Baby Powder.** To make dressing a Barbie doll easier, sprinkle a little Johnson's Baby Powder on the doll's legs (lubricating the rubber), so pants slide on or off more readily.

Baseball Mitts

- **Alberto VO5 Conditioning Hairdressing.** To break in a brand-new baseball mitt, rub a dollop of Alberto VO5 Conditioning Hairdressing into the center of the glove, place a baseball in the glove, fold the mitt around it, and secure with rubber bands. Tuck the glove under a mattress overnight.
- **Gillette Foamy.** To break in a new mitt, rub the center of the glove with Gillette Foamy shaving cream, put a baseball in the mitt, fold the glove around it, secure with rubber bands, and tuck the glove under a mattress overnight.

- **Vaseline Petroleum Jelly.** Vaseline Petroleum Jelly rubbed into a baseball glove softens the leather.
- **Wesson Corn Oil.** Rub a few drops of Wesson Corn Oil into the palm of the glove, place a baseball in the mitt, fold the glove around it, and secure with rubber bands. Tuck the glove under a mattress overnight.

Baseballs

- **Tidy Cats.** To dry a soggy baseball (drenched with water after practicing on a wet field), place the baseball in a bucket, cover it with unused Tidy Cats, and agitate the bucket around. The cat box filler absorbs moisture from baseballs.
- **Wilson Tennis Balls.** To make a practice baseball, cut a small slit in a Wilson Tennis Ball just long enough to fit a penny, and fill the ball with pennies.

Bicycles

- **Alberto VO5 Conditioning Hairdressing.** To lubricate a bicycle chain, use a dab of Alberto VO5 Conditioning Hairdressing.
- **Dawn Dishwashing Liquid.** To find a puncture in a bicycle tire, mix a few drops of Dawn Dishwashing Liquid with water and brush on a leaky tire. The bubbles will indicate the exact location of the puncture.
- **Krazy Glue.** To fix a small puncture in a bicycle tire, remove the inner tube from the tire and locate the hole. Insert the tip of the Krazy Glue applicator into the opening, squeeze out a little glue, remove the applicator, and pinch the rubber together for two minutes. Put the tire back together and inflate.
- **Pam Cooking Spray.** To lubricate a bicycle chain, spray it with Pam Cooking Spray.

- **Scrubbing Bubbles.** To clean a bicycle, spray Scrubbing Bubbles on wheels, spokes, and drive trains. Wait five minutes for the scrubbing bubbles to work their magic, rinse clean, and dry.
- **Vaseline Petroleum Jelly.** To lubricate a bicycle chain, use your finger to run a few dabs of Vaseline Petroleum Jelly along the chain.
- **WD-40.** To prevent mud buildup on a bicycle, spray the bicycle with a thin coat of WD-40 and wipe off the excess.
- **WD-40.** To grease a bicycle chain, spray with WD-40.
- **Wesson Corn Oil.** Use a few drops of Wesson Corn Oil to lubricate the chain on a bicycle.
- **Wilson Tennis Balls.** To prevent a bicycle kickstand from sinking into the ground, carefully cut a small X in the side of a Wilson Tennis Ball and insert the end of the kickstand into the tennis ball. The ball will stop the end of the kickstand from sinking into grass, sand, or mud.

Boating

- **Pampers.** To simplify cleaning boat engine oil that has leaked into the engine pans, unfold a Pampers disposable diaper in each pan, allowing the superabsorbent polymer flakes inside each diaper to absorb the spilled oil.
- **Vaseline Petroleum Jelly.** To prevent snaps on a boat cover from sticking, lightly coat the snaps with Vaseline Petroleum Jelly every four to six months. The petroleum jelly prevents the snaps from rusting.
- **Wilson Tennis Balls.** To make a CB antenna more stationery and prevent it from slapping against the boat windshield, drill a hole through a Wilson Tennis Ball and place the ball over your CB antenna to prevent it from whipping around while boating.

Bowling Balls

- **Huggies Baby Wipes.** To clean a bowling ball, wipe it down with a Huggies Baby Wipe.

Cards

- **Gold Medal Flour.** To clean a deck of playing cards, place the cards inside a paper bag, add four tablespoons Gold Medal Flour, and shake briskly. The flour absorbs the oil from the cards. Remove the cards from the bag and wipe clean.

- **Kingsford's Corn Starch.** Got a deck of playing cards sticky with oil from your fingers? Drop the cards into a paper bag, add four tablespoons Kingsford's Corn Starch, and shake vigorously. The cornstarch absorbs the oil from the cards. Empty the cards from the bag and wipe clean.

- **Turtle Wax.** To prevent playing cards from sticking together, wax the backs of the cards with Turtle Wax and rub with a soft cloth.

Games

- **Cool Whip.** Use empty, clean Cool Whip tubs to hold loose game pieces, such as playing cards or a ball and jacks.

- **Huggies Baby Wipes.** Store loose dice, cards, playing pieces, and small toys in empty Huggies Baby Wipes containers.

- **Maxwell House Coffee.** Maxwell House Coffee cans make perfect storage containers for game pieces.

- **Scotch Packaging Tape.** Reinforce or repair the broken corners of game or puzzle boxes with a strip of Scotch Packaging Tape.

- **Ziploc Storage Bags.** Store loose dice, cards, playing pieces, or jigsaw puzzle pieces in Ziploc Storage Bags.

Golf

- **Alberto VO5 Conditioning Hairdressing.** To make golf clubs shine, clean the shafts with a dab of Alberto VO5 Conditioning Hairdressing on a clean, soft cloth.
- **Cover Girl Continuous Color Classic Red.** To label golf balls, paint a small identifiable mark on the balls with Cover Girl Continuous Color Classic Red Nail Polish.
- **Jet-Dry.** To clean golf balls and increase their range, mix one tablespoon Jet-Dry and two cups water. Rinse golf balls in the solution, then rinse clean and dry. Cleaning residue from the dimples enables the balls to travel further.
- **Parsons' Ammonia.** To clean golf balls, mix one-quarter cup Parsons' Ammonia and one cup water and soak the balls in the mixture. Rinse clean. Remember, the cleaner the dimples, the further the ball travels.
- **Pink Pearl Erasers.** To clean golf balls, rub them with a Pink Pearl Eraser, which you can easily pack in your golf bag.
- **S.O.S Steel Wool Soap Pads.** To clean a golf club, rub the shaft and head gently with a dry S.O.S Steel Wool Soap Pad.

Ice Skates

- **Bounce.** To deodorize smelly ice skates, place a used sheet of Bounce inside the skates. (For more ways to deodorize ice skates, see page 260.)
- **Coca-Cola.** To clean rust from ice skate blades, fill a pan with Coca-Cola and stand the skates so the blades soak in the Real Thing for one hour. Rinse clean.

Ink Stains

- **Crisco All-Vegetable Shortening.** To clean indelible marker or ballpoint ink marks from a toy or doll, rub a dab of Crisco

All-Vegetable Shortening on the ink marks, wait a few minutes, and wipe clean. Repeat if necessary.

- **Jif Peanut Butter.** To wipe ballpoint ink marks from a toy or doll, smear Jif Peanut Butter (creamy, not chunky) on the marks, wait a few minutes, and wipe off.
- **Noxzema Deep Cleansing Cream.** To remove permanent marker from toys or dolls, smear Noxzema Deep Cleansing Cream on the marks and wipe off the ink.

Pool Balls

- **Miracle Whip.** To clean discolored pool balls, coat the balls with Miracle Whip and wipe clean with a soft cloth.

Roller Skates and Skateboards

- **Alberto VO5 Conditioning Hairdressing.** Lubricate roller skate or skateboard wheels with a dab of Alberto VO5 Conditioning Hairdressing.
- **Pam Cooking Spray.** To lubricate the wheels of roller skates or skateboards, spray them with Pam Cooking Spray.
- **Vaseline Petroleum Jelly.** Smear Vaseline Petroleum Jelly around the cylinders on the wheels of roller skates or skateboards so they roll faster.
- **WD-40.** Lubricate roller skate or skateboard wheels with a quick squirt of WD-40.

Sailing

- **Alberto VO5 Conditioning Hairdressing.** To prevent a sailboat's spinnaker pole fittings from jamming or sticking, lubricate them with Alberto VO5 Conditioning Hairdressing.
- **Vaseline.** Lubricate a sailboat's spinnaker pole fittings with Vaseline Petroleum Jelly.

Skiing

- **Colgate Regular Flavor Toothpaste.** To prevent ski goggles from fogging up, coat the insides of the lens with Colgate Regular Flavor Toothpaste, then wipe off, leaving behind a protective film.
- **Gillette Foamy.** To prevent ski goggles from fogging up, spray the inside of the lens with Gillette Foamy shaving cream, then wipe clean.
- **Pledge.** To prevent ski goggles from fogging up, spray the inside of the lens with Pledge, then wipe clean.
- **Scotchgard.** To make a pair of waterproof ski pants, spray a pair of old jeans with Scotchgard. Be sure to wear thermal underwear for warmth.

Sledding

- **Crisco All-Vegetable Shortening.** To speed up a sled, lubricate the bottom of the sled with Crisco All-Vegetable Shortening before sliding down the hillside.
- **Pam Cooking Spray.** To speed up a sled, spray Pam Cooking Spray on the bottom of the sled before taking it out in the snow.
- **Turtle Wax.** To prevent snow from sticking to the bottom of a sled and slowing down your descent, give the bottom of the sled a thick coat of Turtle Wax.
- **Wesson Corn Oil.** To speed up a sled, coat the bottom of the sled with Wesson Corn Oil before hopping aboard.

Sliding Boards

- **Reynolds Cut-Rite Wax Paper.** To resurface a metal sliding board, rub a sheet of Reynolds Cut-Rite Wax Paper on the metal slide.

- **Turtle Wax.** To resurface a metal sliding board, coat the metal with Turtle Wax, polish, and repeat.

Sports Bags

- **Arm & Hammer Baking Soda.** To deodorize a smelly sports bag, sprinkle Arm & Hammer Baking Soda inside the bag to absorb moisture and neutralize offending odors. Let sit for a day or two and then shake out the baking soda.
- **Bounce.** To mask foul smells in a sports bag, place a Bounce sheet in the sack.
- *USA Today.* To deodorize a stinky sports bag, crumple up a few pages of *USA Today*, shove them inside the bag, and let sit overnight. By morning the newsprint will absorb the odors.

String Toys

- **Glad Flexible Straws.** To prevent strings on pull toys from getting tangled, thread the string through one or more Glad Flexible Straws and knot it at the end.

Stuffed Animals

- **Arm & Hammer Baking Soda.** To clean a stuffed animal, sprinkle Arm & Hammer Baking Soda on the stuffed animal, let sit for fifteen minutes, and then brush off.
- **Kingsford's Corn Starch.** To absorb water, juice, or urine from a stuffed animal, rub Kingsford's Corn Starch into the toy, let stand for five minutes, and then brush clean.

Swim Goggles and Masks

- **Colgate Regular Flavor Toothpaste.** To prevent swim goggles and masks from fogging up, coat the insides of the lens with Colgate Regular Flavor Toothpaste, and then wipe off, leaving behind a protective film.

- **Gillette Foamy.** To prevent swim goggles and mask from fogging up, spray the inside of the lens with Gillette Foamy shaving cream, then wipe clean.

Tennis

- **Cover Girl Continuous Color Classic Red.** To label tennis balls, paint a small identifying mark with Cover Girl Continuous Color Classic Red Nail Polish.

Tents and Backpacks

- **Glad Trash Bags.** To waterproof a backpack, cover the backpack with a Glad Trash Bag and cut small slits in the bag for the straps.
- **Oral-B Dental Floss.** To repair rips in tents or backpacks, use Oral-B Dental Floss as a durable, strong thread for tough repairs.
- **Scotchgard.** To waterproof tents and backpacks so they stay dry during a camping trip, spray the camping gear with Scotchgard.

Strange Facts

- In 1752, Benjamin Franklin flew a kite during a thunderstorm, attaching a metal key to the wire he used as line, to prove that lightning is electricity, conducting the most famous and most dangerous kite experiment in history.
- In 1916, John Lloyd Wright, inspired by the interlocking building system used to construct Tokyo's earthquake-proof Imperial Hotel, (designed by his father, architect Frank Lloyd Wright), developed a toy building set comprised of sturdy, interlocking logs made from real wood. Wright named the construction set Lincoln Logs after President Abraham Lincoln,

in honor of the fiftieth anniversary of the end of the Civil War.

- In the 1929 Rose Bowl, University of Southern California defensive lineman Roy Riegels recovered a fumble and ran seventy yards with the football in the wrong direction. A teammate stopped "Wrong Way" Riegels at the one-yard line, enabling Georgia Tech to score a two-point safety and win the game, 8–7.

- On October 25, 1964, Minnesota Viking Jim Marshall picked up a football fumbled by the San Francisco 49ers and ran sixty-six yards the wrong way into his own end zone—scoring two points for the other team.

- In 1984, the Houston Rockets got the number one pick in the NBA draft of college basketball players, choosing seven-foot-tall Hakeem Olajuwon—rather than University of North Carolina jump shooter Michael Jordan. The Portland Trail Blazers made the second pick, selecting seven-foot-tall Sam Bowie. Finally, the Chicago Bulls chose Jordan, making the future basketball superstar the number three NBA pick.

- A nine-foot tall statue of baseball legend Babe Ruth by artist Susan Luery, erected in front of Oriole Park in Baltimore, Maryland, in 1995, depicts Ruth holding a right-handed baseball glove. Babe Ruth was left-handed.

- In 2000 at a Toronto Blue Jays baseball game at the Toronto SkyDome, a device used by vendors to shoot hot dogs to baseball fans, called a Hot Dog Blaster, malfunctioned, showering fans with pieces of hot dogs and buns.

Wallpaper

Cleaning

- **Arm & Hammer Baking Soda.** To clean crayon marks from wallpaper, sprinkle Arm & Hammer Baking Soda on a damp sponge, scrub gently, and wipe clean.
- **Conair Pro Styler 1600.** To clean crayon marks from wallpaper, set a Conair Pro Styler 1600 hair dryer on hot, move the nozzle back and forth over the crayon marks until the wax warms up, and then wipe clean with a paper towel.
- **Murphy Oil Soap.** To remove dried wallpaper paste from wallpaper, mix one tablespoon Murphy Oil Soap and one gallon warm water, dampen a sponge in the solution, and wipe the wallpaper.
- **Play-Doh.** To clean wallpaper, roll a ball of Play-Doh over the walls. The modeling dough lifts grease and grime.
- **Wonder Bread.** To clean wallpaper, cut off the crust from two-day old slices of Wonder Bread and use the mildly abrasive slices of bread to gently rub down the wallpaper.

Removing

- **Clorox Bleach.** After stripping old wallpaper from the walls, use a sponge to wash the walls clean with a mixture of one-quarter cup Clorox Bleach to two gallons water. Let the walls dry for several hours. This cleans off any residue.
- **Downy Fabric Softener.** Remove wallpaper by mixing one capful Downy Fabric Softener with one quart hot water in a plastic bucket, sponge the wallpaper (or apply the solution with a trigger-spray bottle), wait twenty minutes, and peel off the paper.
- **Heinz White Vinegar.** To remove wallpaper, mix equal parts Heinz White Vinegar and hot water in a bucket. Sponge down the wallpaper thoroughly with the mixture or use a clean paint roller to saturate the paper with the vinegar solution. Repeat. Wait two minutes and then peel off the wallpaper in sheets with the greatest of ease. The wallpaper should peel off in sheets.
- **Jet-Dry.** To remove wallpaper, mix four ounces Jet-Dry with one quart hot water in a plastic bucket, sponge the wallpaper, wait twenty minutes, and peel off the paper.
- **Resolve Carpet Cleaner.** To remove stubborn wallpaper from a wall, spray Resolve Carpet Cleaner on the wallpaper, wait a few minutes for the solution to soak into the paper, and then scrape off with a plastic scraper.

Repairing

- **Colgate Regular Flavor Toothpaste.** To glue the peeling corners of wallpaper back in place, use a dab of Colgate Regular Flavor Toothpaste.
- **Elmer's Glue-All.** If the corners of the wallpaper start peeling off the wall, glue the wallpaper back in place with a small dab of Elmer's Glue-All.

- **Uncle Ben's Converted Brand Rice.** To make rice glue to adhere peeling corners of wallpaper back in place, mix one-half cup Uncle Ben's Converted Brand Rice and one-half cup water, stirring until the rice dissolves and the mixture attains the consistency of glue.

Wallpaper Paste

- **Gold Medal Flour** and **C&H Sugar.** To make wallpaper paste, mix one-half cup Gold Medal Flour, one-half cup C&H Sugar, and one cup cold water in a large saucepan. Slowly add in two cups boiling water and stir continuously until stiff. Remove from the heat and cool. Store in an airtight container.

- **McCormick Food Coloring.** Tint wallpaper paste slightly by adding a few drops of food coloring to wallpaper paste so you can see how well you're covering the sheets of wallpaper. Do not use too much food coloring, or the color may bleed through the wallpaper.

- **Mrs. Stewart's Liquid Bluing.** To tint wallpaper paste to make it easier to see when spreading on sheets of wallpaper, mix a few drops of Mrs. Stewart's Liquid Bluing to the wallpaper paste.

Strange Facts

- The Chinese, having invented paper, began gluing rice paper to the walls of their homes as early as 200 BCE.

- Wallpaper became popular during the European Renaissance among the gentry, who wished to decorate the walls of their homes with tapestries like the aristocracy, but could not afford the expensive wall hangings.

- When Pope Clement VII excommunicated King Henry VIII of England in 1533, trade between England and Europe declined sharply. The English aristocracy and gentry, no longer able to import tapestries from Flanders and Arras, switched their allegiance to wallpaper.

- During the rule of Oliver Cromwell in England, the Puritan government halted the production of wallpaper, a luxury item it considered frivolous.

- The 1955 hit song "The Wallflower" (also known as "Dance with Me, Henry") was sung by Georgia Gibbs.

- Brothers Noah and Joseph McVicker originally invented Play-Doh in 1955 as a wallpaper cleaner.

- *Wallpaper* is a term used to describe an image used as a background for a desktop screen on a personal computer.

- The term *wallflower* is slang for a person attending a ballroom dance, who, unwilling to dance or unable to attract a partner, stands against the wall, hoping to blend in with the flowers on the wallpaper

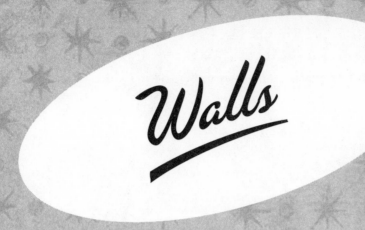

Cleaning

- **Arm & Hammer Baking Soda.** To clean a tile wall, sprinkle Arm & Hammer Baking Soda on a damp sponge, scrub, and rinse clean. (For more ways to clean tile, see page 299.)

- **Huggies Baby Wipes.** To clean food splatters from walls, use a Huggies Baby Wipe.

- **Kingsford's Corn Starch.** To clean grease from walls, sprinkle Kingsford's Corn Starch on a soft cloth and rub the spot until the grease disappears. Cornstarch absorbs grease.

- **Lysol Antibacterial Kitchen Cleaner.** To clean stains from walls, spray the spot with Lysol Antibacterial Kitchen Cleaner and wipe clean.

Crayon Marks

- **Arm & Hammer Baking Soda.** To clean crayon marks from a wall, sprinkle Arm & Hammer Baking Soda on a damp sponge and scrub.

- **Bounty Paper Towels.** Place a sheet of Bounty Paper Towel over the crayon marks and iron the paper towel with a clothes iron set on warm. The iron melts the crayon wax; the paper towel absorbs it.

- **Cascade.** To clean crayon marks from walls, make a paste from one teaspoon Cascade dishwasher detergent and one teaspoon hot water, smear the paste over the crayon marks, wait ten minutes, then wipe clean with a damp cloth.
- **Colgate Regular Flavor Toothpaste.** To clean crayon marks from walls, put some Colgate Regular Flavor Toothpaste on the marks and scrub with a sponge.
- **Conair Pro Styler 1600.** To clean crayon marks from wallpaper, set a Conair Pro Styler 1600 hair dryer on hot, move the nozzle back and forth over the crayon marks until the wax warms up, and then wipe clean with a paper towel.
- **Huggies Baby Wipes.** Wipe crayon marks from walls with a Huggies Baby Wipe.
- **Parsons' Ammonia.** Wearing rubber gloves, scrub crayon marks from a wall with a soft, clean cloth soaked in Parsons' Ammonia. Be sure the room is well ventilated.

- **WD-40.** Remove crayon from painted walls by spraying the marks with WD-40 and wiping the wall clean with a paper towel. Wash the WD-40 residue from the wall with soapy water.

Ink Marks

- **Alberto VO5 Hair Spray.** The acetone in hair spray removes permanent marker from walls. Spray the ink mark with Alberto VO5 Hair Spray and wipe clean.
- **Arm & Hammer Baking Soda.** To clean indelible ink from a wall, sprinkle some Arm & Hammer Baking Soda on a damp cloth and wipe clean.
- **Crisco All-Vegetable Shortening.** Rub a dab of Crisco All-Vegetable Shortening on the ink marks, wait a few minutes, and wipe clean. Repeat if necessary.
- **Lysol Disinfectant.** Spray an indelible ink mark with Lysol Disinfectant and wipe clean with a soft cloth.
- **Murphy Oil Soap.** Murphy Oil Soap removes permanent marker from walls.
- **Smirnoff Vodka.** To clean indelible ink from a wall, saturate a cotton ball with Smirnoff Vodka and wipe clean.

Joint Compound

- **Conair Pro Styler 1600.** To dry joint compound more quickly, set a Conair Pro Styler 1600 hair dryer on high and move the nozzle back and forth over the joint compound.

Mold and Mildew

- **Clorox Bleach.** To clean mold and mildew from outdoor siding, tile, brick, or stucco, mix three-quarters cup Clorox

Bleach per gallon of water. Wearing rubber gloves, scrub the affected area with the solution. Bleach kills and removes mold and mildew.

- **20 Mule Team Borax.** To remove mildew from walls, mix one cup 20 Mule Team Borax in a bucket of warm water and scrub the walls with the solution. Make a fresh batch of the solution, wipe it on the walls, and let dry out for a day or two. Rinse clean with water and let dry.

Paneling

- **Alberto VO5 Conditioning Hairdressing.** To prevent wood paneling from drying out, rub Alberto VO5 Conditioning Hairdressing onto the walls with a clean, soft cloth and buff well, giving the paneling a warm glow.
- **Gillette Foamy.** Use Gillette Foamy shaving cream to clean and polish paneled walls. The shaving cream removes dirt, dust, and grime and simultaneously gives the paneling a beautiful shine.

Plaster

- **Heinz White Vinegar.** To slow the drying time of plaster of Paris, add one tablespoon Heinz White Vinegar to the water when mixing up a new batch of plaster.
- **L'eggs Sheer Energy Panty Hose.** To remove excess plaster after filling a hole, scrub the wall with a balled-up pair of clean, used L'eggs Sheer Energy Panty Hose.

Spackle

- **Arm & Hammer Baking Soda** and **McCormick Food Coloring.** To spackle holes in a wall, mix Arm & Hammer Baking

Soda, a drop of McCormick Food Coloring (to match the color of paint on the wall), and enough water to make a thick paste. Fill the holes with the paste and let dry.

- **Colgate Regular Flavor Toothpaste.** In a pinch, use a small dab of Colgate Regular Flavor Toothpaste to fill in small holes in plaster walls. Let dry thoroughly before painting.

- **Conair Pro Styler 1600.** To dry spackling, set a Conair Pro Styler 1600 hair dryer on low heat and gently wave the nozzle back and forth over the area, being careful to avoid letting the heat crack the spackling.

- **Crayola Chalk.** To fill a hole in the wall, insert a piece of Crayola Chalk into the opening, cut it off even with the wall, and then plaster over it.

- **Elmer's Glue-All.** To fill small nail holes, squirt in drops of Elmer's Glue-All and let dry before painting.

- **Ivory Soap.** To spackle a hole in a wall, rub a bar of Ivory Soap over the hole until the soap fills in the hole even with the wall, let harden, then paint.

- **MasterCard.** A clean, expired credit card makes an excellent substitute for a putty knife for applying spackle to a small hole.

- **S.O.S Steel Wool Soap Pads.** Fill small holes with pieces of an S.O.S Steel Wool Soap Pad, then plaster.

- **Wrigley's Spearmint Gum.** If you don't have any spackle or plaster, chew a stick of Wrigley's Spearmint Gum well (until the sugar is gone) and use small pieces of the gum to seal holes in walls.

Vinyl Siding

- **Thompson's Deck Wash.** Use Thompson's Deck Wash to clean the vinyl siding on the outer walls of your house.

Strange Facts

- According to the book of Joshua in the Hebrew Bible, the Children of Israel walked around the ancient walled city of Jericho seven times and then sounded their trumpets, causing the walls to fall.

- Around 122 CE, Roman emperor Hadrian ordered his legions to build a stone wall spanning eighty miles across the width of Great Britain to prevent the Pictes (ancient tribes living in Scotland) from invading.

- Ancient defensive walls surround hundreds of cities, including Baghdad, Barcelona, Beijing, Casablanca, Florence, Freiberg, Galway, Istanbul, Jerusalem, Moscow, Nuremberg, Paris, Rome, Rothenberg, Stockholm, Vienna, Warsaw, and York.

- The Great Wall of China, stretching some four thousand miles, is visible from orbit around the Earth. However, in 1969, astronaut Alan Bean, who walked on the moon during the *Apollo 12* mission, reported that no trace of any man-made object is visible to the naked eye from the surface of the moon.

- The Berlin Wall, built by the Soviet Union in 1961 to encircle West Berlin and dismantled in 1989, was known in the Communist bloc countries as the "Anti-Fascist Protective Rampart." The Communists built the wall to stop its citizens from emigrating to the West.

- Pink Floyd's 1979 rock album *The Wall* held the number one spot on *Billboard's* charts for fifteen consecutive weeks and includes the number one hit song "Another Brick in the Wall (Part 2)."

- Landlords in Bangkok, Thailand, have used Scotch Transparent Tape to repair cracks in the walls of tenants' apartments.

Washers and Dryers

Baby Clothes

- **Arm & Hammer Baking Soda.** To make baby clothes smell fresh, add one-half cup Arm & Hammer Baking Soda to the baby's laundry.

- **Clorox Bleach.** To remove stains from baby clothes, mix one-quarter cup Clorox Bleach to one gallon water in a plastic bucket. Soak the clothes in the solution for five minutes. Rinse well, then launder as usual.

- **20 Mule Team Borax.** To deodorize baby clothes and eliminate stains, wash baby clothes, linens, bibs, and cotton crib liners in hot water, adding one-half cup 20 Mule Team Borax to your regular laundry detergent. Borax boosts the cleaning power of laundry detergent and deodorizes clothes.

Bleach

- **Arm & Hammer Baking Soda.** To boost the power of bleach and freshen clothes, add one-half cup Arm & Hammer Baking Soda to the wash, along with the normal amount of bleach.
- **Crayola Crayons** and **Reynolds Cut-Rite Wax Paper.** To permanently hide small bleach spots on clothing, color the spots with a Crayola Crayon that matches the color of the fabric and then cover with a sheet of Reynolds Cut-Rite Wax Paper and iron on a low setting.
- **Hydrogen Peroxide.** Instead of using bleach to wash white clothes, add one cup hydrogen peroxide to a load of whites and launder as usual.
- **McCormick Food Coloring.** To permanently hide small bleach spots on clothing, mix McCormick Food Coloring with water to make the proper shade and apply it to the spots.

Blood Stains

- **Heinz White Vinegar.** To clean a blood stain from clothes, saturate the stain with Heinz White Vinegar, wait five minutes, and blot with a clean cloth.
- **Hydrogen Peroxide.** To clean a blood stain from clothes, pour hydrogen peroxide on the stain, let it foam, and then launder as usual. The hydrogen peroxide breaks down the protein in the blood.
- **Ivory Soap.** To clean a blood stain from clothes, rinse the garment with cold water, rub a bar of Ivory Soap over the stain, let sit for five minutes, rub the soap into the spot again, and rinse clean. Repeat if necessary.
- **Jet-Dry.** To clean a blood stain from clothes, saturate the stain with Jet-Dry, wait five minutes, then blot with a clean cloth. Launder as usual.

- **Kingsford's Corn Starch.** To clean a blood stain, cover the spot with a paste made from Kingsford's Corn Starch and cold water. Rub gently, let dry, and then brush clean. The cornstarch absorbs the blood.
- **McCormick Meat Tenderizer.** Cover the blood stain with a paste made from McCormick Meat Tenderizer and cool water. Wait twenty minutes and sponge off with cool water. The enzymes in the meat tenderizer break up the proteins in the blood.
- **Windex.** Spray a blood stain with Windex and rinse clean. Repeat if necessary.

ChapStick

- **Heinz White Vinegar.** If a tube of ChapStick goes through the washer or dryer, staining clothes with wax and oil, wash the clothes with one cup Heinz White Vinegar and your regular detergent.

Chocolate Stains

- **20 Mule Team Borax.** To clean chocolate from clothing, mix one tablespoon 20 Mule Team Borax and one cup warm water and sponge the spot with the solution. Rinse clean with water. If that doesn't work, make a thick paste with borax and water, work the paste into the stain, wait one hour, rinse with warm water, and launder as usual.

Colors

- **Heinz White Vinegar.** To prevent brightly colored clothes from fading or bleeding, before putting the articles in the washing machine, soak them in a bucket of Heinz White Vinegar for ten minutes. The vinegar locks in the color.

- **McCormick Black Pepper.** To stop colors in cotton clothes from running, add one teaspoon McCormick Black Pepper to the first suds in the washing machine.
- **Morton Salt.** To prevent brightly colored clothes from fading or bleeding, add one cup coarse Morton Salt to your detergent in the washing machine.

Crayon

- **Bounty Paper Towels** and **Dawn Dishwashing Liquid.** To remove crayon from clothing, cover the crayon stain with a sheet of Bounty Paper Towel and iron the paper towel. The heat from the iron melts the wax, and the paper towel absorbs it. To remove the pigment from the crayon from the garment, rub a dab of Dawn Dishwashing Liquid into the spot and then throw the item back in your regular wash.

Delicate Hand Washables

- **20 Mule Team Borax.** To wash delicate hand washables, dissolve one-quarter cup 20 Mule Team Borax and two tablespoons detergent in a basin of warm water. Soak the hand washables for ten minutes, rinse in cool water, blot with a towel, lay flat (woolens) or hang to dry away from sunlight and direct heat.

Deodorant Stains

- **Huggies Baby Wipes.** Use a Huggies Baby Wipe to clean deodorant stains from clothes.

Deodorize

- **Heinz White Vinegar.** To deodorize smelly clothes, add one cup Heinz White Vinegar to the wash cycle.

Detergent

- **Arm & Hammer Baking Soda.** To boost the power of your regular laundry detergent, add one-half cup Arm & Hammer Baking Soda with the usual amount of detergent in your regular wash cycle.
- **Johnson's Baby Shampoo.** If you're all out of regular detergent, use one capful Johnson's Baby Shampoo in your regular wash cycle. The baby shampoo gets clothes just as clean as Tide or Cheer, and it makes clothes smell fresh.
- **Parsons' Ammonia.** To clean clothes with half the detergent, add one cup Parsons' Ammonia and half the usual amount of laundry detergent to your wash load. (Remember, never use ammonia with chlorine bleach.)
- **20 Mule Team Borax.** To boost the strength of your regular laundry detergent, add one-half cup 20 Mule Team Borax to each wash load along with the usual amount of detergent. For a large capacity or front-loading machine, add three-quarters cup borax. Borax acts as a water conditioner, boosts the cleaning power of detergent by controlling alkalinity, deodorizes the clothes, and helps remove stains and soil.

Dial

- **Crayola Crayons.** To rejuvenate the worn-out letters and numbers on a washing machine dial, rub the knob with a red or black Crayola Crayon until the indentations of the letters and numbers are filled with colored wax. Then wipe off the excess crayon.

Diapers

- **Arm & Hammer Baking Soda.** To deodorize cloth diapers, mix one-half cup Arm & Hammer Baking Soda and two quarts water in a bucket, soak the diapers in the solution for one hour, then launder as usual.

- **20 Mule Team Borax.** Flush out dirty diapers and soak immediately in a diaper pail filled with warm water and one-half cup 20 Mule Team Borax. Let soak for thirty minutes (or longer) and then wash the diapers in warm water, adding one-half cup borax with the usual amount of detergent. Borax helps deodorize the diapers, eliminate stains, and make the diapers more absorbent.

Disinfectant

- **Heinz White Vinegar.** To kill bacteria in the laundry without using harsh chemicals, add one-quarter cup Heinz White Vinegar during the rinse cycle.
- **Listerine.** To disinfect a washing machine to avoid getting germs from a sick family member, wipe off the surface of the machine with Listerine antiseptic mouthwash and add one-half cup Listerine to the wash cycle.

Double-Knits

- **Canada Dry Club Soda.** To clean a grease stain from double-knit fabrics, pour Canada Dry Club Soda on the spot and scrub gently. Launder as usual.

Down Jackets

- **Wilson Tennis Balls.** To fluff a down jacket tumbling in the dryer, toss a handful of Wilson Tennis Balls into the dryer along with the down jacket. The bouncing balls do all the work.

Drains

- **Wilson Tennis Balls.** To prevent insects from crawling up through the drain in a laundry room floor, unscrew the faceplate from the drain, place a clean, used Wilson Tennis Ball inside the drain to block the hole, and screw the faceplate back in place. When the drain fills with water, the tennis ball will float, allowing water to go down the pipe. When the water is gone, the ball will automatically reseal the hole snugly.

Food Stains

- **Canada Dry Club Soda.** To clean food stains from clothes, blot up the spill, sponge with Canada Dry Club Soda, and launder as usual.
- **Dawn Dishwashing Liquid** and **Heinz White Vinegar.** Mix two teaspoons Dawn Dishwashing Liquid, two teaspoons Heinz White Vinegar, and two quarts warm water. Use the solution to wash food stains from clothes.
- **Huggies Baby Wipes.** To clean a spill from clothes to prevent staining, immediately blot with a Huggies Baby Wipe.
- **Pine-Sol.** To clean food stains from clothes, use a few drops of Pine-Sol on a damp sponge.
- **Resolve Carpet Cleaner.** To clean grape juice stains spills from clothes, spray the spot with Resolve Carpet Cleaner, blot, and rinse thoroughly.
- **Soft Scrub Deep Clean Foaming Cleanser.** To clean food stains from clothes, wet the garments, add Soft Scrub Deep Clean Foaming Cleanser, and let sit until the stains disappear.
- **Windex.** To clean food stains from clothes, immediately spray the spot with Windex, let sit for three minutes, blot, and rinse clean.

Grass Stains

- **C&H Sugar.** To clean grass stains from clothes, make a paste of C&H Sugar and water, cover the grass stain with the mixture, let sit for one hour, and then launder as usual.

- **Karo Corn Syrup.** Rub Karo Corn Syrup onto a grass stain on clothes and launder as usual.

- **Murphy Oil Soap.** To clean grass stains from clothes, rub Murphy Oil Soap into the grass stains and then launder as usual.

- **Smirnoff Vodka.** To remove grass stains from clothes, rub the stain with a clean cloth soaked in Smirnoff Vodka, then rinse thoroughly.

Grease Stains

- **Arm & Hammer Baking Soda.** To clean grease stains from clothes, sprinkle Arm & Hammer Baking Soda over the stain and scrub gently with a wet brush.

- **Coca-Cola.** To clean a grease stain from clothes, pour a can of Coke on the grease stain, let sit for five minutes, and then launder as usual with your regular detergent. The acids in the Real Thing loosen grease stains.

- **Cheez Whiz.** To clean grease from clothes, rub a dollop of Cheez Whiz into the grease stain and run the garment through a regular wash cycle with detergent. The enzymes in Cheez Whiz will help loosen the grease stain.

- **Comet.** Wet the grease stain, sprinkle Comet cleanser over the spot, rub in to form a paste, and let sit overnight. In the morning, rinse clean with warm water.

- **Crayola Chalk.** Rub Crayola Chalk on a grease stain, let the chalk absorb the oil, and then brush off. Launder as usual.

- **Crisco All-Vegetable Shortening.** Rub a dab of Crisco All-Vegetable Shortening into the grease stain and then launder as usual. The shortening breaks down the grease stain.

- **Dawn Dishwashing Detergent.** Rub a few drops of Dawn Dishwashing Liquid into the grease stain and then launder as usual. Dawn cuts through grease. In fact, when a tanker truck flipped over on Interstate 74 in Cincinnati, Ohio, on

April 30, 1998, spilling four tons of inedible industrial animal fat, Cincinnati-based Procter & Gamble donated a tanker truck filled with Dawn Dishwashing Liquid to be sprayed over the oil slick and scrubbed with road sweeper brushes—demonstrating how well Dawn cuts through grease.

- **Formula 409.** Pretreat grease stains on clothes with Formula 409 and launder as usual.
- **Gunk Brake Cleaner.** To clean grease from clothing, spray Gunk Brake Cleaner on the stain, then launder the garment as usual.
- **Johnson's Baby Powder.** To absorb a grease stain from clothes, sprinkle Johnson's Baby Powder over the stain, rub it into the garment, and launder in cold water.
- **Kingsford's Corn Starch.** Pour Kingsford's Corn Starch over the grease spot, let sit overnight so the cornstarch can absorb the grease, brush off, and then launder as usual.
- **Lestoil.** To clean grease from clothing, rub Lestoil into the spot and launder as usual.
- **Pine-Sol.** To clean grease from clothing, rub Pine-Sol on the stain, then launder the garment as usual.
- **Resolve Carpet Cleaner.** Spray Resolve Carpet Cleaner on a grease stain on clothes, let soak, then launder as usual with your regular detergent.
- **WD-40.** Spray WD-40 directly on a grease stain on clothing, let is soak for a few minutes, and then launder the garment with your regular detergent.

Gum

- **Cutex Nail Polish Remover.** To clean chewing gum from clothes, saturate a cotton ball with Cutex Nail Polish Remover and use it to dab the gum. The acetone in the nail polish remover dissolves the adhesives in the chewing gum. (Be sure to test an inconspicuous spot on the clothing to make certain the fabric is colorfast.)

- **Jif Peanut Butter.** If you forgot to check your kids' pockets and wind up with chewing gum melted all over the inside of the clothes dryer, use a dab of Jif Peanut Butter (creamy, not chunky) to remove the gum from inside walls of the clothes dryer drum.

- **Jif Peanut Butter.** To remove chewing gum from clothes, rub a dab of Jif Peanut Butter over the spot, let sit for a few minutes, and then work out the gum with a comb. The oils in the peanut butter dissolve the gums in the chewing gum.

- **Noxzema Deep Cleansing Cream.** Rub a dollop of Noxzema Deep Cleansing Cream into chewing gum stuck in clothes, let sit for a few minutes, and then work out the gum with a comb. The cold cream dissolves the gums in the chewing gum.

- **WD-40.** To get chewing gum out of clothes, spray WD-40 on the spot, wait a few minutes, and wipe clean. The petroleum distillates in the WD-40 dissolve the gums in the chewing gum. Then launder as usual.

Ink Stains

- **Alberto VO5 Hair Spray.** To remove an ink spot from clothes, spray Alberto VO5 Hair Spray on the stain, blot until the stain comes up, and wash. The acetone in Alberto VO5 Hair Spray removes indelible marker and ballpoint pen marks from fabrics.

- **Colgate Regular Flavor Toothpaste.** Squeeze Colgate Regular Flavor Toothpaste on the ink stain, add some water, scrub, and rinse thoroughly.

- **Fantastic.** If you accidentally leave a pen in a pocket and get ink stains all over the inside of the drum of the dryer, unplug the machine, spray the stains with Fantastic, and rub gently with a cloth. Wipe clean with a damp cloth. Then toss some clean rags in the dryer, plug in the machine again, and run the dryer for twenty minutes.

- **Huggies Baby Wipes.** To clean ink stains from fabric, wipe the spot with a Huggies Baby Wipe.

- **Purell Instant Hand Sanitizer.** Saturate the ink stain with Purell Instant Hand Sanitizer and blot with a paper towel. Repeat if necessary.

- **ReaLemon.** While the ink stain is still wet, saturate the spot with ReaLemon lemon juice (which causes the ink stain to spread) and immediately launder the garment with regular detergent in cold water.

- **Soft Scrub Deep Clean Foaming Cleanser.** To clean ink stains from clothes, spray the spot with Soft Scrub Deep Clean Foaming Cleanser, wait a few minutes, and then launder as usual.

- **Tide.** To clean ink stains from the inside of the drum of the dryer, unplug the machine, mix equal parts liquid Tide laundry detergent and water, and use a soft, clean cloth to apply the mixture to the stains and scrub gently. Wipe clean with a damp cloth. Then toss some clean rags in the dryer, plug in the machine again, and run the dryer for twenty minutes.

Jeans

- **Morton Salt.** To soften a new pair of jeans, add one-half cup Morton Salt to your detergent in the washing machine.

- **Downy Fabric Softener.** To soften a new pair of jeans, fill your washing machine with water, add one capful Downy

Fabric Softener, soak the jeans overnight, then run through the rinse cycle and dry.

Linen Tablecloths

- **Cascade.** To clean stains from a linen tablecloth, pour liquid Cascade dishwasher detergent over the stains and launder as usual.

Lint

- **Heinz White Vinegar.** To prevent lint from clinging to clothes, add one cup Heinz White Vinegar to each wash load.
- **Jet-Dry.** To prevent lint from clinging to clothes, add four ounces Jet-Dry to each wash load in lieu of fabric softener. Jet-Dry also removes the soap from the clothes, which helps people who have allergic reactions to detergent. The Jet-Dry does double duty in the washing machine, simultaneously cleaning soap scum from the tubes and pipes in the washing machine.
- **L'eggs Sheer Energy Panty Hose.** Toss a pair of L'eggs Sheer Energy Panty Hose into the dryer with your wet clothes to prevent lint from clinging to clothes.

Lint Catcher

- **L'eggs Sheer Energy Panty Hose.** To capture lint from a washing machine drain, cut the foot off of a used pair of L'eggs Sheer Energy Panty Hose and attach it to the end of the washer hose with a strong rubber band. The nylon screen catches all the lint as it exits, preventing the lint from clogging the drain and pipes. To clean out the lint, remove the panty hose foot and turn it inside-out.

Lipstick Stains

- **Alberto VO5 Hair Spray.** To clean lipstick from clothes, spray Alberto VO5 Hair Spray on the stain, let sit overnight, and then launder the garment as usual. The acetone in the hairspray dissolves the lipstick.
- **Colgate Regular Flavor Toothpaste.** To remove lipstick stains from clothes, rub a dab of Colgate Regular Flavor Toothpaste into the stain. Launder as usual.
- **Crisco All-Vegetable Shortening** and **Canada Dry Club Soda.** To clean lipstick stains from linen napkins, rub a dab of Crisco All-Vegetable Shortening into the spot and then rinse the stain with Canada Dry Club Soda. Launder as usual.
- **Smirnoff Vodka.** Saturate lipstick stains on fabric with Smirnoff Vodka and launder as usual. The alcohol dissolves the lipstick's oily base.
- **Vaseline Petroleum Jelly.** To remove lipstick stains from clothes, rub a dab of Vaseline Petroleum Jelly into the stain and launder as usual.

Makeup

- **Huggies Baby Wipes.** To clean makeup from clothes, rub the stain with a Huggies Baby Wipe.

Mold and Mildew

- **Coca-Cola.** To clean mold and mildew from clothes, pour a two-liter bottle of Coca-Cola into the washing machine, add your regular detergent, let the machine fill with water, and let the clothes soak for thirty minutes before running them through the regular cycle. The acids in the Real Thing help clean the mold and mildew from clothes.

Moving

- **WD-40.** To move a washer or dryer without scratching the vinyl or tile floor, spray WD-40 on the floor in front of the washer or dryer so the appliance glides easily. To push the washer or dryer back in place, spray a line of WD-40 on the vinyl along the trail where the legs slid out. Afterward, simply buff the floor with a paper towel to clean up any residue.

Paint Stains

- **Parsons' Ammonia.** To clean dry paint from clothes, mix equal parts Parsons' Ammonia and turpentine, saturate the spot, and then launder with warm water. (Remember, never use ammonia with chlorine bleach.)
- **Smirnoff Vodka.** To clean acrylic paint from clothing, saturate the stain with Smirnoff Vodka, let sit for a few minutes, and then blot with a dry cloth.

Perspiration Stains

- **Heinz White Vinegar.** To clean perspiration stains from sheets, towels, and clothes, mix one part Heinz White Vinegar to four parts water, apply the solution to the stains, and then rinse clean.
- **Parsons' Ammonia.** To clean perspiration stains from sheets, towels, and clothes, pour one cup Parsons' Ammonia in your washing machine, add your regular detergent, and launder as usual. (Remember, never use ammonia with chlorine bleach.)

Ring-around-the-Collar

- **Clairol Herbal Essences.** To clean ring-around-the-collar (which is sebum oil stains), rub Clairol Herbal Essences Shampoo into the fabric and rinse clean.

- **Crayola Chalk.** Mark ring-around-the-collar stains heavily with white Crayola Chalk. The chalk absorbs the sebum oil in the stain.
- **McCormick Cream of Tartar.** To clean ring-around-the-collar, wet the collar with warm water, rub in McCormick Cream of Tartar, and then launder the garment as usual.
- **Parsons' Ammonia** and **Tide.** Mix one tablespoon Parsons' Ammonia, one-half teaspoon Tide laundry detergent, and one cup warm water. Rub the solution into the collar, let sit for thirty minutes, and launder as usual. (Remember, never use ammonia with chlorine bleach.)
- **Skin So Soft Body Lotion.** Skin So Soft Body Lotion removes the dirt rings in collars when rubbed into the fabric before washing.

Rust Stains

- **McCormick Alum** and **McCormick Cream of Tartar.** To remove rust stains from washable fabrics, mix one teaspoon McCormick Alum, one teaspoon McCormick Cream of Tartar, and enough water to make a paste. Rub the paste into the rust stain, wait five minutes, and then rinse with warm water.
- **McCormick Cream of Tartar.** To remove rust stains from fabric, make a paste from McCormick Cream of Tartar and hot water, rub it into the stain, let sit, then launder as usual.
- **ReaLemon.** To clean rust stains from clothes, add one cup ReaLemon lemon juice to the washer.

Scorch Marks

- **Heinz White Vinegar.** To clean light scorch marks from fabrics, gently rub Heinz White Vinegar on the mark and then wipe with a clean cloth.

Soap Scum

- **Arm & Hammer Baking Soda.** To clean soap scum from a washing machine, do a load of laundry using one cup Arm & Hammer Baking Soda instead of your regular detergent. The soap buildup inside the washing machine will clean the clothes, and the baking soda eliminates the remaining buildup.
- **Heinz White Vinegar.** To clean the hoses and unclog soap scum from a washing machine, once a month pour one cup Heinz White Vinegar into the washing machine and run the machine through a normal cycle, without any clothes inside.
- **Jet-Dry.** To clean soap scum from the tubes and pipes of a washing machine, fill the washer with water, add four ounces Jet-Dry, and then run the machine through its regular cycle.

Stains

- **Cascade.** To clean stubborn stains from clothes (blood, grass, grease, ink, or mildew), dissolve one-half cup Cascade dishwasher detergent in a bucket of very hot water, soak the garment overnight, and launder as usual.
- **Dawn Dishwashing Liquid** and **Oral-B Toothbrush.** To clean stains from clothes, squirt a dollop of Dawn Dishwashing Liquid on the spot, scrub with a clean, used Oral-B Toothbrush, and launder as usual.
- **Formula 409.** To clean tomato sauce stains, fruit stains, or coffee stains from clothes, spray Formula 409 on the trouble area, let sit for two minutes, and launder as usual.
- **Murphy Oil Soap.** To clean stains from clothes, dampen the stains, apply a few drops of Murphy Oil Soap full strength, and launder as usual.
- **Spic and Span.** To clean dirt stains from clothes, mix one teaspoon Spic and Span with enough water to make a paste, apply to the stain, and launder as usual.

Static Cling

- **Wilson Tennis Balls.** To reduce static cling, throw a couple of Wilson Tennis Balls into the dryer while the clothes are tumbling.

Suds

- **Downy Fabric Softener.** If you accidentally pour too much detergent in your washer, creating excessive suds, add one capful Downy Fabric Softener to the wash load.
- **Heinz White Vinegar.** To remove excess soap from clothes in the washing machine, add one cup Heinz White Vinegar to the rinse cycle.
- **Jet-Dry.** To dissolve excess soap suds in your washing machine, add one tablespoon Jet-Dry to the wash load.

Suede

- **Maxwell House Coffee.** To cover spots on black suede, make a cup of Maxwell House Coffee and sponge the black coffee on the trouble area.

Tar Stains

- **Crisco All-Vegetable Shortening.** Scrape off as much tar as possible from the garment, place a dollop of Crisco All-Vegetable Shortening over the spot, wait three hours, wipe off the shortening and tar, and launder the item as usual.

Whiter Whites

- **Arm & Hammer Baking Soda.** To whiten whites, add one-half cup Arm & Hammer Baking Soda, along with the normal amount of regular detergent. The baking soda boosts the power of the detergent.

- **Cascade.** To whiten white polyester, mix one cup Cascade dishwasher detergent and one gallon warm water in a plastic bucket. Soak the clothes in this mixture overnight, and then launder as usual. The phosphates in Cascade remove the gray soap buildup from white polyester.
- **Cascade, Clorox Bleach,** and **Heinz White Vinegar.** To get your whites whiter than white, mix one-half cup Cascade dishwasher detergent, one-half cup Clorox Bleach, and one gallon hot water in a plastic bucket and soak the white clothing in this solution overnight. In the morning, pour the entire contents of the bucket into the washing machine and launder as usual, adding one-half cup Heinz White Vinegar to the rinse water.
- **Nestlé Carnation NonFat Dry Milk.** To whiten white clothes, mix one cup Nestlé Carnation NonFat Dry Milk in a bucket of hot water and soak the clothes in the milky solution overnight. In the morning, discard the liquid and launder the clothes as usual.

Wool

- **Heinz White Vinegar.** To deodorize a wool sweater, wash the sweater, then rinse in equal parts Heinz White Vinegar and water to eliminate the odor.

Strange Facts

- In the 1920s, scientists at Procter & Gamble discovered synthetic surfactants that suspended dirt and grease from clothes until it could be washed away. A decade later, Procter & Gamble scientists discovered special chemical compounds called "builders" that help surfactants penetrate clothes fibers more deeply, allegedly "making them more effective than soap flakes, even on tough greasy stains." Procter & Gamble introduced Tide in 1946 as the "New Washday Miracle." Before the advent of Tide, Americans used soap flakes to clean clothes.

- In 1934, Andrew Clein opened the world's first coin-operated Laundromat in Fort Worth, Texas.

- *Consumer Reports* claims, "No laundry detergent will completely remove all common stains," and reports very little difference in performance between major name brand powdered detergents.

- Wal-Mart sells 227,592,400 clothespins each year—enough to give every citizen of New York City thirty clothespins.

- The Leo Burnet Advertising Agency created the Maytag Repairman, a character who never gets any repair calls for Maytag washers (because the dependable machines never break down) and calls himself the "loneliest man in town." Actor Jesse White, who starred as the asylum attendant in the 1950 movie *Harvey* and played Jesse Leeds on the television comedy *The Danny Thomas Show*, played the Maytag Repairman in television commercials from 1967 to 1988. Actor Gordon Jump, who starred as Arthur Carlson on the hit television sitcom *WKRP in Cincinnati*, took over the role of the Maytag Repairman, until his death in 2003.

- In the 1985 Academy Award–nominated movie *My Beautiful Laundrette*, a Pakistani immigrant, given the job of managing a run-down Laundromat, teams up with a friend to redecorate the store and turns it into a thriving business.

Windows and Doors

Artificial Snow

- **Budweiser** and **Epsom Salt.** Rather than decorating a window with aerosol snow, mix stale Budweiser beer with Epsom Salt until the beer cannot hold any more Epsom Salt. Apply the mixture to the glass with a sponge. When it dries, the window will be frosted.

- **Pam Cooking Spray.** Before decorating windows with artificial snow, spray the glass with a light coat of Pam Cooking Spray. When you're ready to clean the artificial snow from the windows, the decorative spray will wipe away easily.

- **WD-40.** Spray windows with a light coat of WD-40 before spraying with artificial snow so the decorative spray will wash off more readily.

Brass Hardware

- **Alberto VO5 Hair Spray.** To prevent tarnish from forming on freshly polished brass doorknobs and hinges, spray Alberto VO5 Hair Spray on the brass object to add a protective coating.

- **Bounce.** Polish brass doorknobs and hinges with a clean, used Bounce dryer sheet.

- **French's Mustard.** Cover the brass object with French's Mustard, wait ten minutes, then rinse clean with water. The vinegar in the mustard helps clean the tarnish from the brass.

- **Gold Medal Flour, Morton Salt,** and **Heinz White Vinegar.** Mix equal parts Gold Medal Flour and Morton Salt and add one teaspoon Heinz White Vinegar to make a thick paste. Spread a thick layer of the salty flour on doorknobs and hinges and let dry. Rinse and wipe off paste. The vinegar helps clean the tarnish from the brass, and the salty dough is a mild abrasive.

- **Heinz Ketchup.** Cover the brass object with Heinz Ketchup, let sit for ten minutes, then rinse clean. The acids from the tomatoes and the acetic acid from the vinegar clean brass.

- **Kool-Aid.** Mix the contents of one packet of any flavor Kool-Aid with two quarts water and soak your brass in the fruit-flavored drink. The citric acid cleans brass. (Be sure to discard the Kool-Aid afterward so nobody accidentally drinks it.)

- **Lea & Perrins Worcestershire Sauce.** To clean tarnish from brass, apply Lea & Perrins Worcestershire Sauce with a damp cloth, rub gently, and then rinse clean.

- **Morton Salt** and **ReaLemon.** Make a paste from Morton Salt and ReaLemon lemon juice, scrub gently, and then rinse with water.

- **Parsons' Ammonia.** Scrub brass lightly with a soft brush dampened with Parsons' Ammonia.

Curtains

- **Alberto VO5 Hair Spray.** To stiffen ruffled curtains, hold the fabric taut and spray with Alberto VO5 Hair Spray.

- **Bounce.** To prevent nylon curtains from clinging, rub a hot iron over a clean, used sheet of Bounce fabric softener and then iron the nylon curtains. The antistatic elements from the Bounce will prevent the curtains from clinging to themselves.

- **Epsom Salt.** To stiffen and whiten curtains, wash the curtains with your regular detergent in the washing machine and add one cup Epsom Salt to the final rinse water.

- **Scotch Packaging Tape.** To tag the pull cord that opens the drapes, wrap a half-inch piece of Scotch Packaging Tape at eye level to create a transparent flag around the appropriate cord.

- **Wilson Tennis Balls.** To make unique curtain rods, mount a wooden dowel above the window, cut a hole (the diameter of the dowel) in two Wilson Tennis Balls, cover the balls with fabric, and place one on each end of the dowel.

Dents

- **Maybelline Express Finish Clear Nail Polish.** To repair a small dent in a window, fill the hole with a few drops of Maybelline Express Finish Clear Nail Polish and let dry. Repeat as many times as necessary to fill the nick.

Door Hinges

- **Alberto VO5 Conditioning Hairdressing.** To lubricate squeaky door hinges, apply a dab of Alberto VO5 Conditioning Hairdressing to the pin.

- **Gillette Foamy.** Spraying the hinge pin with Gillette Foamy shaving cream lubricates it and eliminates squeaking.

- **Pam Cooking Spray.** For a nontoxic lubricant for door hinges, spray the pin with Pam Cooking Spray.
- **Pledge.** Lubricate door hinges with a quick spritz of Pledge furniture polish and wipe off the excess.
- **Vaseline Petroleum Jelly.** Rub a dab of Vaseline Petroleum Jelly into the pins of door hinges to stop the squeaking.
- **WD-40.** Spray the pin in the door hinge with WD-40 and wipe off the excess.

Frozen Windows

- **Conair Pro Styler 1600.** To thaw a window frozen shut, use a Conair Pro Styler 1600 hair dryer to blow warm air around the frame of the window to defrost the tracks.

Glass

- **Saran Wrap.** To temporarily repair a small hole in a window, tape a piece of Saran Wrap over the break to keep out wind, rain, or snow.
- **Scotch Packaging Tape.** To remove a broken window pane, put on a pair of protective gloves, crisscross Scotch Packaging Tape on both sides of the broken glass, tap the inside edges with a hammer until the pane breaks free, and peel off the tape to remove any shards.
- **Wrigley's Spearmint Gum.** To repair a loose pane of glass temporarily, use a wad of well-chewed Wrigley's Spearmint Gum as window putty.

Hard Water Stains

- **Downy Fabric Softener.** To clean hard water stains from windows, cover the stains with full-strength Downy Fabric Softener, wait ten minutes, then wipe with a damp cloth.

- **Jet-Dry.** To clean hard water stains from windows, cover the stains with full-strength Jet-Dry, wait ten minutes, then wipe with a damp cloth.
- **Pam Cooking Spray** and **Dawn Dishwashing Liquid.** To clean mineral deposits from windows, spray the glass with Pam Cooking Spray. Wait five minutes and then wash clean with a few drops of Dawn Dishwashing Liquid in a bucket of water.
- **Rain-X.** To prevent mineral deposits from adhering to windows, treat the glass with Rain-X.

Leaks

- **Conair Pro Styler 1600.** To find out if a window is leaking heat, hold a lit candle just inside the window, while someone else goes outside with a Conair Pro Styler 1600 hair dryer and blows air along the frame. If the flame flickers, the window needs caulking.
- **Kleenex Tissues.** To determine if cold air is getting into the house around doors and windows, hold a Kleenex Tissue along the frame of the door or window. Incoming air will cause the tissue to move.

Locks

- **Pam Cooking Spray.** If the key doesn't slide easily into the keyhole or the lock doesn't open, spray the teeth of the key with Pam Cooking Spray and slide the key in and out of the lock repeatedly to lubricate the tumblers.
- **Vaseline Petroleum Jelly.** To get a key to work in a lock, rub a dab of Vaseline Petroleum Jelly on your key before inserting it into the lock. The petroleum jelly will lubricate the tumblers so the lock opens easily.

- **WD-40.** If a lock gets jammed when you insert the key, spray a small amount of WD-40 into the keyhole and insert the key several times to coat the tumblers with the petroleum distillate.

Mini-Blinds

- **Playtex Living Gloves** and **Bounce.** Cleaning those one-inch mini-blinds can be a mini-pain. The easiest way to clean them is to put on a pair of Playtex Living Gloves (so you won't cut up your fingers) and then wipe down the blinds with clean, used sheets of Bounce. The antistatic elements in Bounce lift up all that dust and prevent it from settling as quickly.
- **Scrubbing Bubbles.** Take down filthy mini-blinds, place them in the bathtub, and spray them with Scrubbing Bubbles. Let sit for ten minutes so the scrubbing bubbles can do their job. Rinse clean with hot water.
- **Smirnoff Vodka.** Another way to clean those mini-blinds with mini-effort is to put on a pair of cotton gloves, dip your fingers in a mixture of equal parts Smirnoff Vodka and water, and clean away. (Imbibing the vodka while cleaning the blinds also seems to make the job go faster, but you didn't hear that from me.)

Plexiglas

- **Colgate Regular Flavor Toothpaste.** To hide scuff marks on clear Plexiglas acrylic glass, use a dab of Colgate Regular Flavor Toothpaste to polish the sheet of glass.

Screens

- **Cascade.** Dissolve one-quarter cup Cascade dishwasher detergent in one gallon of very hot water, and use a large scrub brush dipped in the solution to scrub window screens. Rinse clean with a garden hose.

- **Downy Fabric Softener.** Mix four tablespoons Downy Fabric Softener in a gallon of water and wash the screens with the solution. The surfactants in Downy boost the solvency of water, washing the dirt from window screens.

- **L'eggs Sheer Energy Panty Hose.** To clean dust from window screens, ball-up a clean, used pair of L'eggs Sheer Energy Panty Hose and rub it over the screens. The nylon is a mild abrasive that cleans dust and dirt from screens.

- **Maybelline Express Finish Clear Nail Polish.** To prevent insects from getting into your home through small holes in a window screen, seal the holes shut with a few dabs of Maybelline Express Finish Clear Nail Polish.

Shades

- **Maybelline Express Finish Clear Nail Polish.** To repair a small tear in a window shade, cover the tear on the back of the shade with a small piece of masking tape and give the tear on the front of the shade a coat of Maybelline Express Finish Clear Nail Polish.

- **Reynolds Wrap.** If you're a night owl or someone who works the night shift and prefers to sleep by day, make window shades that block out the daylight by placing Reynolds Wrap over windows.

Sliding Doors

- **Pledge.** To make sliding doors glide back and forth more easily, spray Pledge furniture polish in the track of the sliding door. The waxy polish helps keep dirt out and lubricates the track.

- **WD-40** and **Q-Tips Cotton Swabs.** To clean sliding door tracks, spray WD-40 into the grooves and wipe with Q-Tips Cotton Swabs. The WD-40 also lubricates the track so the door slides easier.

Venetian Blinds

- **Bounce.** Wipe the blinds with a clean, used sheet of Bounce. The antistatic elements in Bounce seem to magnetically collect the dust from the blinds and also keep dust from resettling.
- **Cascade.** To clean filthy Venetian blinds, sprinkle one-half to one cup Cascade dishwasher detergent into a bathtub filled with warm water. Place the Venetian blinds in the tub and let soak for five to ten minutes. Run a sponge or cloth over each blind. Rinse clean with a hand-held shower nozzle or take the blinds outside, hang them on a clothesline, and rinse with water from a hose.

Window Cleaner

- **Canada Dry Club Soda.** To clean windows, fill a trigger-spray bottle with Canada Dry Club Soda and wipe with a soft, dry cloth.
- **Cascade.** To clean grease and grime from windows, dissolve two tablespoons Cascade dishwasher detergent in a bucket of hot water. Use a clean mop dipped in the solution to wash the windows outside. Rinse with water from a hose. The surfactants in Cascade let the windows dry without leaving behind streaks or spots.
- **Downy Fabric Softener.** Mix one-third cup Downy Fabric Softener and one gallon water, fill a trigger-spray bottle with the solution, spray a two-foot square section of the window, wait ten seconds, and buff dry with a crumpled-up sheet of newspaper.

- **Heinz White Vinegar.** Fill a sixteen-ounce trigger-spray bottle with one cup Heinz White Vinegar and one cup water. Spray the solution on the glass and wipe with a crumpled-up sheet of newspaper.

- **Jet-Dry.** To clean windows, fill a clean, empty sixteen-ounce trigger-spray bottle with water, add one tablespoon Jet-Dry, and shake well. Spray glass and wipe with a crumpled-up sheet of newspaper.

- **Kingsford's Corn Starch** and **Dawn Dishwashing Liquid.** To make a powerful window cleanser, mix one teaspoon Kingsford's Corn Starch and one teaspoon Dawn Dishwashing Liquid in a gallon of water. Saturate a clean cloth with the sudsy water, wash the window with it, and dry with a clean cloth. The cornstarch prevents streaks.

- **Kingsford's Corn Starch, Heinz White Vinegar,** and **Parsons' Ammonia.** In a bucket, mix together two tablespoons Kingsford's Corn Starch, one-half cup Heinz White Vinegar, one-half cup Parsons' Ammonia, and one gallon warm water. Saturate a clean cloth with the milky solution, wash the window with it, and dry with a clean cloth. The cornstarch prevents streaks.

- **L'eggs Sheer Energy Panty Hose.** To clean windows, use a clean, used, balled-up pair of L'eggs Sheer Energy Panty Hose.

- **McCormick Cream of Tartar.** Dissolve one teaspoon McCormick Cream of Tartar in two cups of water in a sixteen-ounce trigger-spray bottle, spray the solution on windows, and wipe with a crumpled-up sheet of newspaper.

- **Mr. Coffee Filters.** Clean windows with Mr. Coffee Filters, made from 100 percent virgin paper that doesn't leave any lint behind.

- **Mrs. Stewart's Liquid Bluing.** Add a few drops of Mrs. Stewart's Liquid Bluing in a bucket of water and use the solution to clean a window.

- **Pledge.** To keep windows shiny and clean, spray the glass with Pledge furniture polish and buff with a clean cloth.
- **Rain-X.** Treating the windows on your house with Rain-X prevents dirt and grime from adhering to the glass.
- **Smirnoff Vodka** and **Dawn Dishwashing Liquid.** Fill a sixteen-ounce trigger-spray bottle with one cup Smirnoff Vodka and one cup water, add a couple of drops of Dawn Dishwashing Liquid, and shake well to make a first-rate window cleanser.
- **20 Mule Team Borax** and **Parsons' Ammonia.** To make an effective window cleanser, mix one-quarter cup 20 Mule Team Borax, one-half cup Parsons' Ammonia, and two gallons water.
- *USA Today.* Use crumpled-up pages of *USA Today* and any glass cleanser listed in this section to clean windows without leaving behind unsightly streaks.

Window Sills

- **Huggies Baby Wipes.** To clean dust and grime from a window sill, wipe the sill with a Huggies Baby Wipe.

Window Tracks

- **Alberto VO5 Conditioning Hairdressing.** Lubricate window tracks with a dab of Alberto VO5 Conditioning Hairdressing.
- **ChapStick.** Rub ChapStick on the tracks so the window slides open and shut easily.
- **Ivory Soap.** To lubricate window tracks, rub a bar of Ivory Soap along the runners.
- **Pam Cooking Spray.** To prevent a window from sticking, lubricate the channels with Pam Cooking Spray.
- **Vaseline Petroleum Jelly.** Lubricate window tracks by running a dollop of Vaseline Petroleum Jelly along the runners.
- **WD-40.** To make a window slide opened and closed with greater ease, spray WD-40 along the channels of the window and wipe off the excess.

Strange Facts

- The ancient Chinese philosopher Lao-tzu wrote in the *Tao Te Ching*, "One may know the world without going out of doors. One may see the Way of Heaven without looking through the windows."

- April 19, 1965, marked the opening of the Houston Astrodome, built for $30 million. The 4,596 transparent plastic panels in the dome itself allowed sunlight in, but not without creating massive glare. Ultimately, the only way to eliminate the glare was to paint the panels a dark color, keeping out the sunlight entirely.

- Singer and songwriter Jim Morrison, a huge fan of the work of poet William Blake, named his rock band the Doors after a line in William Blake's 1790 poem *The Marriage of Heaven and Hell*: "If the doors of perception were cleansed everything would appear to man as it is, infinite." This line also inspired writer Aldous Huxley to title his 1954 book *The Doors of Perception*, which begins with the line from the poem.

- In 1973, winds and bad engineering caused hundreds of windows to blow out of Boston's newly built John Hancock Building, designed by renowned architect I. M. Pei. All 10,340 windows had to be replaced.

- In March 1982, nine inmates at the newly opened, $11.2 million computer-controlled Baltimore County detention facility, billed as "the most modern jail in the United States," escaped by kicking out an "unbreakable" window.

- The elegant restaurant on the top two floors of the north tower of the World Trade Center in New York City was called "Windows on the World."

✳ ✳ ✳ ✳ ✳ ✳ ✳ ✳ ✳ ✳ ✳ ✳ ✳ ✳ ✳ ✳
✳   ✳
✳   For more offbeat uses for brand-name products,   ✳
✳   visit Joey Green on the Internet at: ✳
✳   ✳
✳   www.wackyuses.com   ✳
✳   ✳
✳ ✳ ✳ ✳ ✳ ✳ ✳ ✳ ✳ ✳ ✳ ✳ ✳ ✳ ✳ ✳

Acknowledgments

At Rodale, I am grateful to my editor, Karen Bolesta, for championing my cause and making this book a labor of love. I am also deeply indebted to my agent, Stephanie Tade; researcher, Debbie Green; expert copy editor, Jennifer Bright Reich; designer, Anthony Serge; project editor, Lois Hazel; and illustrator, Connie Stern.

A very special thanks to my manager, Barb North, and the hundreds of people who have visited my website and taken the time to send me e-mails sharing their ingenious tips for the brand-name products we all know and love.

Above all, all my love to Debbie, Ashley, and Julia.

Bibliography

Sources

- *All-New Hints from Heloise* by Heloise (New York: Perigee, 1989)
- *America's Stupidest Business Decisions* by Bill Adler (New York: Quill, 1997)
- *Another Use For* by Vicki Lansky (Deephaven, Minnesota: Book Peddlers, 1991)
- *Ask Anne & Nan* by Anne Adams and Nancy Walker (Brattleboro, Vermont: Whetstone, 1989)
- *The Bag Book* by Vicki Lansky (Deephaven, Minnesota: Book Peddlers, 2000)
- *Baking Soda Bonanza* by Peter A. Ciullo (New York: Harper-Perrenial, 1995)
- *The Blunder Book* by M. Hirsh Goldberg (New York: Quill, 1984)
- *The Book of Lists* by David Wallechinsky, Irving Wallace, and Amy Wallace (New York: William Morrow, 1977)
- *The Book of Lists 2* by Irving Wallace, David Wallechinsky, Amy Wallace, and Sylvia Wallace (New York: William Morrow, 1980)
- *The Dictionary of Misinformation* by Tom Burnam (New York: Thomas Y. Crowell, 1975)
- *Dictionary of Trade Name Origins* by Adrian Room (London: Routledge & Kegan Paul, 1982)
- *Familiar Quotations, Fifteenth Edition* by John Bartlett, edited by Emily Morison Beck (New York: Little, Brown, 1980)

- *Famous American Trademarks* by Arnold B. Barach (Washington, D.C.: Public Affairs Press, 1971)
- *The Film Encyclopedia* by Ephraim Katz (New York: Perigee, 1979)
- *The Guinness Book of World Records* (New York: Bantam, 1998)
- *Hints from Heloise* by Heloise (New York: Arbor House, 1980)
- *Home Maintenance for Dummies* by James Carey and Morris Carey (Foster City, California: IDG Books Worldwide, 2000)
- *Household Hints & Formulas* by Erik Bruun (New York: Black Dog and Leventhal, 1994)
- *Household Hints & Handy Tips* by *Reader's Digest* (Pleasantville, New York: Reader's Digest Association, 1988)
- *Household Hints for Upstairs, Downstairs, and All Around the House* by Carol Reese (New York: Henry Holt and Company, 1982)
- *How the Cadillac Got Its Fins* by Jack Mingo (New York: HarperCollins, 1994)
- *Make It Yourself* by Dolores Riccio and Joan Bingham (Radnor, Pennsylvania: Chilton, 1978)
- *Mary Ellen's Best of Helpful Hints* by Mary Ellen Pinkham (New York: Warner/B. Lansky, 1979)
- *Mary Ellen's Greatest Hints* by Mary Ellen Pinkham (New York: Fawcett Crest, 1990)
- *New Complete Do-It-Yourself Manual* by the editors of *Reader's Digest* (Pleasantville, New York: Reader's Digest, 1991)
- *The Origins of Everyday Things* by the editors of *Reader's Digest* (London: Reader's Digest, 1999)
- *The Oxford Companion to English Literature, Fourth Edition,* edited by Sir Paul Harvey (Oxford: Claredon Press, 1973)

- *The Oxford Dictionary of Modern Quotations* by Tony Augarde (Oxford: Oxford University Press, 1991)
- *Panati's Extraordinary Origins of Everyday Things* by Charles Panati (New York: HarperCollins, 1987)
- *Popular Mechanics Home Answer Book*, edited by Steven Willson (New York: Hearst Books, 1991)
- *Practical Problem Solver* by *Reader's Digest* (Pleasantville, New York: Reader's Digest, 1991)
- *Reader's Digest Book of Facts* (Pleasantville, New York: Reader's Digest, 1987)
- *Reader's Digest The Family Handyman Helpful Hints: Quick & Easy Solutions, Time-Saving Tips, Tricks of the Trade* by the Editors of *Reader's Digest* (Pleasantville, New York: Reader's Digest Association, 1995)
- *Ripley's Believe It Or Not! Encyclopedia of the Bizarre* by Julie Mooney and the editors of *Ripley's Believe It Or Not!* (New York: Black Dog & Leventhal, 2002)
- *Rodale's Book of Hints, Tips & Everyday Wisdom* by Carol Hupping, Cheryl Winters Tetreau, and Roger B. Yepsen, Jr. (Emmaus, Pennsylvania: Rodale Press, 1985)
- *Strange Stories, Amazing Facts* (Pleasantville, New York: Reader's Digest, 1976)
- *Symbols of America* by Hal Morgan (New York: Viking, 1986)
- *Time Almanac Reference Edition 1994*, (Washington, D.C.: Compact Publishing, 1994)
- *Why Did They Name It...?* by Hannah Campbell (New York: Fleet, 1964)
- *The Woman's Day Help Book* by Geraldine Rhoads and Edna Paradis (New York: Viking, 1988)
- *The World Almanac and Book of Facts 2000* (Matwah, New Jersey: World Almanac Books, 2000)
- *The World Book Encyclopedia* (Chicago: World Book, 1985)

Trademark Information

"A1" is a registered trademark of Kraft Foods.

"Albers" is a registered trademark of Nestlé.

"Alberto VO5`` is a registered trademark of Alberto-Culver USA, Inc.

"Alka-Seltzer" is a registered trademark of Miles, Inc.

"Arm & Hammer" and "Clean Shower" are registered trademarks of Church & Dwight Co, Inc.

"Armor All" is a registered trademark of The Armor All Products Corp.

"Aunt Jemima" is a registered trademark of the Quaker Oats Company.

"Avery" is a registered trademark of Avery Dennison Corporation.

"Band-Aid" is a registered trademark of Johnson & Johnson.

"Bayer" is a registered trademark of Bayer Corporation.

"Bioré" is a registered trademark of Kao Brands Company.

"Bon Ami" is a registered trademark of Bon Ami Company.

"Bounce" is a registered trademark of Procter & Gamble.

"Bounty" is a registered trademark of Procter & Gamble.

"Bubble Wrap" is a registered trademark of Sealed Air Corporation.

"Budweiser" is a registered trademark of Anheuser-Busch, Inc.

"C&H" is a registered trademark of C&H Sugar Company, Inc.

"Campbell's" is a registered trademark of Campbell Soup Company.

"Canada Dry" is a registered trademark of Cadbury Beverages Inc.

"Car-Freshner" is a registered trademark of Car-Freshener and Julius Sämaay Ltd.

"Carnation" and "Nestlé" are registered trademarks of are registered trademarks of Société des Produits Nestlé S.A., Vevey, Switzerland.

"Cascade" is a registered trademark of Procter & Gamble.

"ChapStick" is a registered trademark of A. H. Robbins Company.

"Cheez Whiz" is a registered trademark of Kraft Foods.

"Clairol," "Herbal Essences," and "Nice 'n Easy" are registered trademarks of Clairol.

"Clean and Clear" is a registered trademark of Johnson & Johnson Consumer Companies, Inc.

"Clorox" is a registered trademark of the Clorox Company.

"Close-Up" is a registered trademark of Chesebrough-Ponds USA, Co.

"Coca-Cola" and "Coke" are registered trademarks of the Coca-Cola Company.

"Colgate" is a registered trademark of Colgate-Palmolive.

"Comet" is a registered trademark of Procter & Gamble.

"Con-Tact" is a registered trademark of Rubbermaid, Incorporated.

"Conair" and "Pro Styler" are registered trademarks of Conair Corporation.

"Cool Whip" is a registered trademark of Kraft Foods.

"Coppertone" is a registered trademark of Schering-Plough HealthCare Products, Inc.

"Country Time" and "Country Time Lemonade" are registered trademarks of Kraft Foods.

"Cover Girl" and "Continuous Color" are registered trademarks of Procter & Gamble.

"Crayola" is a registered trademark of Binney & Smith Inc.

"Cream of Wheat" is a registered trademark of Nabisco.

"Crisco" is a registered trademark of the J. M. Smucker Co.

"Cutex" is a registered trademark of MedTech.

"Dannon" is a registered trademark of the Dannon Company.

"DAP" is a registered trademark of DAP, Inc.

"Dawn" is a registered trademark of Procter & Gamble.

"Depend" is a registered trademark of Kimberly-Clark Worldwide, Inc.

"Dial" is a registered trademark of Dial Corp.

"Dixie" is a registered trademark of James River Corporation.

"Downy" is a registered trademark of Procter & Gamble.

"Easy-Off" is a registered trademark of Reckitt Benckiser Inc.

"Efferdent" is a registered trademark of Warner-Lambert.

"Elmer's Glue-All" and Elmer the Bull are registered trademarks of Borden.

"Ex-lax" is a registered trademark of Novartis Consumer Health, Inc.

"Fantastik" is a registered trademark of S.C. Johnson & Son, Inc.

"Febreze" is a registered trademark of Procter & Gamble.

"Formula 409" is a registered trademark of the Clorox Company.

"Forster" is a registered trademark of Diamond Brands, Inc.

"French's" is a registered trademark of Reckitt Benckiser Inc.

"Frisbee" is a registered trademark of Mattel, Inc.

"Gain" is a registered trademark of Procter & Gamble.

"Gatorade" is a registered trademark of the Gatorade Company.

"Gerber" is a registered trademark of Gerber Products Company.

"Geritol" is a registered trademark of GlaxoSmithKline.

"Gillette" is a registered trademark of Procter & Gamble.

"Glad" is a registered trademark of First Brands Corporation.

"Glade" is a registered trademark of S.C. Johnson & Son, Inc.

"Gold Medal" is a registered trademark of General Mills, Inc.

"Goodyear" is a registered trademark of Goodyear, Inc.

"Gunk" is a registered trademark of Radiator Specialty Company.

"Hartz" is a registered trademark of Hartz Mountain Company.

"Heinz" is a registered trademark of H.J. Heinz Company.

"Hershey's" is a registered trademark of Hershey Foods Corporation.

"Huggies" is a registered trademark of Kimberly-Clark Corporation.

"Hunt's" is a registered trademarks of Hunt-Wesson, Inc.

"Ivory" is a registered trademark of Procter & Gamble.

"Jell-O" is a registered trademark of Kraft Foods.

"Jet-Dry" is a registered trademark of Reckitt Benckiser, Inc.

"Jif" is a registered trademark of the J. M. Smucker Co.

"Johnson's" and "Johnson & Johnson" are registered trademarks of Johnson & Johnson.

"Joy" is a registered trademark of Procter & Gamble.

"Karo" is a registered trademark of CPC International Inc.

"Kikkoman" is a registered trademark of Kikkoman Corporation.

"Kingsford" is a registered trademark of Kingsford Products Company.

"Kingsford's" is a registered trademark of ACH Food Companies.

"Kiwi" is a registered trademark of Sara Lee Corporation.

"Kleenex" is a registered trademark of Kimberly-Clark Corporation.

"Kool-Aid" is a registered trademark of Kraft Foods.

"Krazy" is a registered trademark of Borden, Inc.

"Land O Lakes" is a registered trademark of Land O Lakes, Inc.

"Lea & Perrins" is a registered trademark of H. J. Heinz Company.

"Lestoil" is a registered trademark of the Clorox Corporation.

"Lipton," "The 'Brisk' Tea," and "Flo-Thru" are registered trademarks of Unilever.

"Liquid Paper" is a registered trademark of Liquid Paper Corporation.

"Listerine" is a registered trademark of Warner-Lambert.

"Lubriderm" is a registered trademark of Warner-Lambert.

"Lysol" is a registered trademark of Reckitt Benckiser Inc.

"L'eggs" and "Sheer Energy" are registered trademarks of Sara Lee Corporation.

"Massengill" is a registered trademark of SmithKlein Beecham.

"MasterCard" is a registered trademark of MasterCard International Incorporated.

"Maxwell House" and "Good to the Last Drop" are registered trademarks of Maxwell House Coffee Company.

"Maybelline" and "Express Finish" are registered trademarks of L'Oréal USA, Inc.

"McCormick" is a registered trademark of McCormick & Company, Incorporated.

"Mennen" is a registered trademark of the Mennen Co.

"Miracle Whip" is a registered trademark of Kraft Foods.

"Morton" is a registered trademark of Morton International, Inc.

"Mott's" is a registered trademark of Mott's Inc.

"Mr. Clean" is a registered trademark of Procter & Gamble.

"Mr. Coffee" is a registered trademark of Mr. Coffee, Inc.

"Mrs. Stewart's" is a registered trademark of Luther & Ford Company.

"Murphy" is a registered trademark of Colgate-Palmolive Company.

"Nair" is a registered trademark of Church & Dwight Co., Inc.

"Nestea" and "Nestlé" are registered trademarks of Société des Produits Nestlé S.A., Vevey, Switzerland.

"NoSalt" is a registered trademark of RCN Products, Inc.

"Noxzema" is a registered trademark of Procter & Gamble.

"Old Spice" is a registered trademark of Procter & Gamble.

"Oral-B" is a registered trademark of Oral-B Laboratories.

"OxiClean" is a registered trademark of Church & Dwight Co., Inc.

"Pam" is a registered trademark of American Home Foods.

"Pampers" is a registered trademark of Procter & Gamble.

"Parsons'" is a registered trademark of Church & Dwight Co., Inc.

"Pine-Sol" is a registered trademark of the Clorox Company.

"Pink Pearl" is a registered trademark of Sanford.

"Play-Doh" is a registered trademark of Hasbro, Inc.

"Playtex" and "Living" are registered trademarks of Playtex Products, Inc.

"Pledge" is a registered trademark of S.C. Johnson & Sons, Inc.

"Pond's" is a registered trademark of Unilever.

"Post-it" is a registered trademark of 3M.

"Preparation H" is a registered trademark of Whitehall-Robbins.

"Pringles" and "Potato Crisps" are registered trademarks of Procter & Gamble.

"Procter-Silex" is a registered trademarks of Procter-Silex.

"Purell" is a registered trademark of Johnson & Johnson Consumer Companies, Inc.

"Q-Tips" is a registered trademark of Chesebrough-Pond's USA Co.

"Quaker Oats" is a registered trademark of the Quaker Oats Company.

"Rain-X" is a registered trademark of Unelko Corporation.

"ReaLemon" is a registered trademark of Borden.

"Red Devil" is a registered trademark of Reckitt Benckiser Inc.

"Resolve" is a registered trademark of Reckitt Benckiser Inc.

"Reynolds," "Reynolds Wrap," and "Cut-Rite" are registered trademarks of Reynolds Metals.

"Rit" is a registered trademark of BestFoods.

"Ronsonol" is a registered trademark of the Ronson Consumer Products Corporation.

"Rubbermaid" is a registered trademark of Newell Rubbermaid Inc.

"S.O.S" is a registered trademark of the Clorox Company.

"Saran" and "Saran Wrap" are registered trademarks of S.C. Johnson & Sons, Inc.

"Scotch," Scotch-Brite," and "Scotchgard" are registered trademarks of 3M.

"Scrubbing Bubbles" is a registered trademark of S.C. Johnson & Sons, Inc.

"Sea Breeze" is a registered trademark of Sea Breeze.

"7-UP" is a registered trademark of Dr Pepper/Seven-Up, Inc.

"Shout" is a registered trademark of S.C. Johnson & Sons, Inc.

"Silly Putty" is a registered trademark of Binney & Smith Inc.

"Simple Green" is a registered trademark of Sunshine Makers, Inc.

"Skin So Soft" is a registered trademark of Avon Products.

"Slinky" is a registered trademark of James Industries.

"Smirnoff" is a registered trademark of United Vintners & Distributors.

"Soft Scrub" is a registered trademark of Dial Corp.

"SPAM" is a registered trademark of Hormel Foods Corporation.

"Spic and Span" is a registered trademark of Procter & Gamble.

"Spray 'n Wash" is a registered trademark of Reckitt Benckiser Inc.

"Star" is a registered trademark of Star Fine Foods.

"Stayfree" is a registered trademark of McNeil-PPC, Inc.

"Stridex" is a registered trademark of Blistex, Inc.

"SueBee is a registered trademark of Sioux Honey Association.

"Super Soaker" is a registered trademark of Hasbro.

"Tabasco" is a registered trademark of McIlhenny Company.

"Tampax" is a registered trademark of Tambrands, Inc.

"Tang" is a registered trademark of Kraft Foods.

"Thompson's" is a registered trademark of the Thompson's Company.

"Tide" is a registered trademark of Procter & Gamble.

"Tidy Cats" is a registered trademark of the Ralston Purina Company.

"Tupperware" is a registered trademark of Tupperware Worldwide.

"Turtle Wax" is a registered trademark of Turtle Wax, Inc.

"20 Mule Team" and "Borax" are registered trademarks of United States Borax & Chemical Corporation.

"Uncle Ben's" and "Converted" are registered trademarks of Uncle Ben's, Inc.

"USA Today" is a registered trademark of Gannett News Service.

"Vaseline" is a registered trademark of the Chesebrough-Pond's USA.

"Velcro" is a registered trademark of Velcro Industries.

"WD-40" is a registered trademark of the WD-40 Company.

"Welch's" is a registered trademark of Welch Foods Inc.

"Wesson" is a registered trademark of Hunt-Wesson, Inc.

"Westley's" is a registered trademark of Blue-Coral Sick 50, Ltd.

"Wilson" is a registered trademark of Wilson Sporting Goods Co.

"Windex" is a registered trademark of S. C. Johnson & Sons, Inc.

"Wish-Bone" is a registered trademark of Unilever.

"Wonder" is a registered trademark of Interstate Brands Corporation.

"Wrigley's," "Juicy Fruit," and "Wrigley's Spearmint" are registered trademarks of Wm. Wrigley Jr. Company.

"Ziploc" is a registered trademark of S.C. Johnson & Son, Inc.

Index

Arm & Hammer Clean Shower
for cleaning
carpet stains, 30
mirrors, 211
mold and mildew, 235
rust from tools, 318
sinks, 281, 285
small appliances, 287
vinyl floors, 121
as drain unclogger, 93–94
for prolonging life of sharp tools, 310
Arm & Hammer Super Washing Soda, as
automatic dishwashing soap, 88
Armor All
as furniture polish, 140, 235
for preventing soap scum in shower, 272
as TV screen cleaner, 104
for waxing car, 53

Bayer Aspirin for reviving
cut flowers, 126
dead car battery, 36
Bioré Facial Cleansing Cloths, for
preventing fogging, 107
Bounce
for absorbing pipe condensation, 252
for cleaning
artificial flowers, 125
cathode-ray computer screen, 102
cobwebs and dust from ceilings, 67
cookware, 192
dead lovebugs from car, 40
eyeglasses, 108
microwave ovens, 289
mini-blinds, 373
mirrors, 211
sawdust, 319
soap scum from shower, 272
tile, 121, 299
Venetian blinds, 375
for dusting furniture, 135
for eliminating
excess suds in dishwasher, 89
static electricity, 81, 104, 312
for keeping cats off furniture, 60
as lawn mower air filter, 313
for picking up shed pet hair, 63
for preventing
laser printer jams, 101
nylon curtains clinging, 370
planters leaking soil, 163
for repelling pests, 240, 241
as Swiffer sheet substitute, 119
Bounty Paper Towels
for cleaning
candle wax, 19–20, 24
crayon, 344, 352
hair dye from carpet, 26
ovens, 296
steam iron, 70

as garbage can deodorizer, 154
for preserving wooden kitchenware, 196,
200, 201
for preventing
cast iron rusting, 189
wet book pages wrinkling, 13
for revitalizing wilted flowers, 130
seasoning cast iron using, 190
Budweiser
artificial snow made with, 368
fertilizer using, 204
as leather upholstery cleaner, 52
for luring insects from barbecue, 4
as slug and snail killer, 176

Campbell's Tomato Juice, for deodorizing
skunk smell, 64
Canada Dry Club Soda
for cleaning
car battery corrosion, 36
carpet stains, 28, 29, 30, 33, 64
cast iron, 189
clothing stains, 354, 355, 361
countertops, 20
glass, 55, 375
jewelry, 180
porcelain sinks, 283
loosening rust with, 316, 318
polishing chrome with, 280
watering houseplants with, 167
C&H Sugar
for cleaning grass stains, 355
glue made with, 157
as hand cleaner, 313
for insect control, 171, 172, 173
for prolonging life of flowers, 127
wallpaper paste made with, 341
Cascade
for cleaning
barbecue grill, 2
bathtubs, 6–7, 10
clothing stains, 364
coffee or tea stains from cups, 192
cookware, 192
crayon marks from wall, 344
linen tablecloth, 360
oil spots from driveway, 150
patio furniture, 235
sinks, 282, 284
small appliances, 287
soap scum from shower, 272
stoves and ovens, 294, 296
thermos bottles, 199
tile, 121, 299
toilets, 303
vases, 128
Venetian blinds, 375
windows and screens, 373–74, 375
fixing leaky radiator with, 48
whitening clothes with, 366

401

About the Author

Joey Green—author of *Polish Your Furniture with Panty Hose, Paint Your House with Powdered Milk, Wash Your Hair with Whipped Cream,* and *Clean Your Clothes with Cheez Wiz*—got Jay Leno to shave with Jif Peanut Butter on *The Tonight Show*, Rosie O'Donnell to mousse her hair with Jell-O on *The Rosie O'Donnell Show*, and had Katie Couric drop her diamond engagement ring in a glass of Efferdent on *Today*. He has been seen polishing furniture with SPAM on *NBC Dateline*, cleaning a toilet with Coca-Cola in the *New York Times*, and washing his hair with Reddi-wip in *People*.

Green, a former contributing editor to *National Lampoon* and a former advertising copywriter at J. Walter Thompson, is the author of more than forty books, including *Marx & Lennon: The Parallel Sayings, Weird Christmas,* and *The Zen of Oz: Ten Spiritual Lessons from Over the Rainbow*. A native of Miami, Florida, and a graduate of Cornell University, he wrote television commercials for Burger King and Walt Disney World and won a Clio Award for a print ad he created for Eastman Kodak. He backpacked around the world for two years on his honeymoon and lives in Los Angeles with his wife, Debbie, and their two daughters, Ashley and Julia.